RE-IMAGINING THE RESEARCH PROCESS

CONVENTIONAL & ALTERNATIVE METAPHORS

RE-IMAGINING THE RESEARCH PROCESS

CONVENTIONAL & ALTERNATIVE METAPHORS

MATS ALVESSON & JÖRGEN SANDBERG

$SAGE

Los Angeles | London | New Delhi
Singapore | Washington DC | Melbourne

Los Angeles | London | New Delhi
Singapore | Washington DC | Melbourne

SAGE Publications Ltd
1 Oliver's Yard
55 City Road
London EC1Y 1SP

SAGE Publications Inc.
2455 Teller Road
Thousand Oaks, California 91320

SAGE Publications India Pvt Ltd
B 1/I 1 Mohan Cooperative Industrial Area
Mathura Road
New Delhi 110 044

SAGE Publications Asia-Pacific Pte Ltd
3 Church Street
#10-04 Samsung Hub
Singapore 049483

Editor: Ruth Stitt
Assistant editor: Jessica Moran
Production editor: Manmeet Kaur Tura
Copyeditor: Sarah Bury
Proofreader: Elaine Leek
Indexer: Cathryn Pritchard
Marketing manager: Lucia Sweet
Cover design: Naomi Robinson
Typeset by: C&M Digitals (P) Ltd, Chennai, India
Printed in the UK

Library of Congress Control Number: 2021932853

British Library Cataloguing in Publication data

A catalogue record for this book is available from
the British Library

ISBN 978-1-5297-3215-3
ISBN 978-1-5297-3214-6 (pbk)

At SAGE we take sustainability seriously. Most of our products are printed in the UK using responsibly
sourced papers and boards. When we print overseas we ensure sustainable papers are used as measured
by the PREPS grading system. We undertake an annual audit to monitor our sustainability.

CONTENTS

LIST OF TABLES

PREFACE

Like many others we often doubt the meaningfulness and relevance of social research. Many, if not most academics follow established scientific ways for doing and conducting research, but their results are often predicable and boring. Conventional ideas and rules for doing social research are helpful, but also constraining and seem to work against imagination, creativity and thus interesting results. As Murray Davis has emphasized, social science needs to be seen as interesting in order to have influence. We think we can do much better than we currently do, and suggest that working with alternative metaphors for the research process can be very helpful in generating more imaginative and interesting research. It can lead to mind-stretching and rejuvenated research through re-imagining various key elements in the research process. This is what we set out to do in this book.

We would like to thank Ron Barnett, Yvonne Billing, Martin Blom, Yiannis Gabriel, Rolf Lind and Roland Paulsen for helpful comments on a draft of the book.

Some of the ideas in this book first appeared in Alvesson, M., & Sandberg, J. (2018). Metaphorizing the research process: Reflexivity, imagination and novelty. In C. Cassell, A. Cunliffe & G. Grandy (Eds.), *The Sage handbook of qualitative business and management research methods: Methods and challenges* (pp. 486–505). London: Sage.

Mats Alvesson and Jörgen Sandberg

Lund and Brisbane January 2021

ABOUT THE AUTHORS

Mats Alvesson holds a chair in the Business Administration department at Lund University in Sweden and is also part-time professor at University of Queensland (UQ) Business School, Australia and at City University, London, UK. He has done extensive research and published widely in the areas of qualitative and reflexive methodology, critical theory, organizational culture, knowledge work, identity in organizations, gender, organizational change, leadership, etc. His latest books include *Reflexive leadership: Organizing in an imperfect world* (with Blom and Sveningsson, Sage, 2017) and *Return to meaning: A social science with something to say* (with Gabriel and Paulsen, Oxford University Press, 2017).

Jörgen Sandberg is Professor in the University of Queensland (UQ) Business School, Australia, and at Warwick Business School, UK, as well as Co-Lead of Practice and Process Studies, a multidisciplinary research group within the UQ Business School. He has researched and published extensively in the areas of competence and learning in organizations; practice, process, sensemaking theory; theory development; philosophy of science; and research methodology. His most recent books include *Skillful performance: Enacting capabilities, knowledge, competence and expertise in organizations* (with Rouleau, Langley and Tsoukas, Oxford University Press, 2017), and *Constructing research questions: Doing interesting research* (with Alvesson, Sage, 2013). He also serves on the editorial boards for *Academy of Management Review*, *Journal of Organizational Behavior* and *Organization Studies*.

INTRODUCTION: MAKING RESEARCH MORE IMAGINATIVE AND INTERESTING

Thinking about how we can improve the way we develop knowledge is a key concern in academia. Often such thinking means learning how to conduct research in a rational and reliable way. The use of scientific methods is thus a cornerstone in the activities of the social researcher. Although following strict methodological guidelines is most salient in quantitative studies, it is also common in most qualitative research. Rationality and rigour are seen as the foundation for developing scientific knowledge and social research are seldom on the safe side when it comes to demonstrating these virtues. The messiness and indeterminacy of many social phenomena, as well as the importance of the researcher's paradigmatic background and his or her idiosyncrasies, make both the doings and the results of social research ambiguous. There are also situation-specific influences on responses from those being studied: they may produce different accounts about an issue depending on how the interviewer is perceived. For example, a young ethnic woman with an accent from a sociology department or an older white man with an upper-middle-class background from a business school may trigger different responses even if the interview questions are the same. Much social research is disputed or disputable. Relying on responses to a questionnaire or what people say in interviews may be seen as a rather uncertain foundation for establishing the truth. But as they are established methods, researchers tend to use them regularly without much signs of doubt or worry. However, rather than denying or marginalizing the ambiguity and messiness of social research it could be acknowledged, and options for thinking seriously about and dealing with it could be considered. Such considerations call for reflexivity rather than a recipe-following view on research.

BEYOND CONVENTIONALISM

A usually safe way of demonstrating credibility is to follow established ways of doing and conducting research. This is sometimes done without too much thinking outside the conventional lines of approaching the research task. Conservativism and conventionalism provide a lot of protection and a high degree of comfort for the researcher. The established ways of conducting research are seen as proven and reliable. They are institutionalized and taken for granted, and by complying with the dominant norms, researchers can significantly reduce the risk for serious critique and questioning of their research. The tendency to isomorphism – the gravitation over time to a singular, common form – is often strong in social life and research is no exception. Established methodology textbooks and articles published in leading journals then tend to look very similar. Leading journals set the norm. This facilitates a sense of social order and safe navigation but also means a closing of the academic mind.

This order and closing are both good and bad. Good because this means that there are clear standards and guidelines for thinking about, doing, writing, reading and evaluating research, at least journal articles. Anxiety and stress are reduced. Bad because all this means a lack of imagination, creativity and many missed opportunities to improve knowledge development in social research. (And probably in other areas as well, but here we are only interested in social science studies, in particular qualitative research.)

This book is about helping researchers reduce the risk of missing interesting opportunities in doing and writing research. We identify conventions in thinking about the research process and point out alternatives. The book provides an inventory of metaphors (images) of the research process and its key elements that will aid reflexivity in conducting more imaginative and interesting research. We are less interested in explicit metaphors for embellishing specific language than in implicit metaphors underlying our thinking about research. For example, society may be seen as a hyper-community, as a system, or as negotiated order reducing conflict. Similarly, an academic school may be viewed as a knowledge-maximization vehicle, a status-enhancement movement or a site for guild thinking. These metaphors may not be explicit in texts indicating the underlying meanings, but rather implicit and therefore require in-depth readings to be carved out or spotted. (Here we use different explicit metaphorical expressions – read, carve, spot – but point out one underlying metaphor/image for how to interpret implicit, underlying metaphors.)

An awareness of metaphors enables researchers to consider a range of options, being more imaginative and thus capable of choosing paths that s/he assess to be more interesting and lead to better results and texts. This metaphorical reflexivity can be helpful to researchers in not just improving and developing their research, but also for themselves as researchers and academics more broadly, including as teachers and in interaction with practitioners or the public. We want to encourage increased mind-stretching, facilitate more imagination, more independent choices and, as a result, hopefully, more varied, imaginative and interesting research. We are therefore less worried about rationality, rigour, reliability, legitimacy and predictability in research than we are eager to promote reflexivity, imagination, originality and creativity. We believe that doing more of the latter can lead to a greater chance of producing research texts, such as journal articles, essays, books and book chapters that bring about positive reader experiences, thus making research more impactful. In order for research to have an impact typically requires significant readership, and readers are strongly inclined to read texts they find interesting (Davis, 1971). Contemporary social science often scores badly in this respect.

RIGOUR AND/VERSUS IMAGINATION

Our emphasis on reflexivity and imagination does not mean that we do not care about virtues like rigour and techniques. They are obviously very important in all kinds of research, which have also been written about at great length. Our concern in this book is instead about how to rethink how we do research, and to facilitate imaginative research. We see massive problems within contemporary academia in this respect – a surplus of reasonable rigorous and predictable studies and a shortage of original and interesting work. We feel that social science studies need more good ideas and perhaps less focus on data management. We are – as we will show – not alone in finding a disturbing lack of non-predictable studies and texts in an age characterized by the massification of research and research outlets.

Our stance does not mean that we see the mentioned alternative ideals as simply good and unproblematic. A call for imagination may lead to efforts and results that are far from satisfactory. Trying to be imaginative may lead to bad ideas. The risk of failure and embarrassment is high, and many may be well advised to stick to an established route rather than pursuing risky detours. But risk aversion should not be the primary motive for doing research. And bearing the risks of promoting ideals like imagination and creativity should not prevent us from suggesting how researchers can consider new research avenues and make more informed choices when conducting and reporting research. Although some researchers should rely on more standard procedures than their imagination for doing research, many can probably be a bit more creative and original in their projects.

How to come up with ideas and frameworks for increasing the likelihood of producing work that is more non-standardized and interesting may be seen as very difficult, but we do not see this as mission impossible. Others have offered good ideas before us (e.g. Abbott, 2004; Weick, 1989). We propose the use of metaphors to identify, articulate and challenge the underlying images behind various elements of the research process, such as the purpose of research, design and contribution. As we will show, it is possible to consider and contrast different metaphors for various parts of the research process and, based on that, encourage more thoughtful decisions by the researcher. For example, one may view the purpose of research as building theory, establishing facts, or telling stories. Data may be conceptualized as a mirror of reality, as complicated clues for understanding, or as a trigger of ideas. The researcher's identity or role may be seen as a fact-finder or as a vehicle for giving voice to the subjects of study. The contribution of a study may be viewed as bricklaying – you add knowledge to existing knowledge – or as conversation starter – you introduce a new theme of interest. In this regard, it can be argued that metaphors are 'thought-leaders' taking us into new territory and providing us with the tools to order and comprehend it (Yob, 2003: 133).

In this book we identify and articulate metaphors that commonly guide the way we conduct research and, importantly, propose metaphors that offer alternative ways of thinking about various parts of the research process. The reader is then offered a range of more or less accepted metaphors or images of key elements of the research process. Grasping and considering a spectrum of metaphors of the main parts of the research process may stimulate researchers and lead to increased awareness, more informed choices, a heightened creative spirit and – hopefully – result in the generation of more imaginative and interesting research. But we also want to encourage the reader to think for him- or herself, to develop and play around with and apply metaphors that s/he finds can lead to better research, in one sense or another.

We do believe that the identification and presentation of a range of metaphors for all key elements of the research process may lead to an increased awareness of what is available, and also to some less well-known ways of thinking about research: both in terms of thinking about and actually doing research in more interesting ways, and how the researcher can develop him- or herself as a reflexive person. The latter means a self-critical, flexible and imaginative mindset in relationship to the research process and its key elements, as well as in relationship to the social forces within and outside academia that form and frame research, as well as the researcher as a disciplined subject.

Through clearly indicating a spectrum of options, conceptualized as metaphors, our hope is that the reader can make more informed, reflexive and autonomous decisions and engage in research paths that will lead to more varied, imaginative and hopefully more interesting (as experienced by the reader) research. This may mean anything from modifications of parts of the research process to the entire enterprise.

OUR AIM

The overall aim of this book is thus to encourage researchers to become more thoughtful and creative in their way of conducting and reporting their research. This is accomplished by challenging the dominance of certain conventions and templates for doing and reporting primarily qualitative research, but also to a considerable degree social research in general. In particular, we want to open up an awareness and encourage researchers to consider and to use alternative metaphors for conducting research: from how to think about the overall purpose of research to how to write research texts. In a sense, the book aims for emancipation or at least to loosen up the methodological straitjackets of research: encouraging an opening up of the academic methodological mind, which too often is locked into a particular path of the 'musts' of doing research. We do so by elaborating and proposing a metaphorical framework – a kaleidoscope of metaphors – that can be used for identifying and problematizing the taken-for-granted and (often dead) metaphors under-lying the research process. We are particularly interested in root metaphors, that is, basic images of the research process and its key elements, which we contend significantly guide and shape researchers' thinking and ideas about how to conduct research.

As we discuss in Chapter 1, current attempts for boosting the development of more interesting and imaginative research have commonly focused on single elements of the research process (e.g. object of study, existing literature, theory, methods, writing, con-tribution). We suggest a broader route. Our key point in this book is that metaphorizing the major elements of the entire research process provides a more comprehensive and imagination-stimulating approach for opening up what often appears to be tunnel-vision views of how to conduct research. Specifically, we aim to make a case for the value of a systematic, self-critical and reflexive metaphorization of the entire spectrum of the key elements of the research process. We contend that such a broad metaphorization of the research process has the potential to increase the chances of researchers to generate more novel, interesting and influential ideas and engaging research texts by (a) stimulating provocations and insights about what research may be about and how to accomplish it, (b) encouraging the researcher to think differently and more actively about several issues that normally are taken for granted or normalized in research, and (c) to reflect upon and sometimes reconsider him- or herself as an academic, with certain inclinations, compe-tences and blinkers. Creating and working with new metaphors for research obviously does not guarantee any good studies or valuable contributions, but we believe it will help researchers to increase the likelihood of good outcomes of their research efforts.

We aim for a broad readership and believe that both newcomers to the field of social research and more experienced researchers may benefit from the book. Young people may become less inclined to be socialized into research micro-tribes, conventions and/or see-ing a dominant approach as the natural, inevitable and only way for conducting research. More senior people may get some inspiration to reconsider and break out of old habits, which lead many of their studies and publications to look like clones.

OUTLINE OF THE BOOK

The book consists of three parts. In *Part I: Setting the scene and metaphorical reflexivity*, we elaborate the basis for the metaphorical kaleidoscope that helps researchers to think in more imaginative and creative ways about conducting and reporting research. A kaleido-scope consists of several lenses that can be combined in multiple ways to produce different pictures. For us, this means trying to work with different metaphors of the key elements of the research process. We start out in Chapter 1 by describing the contemporary situation of social research in terms of general accomplishments, or rather shortcomings, in gen-erating research of significant value. We identify how metaphors underlying dominant conventions and templates for conducting research create cognitive and social straitjackets that obstruct researchers from approaching the research process in more imaginative and creative ways. Conventional templates for research certainly work well for many researchers and projects, but they tend to close the mindset and restrict choices and, thus, risk preventing more interesting research possibilities. In Chapter 2, we approach the subject matter by describing some key characteristics of metaphors and assessing their pros and cons in the research process (hereafter RP) – the advantage and possible disadvantage of highlighting them – as well as their (un)avoidability in studies. In Chapter 3, we discuss the topic of reflexivity, its meanings and use in research. We thereafter in Chapter 4 relate reflexivity to metaphors and discuss how access to a variety of metaphors aids reflexivity and thinking carefully about the underlying images of research, which trigger awareness of metaphors in use and may encourage alternatives.

In *Part II: Re-imagining the research process*, we elaborate and populate the kaleidoscope with a spectrum of metaphors of the key elements of RP. In Chapter 5, we metaphorize the main *grounding* elements of the research process, namely, the overall purpose of research, the role (or identity) of the researcher, the research collective, and the view of the phenomenon to be studied. In Chapter 6, we address the *framing* elements of the research process in terms of the literature review, theory and design. In Chapter 7, the theme is what we call the *processing* elements and here we include method, data (collection) and analysis. Finally, in Chapter 8, we metaphorize the *delivering* elements of the research process: writing and contribution, that is, elements more salient during the later stages of a research project.

In *Part III: A kaleidoscope of RP metaphors*, we formalize the kaleidoscope of RP metaphors and illustrate how it can be used in research. In Chapter 9, we pull together our ideas from Chapters 5–8 and present a set of guidelines for putting the kaleidoscope to work. Then, in Chapter 10, we illustrate how the framework can be used for generating alternative ways of conducting research by applying it to two examples: one study of how technology is structuring work and another on the changing identity of medical students in residence, that is, the stage before they become full doctors. Finally, in Chapter 11, we discuss how applying the metaphorical kaleidoscope can contribute to the development of more imaginative and interesting research and writing. But we also temper our otherwise great, and perhaps the reader's, enthusiasm through pointing at potential problems with the proposed metaphor-focused route. Unfortunately, there is no such thing as a free lunch – or a risk-free route to creativity and originality – and a metaphor approach may also have its costs. Reflexivity means that one is well aware of the problems of what one is doing and realizes that an excellent meal may be followed by a huge price.

I

SETTING THE SCENE AND
METAPHORICAL REFLEXIVITY

1

CONVENTIONS AND TEMPLATES: A STRAITJACKET FOR INNOVATIVE RESEARCH

HAS SOCIAL SCIENCE RESEARCH LOST ITS MOJO?

Universities are globally a growth business. In many countries almost half of the young population take some kind of university degree – sometimes in topics that few people would have seen as particularly academically oriented some decades ago, such as nursing, tourism or beverage management. With the expansion of the higher education sector and the strong belief in the knowledge society, we have witnessed a dramatic increase in social science research, not least in qualitative research – our key interest in this book. There are not only 'good' motives for this expansion in research: it is also very much about status and legitimacy. In a crowded higher education market, it is important to have a favourable position compared to competitors, and here it is vital to show that institutions, at least for those aspiring to be seen as high up on the status (and ranking) ladder, are research intensive. This leads to massification research. In the past, being a university and doing teaching were a sufficient source of status, now an intensive positioning game has taken over. For many institutions and people, it is more a matter of not appearing or feeling inferior.

Nevertheless, given the expansion in research on a variety of topics, one would assume a plurality of large and lively social science research fields, comprising an enormous variety of perspectives, methodologies and research styles. One would perhaps assume that this would offer fellow researchers, professionals, political and organizational decision makers and the educated public a wealth of interesting and novel studies of great value. Even though a quantitative expansion may not lead to a corresponding increase in significant research contributions, one could expect it would lead to at least some more really valuable, and impactful, knowledge contributions. This does not, however, seem to be the case. Although there are many views on this, and across different disciplines there is probably variation, we see many signs of great disappointment with the state of the art of social science research.

Many agree that despite all the good work being produced, contemporary social science is frequently accused of being dull, narrow, incremental and irrelevant (e.g. Abbott, 2004; Alvesson, Gabriel & Paulsen, 2017; Tourish, 2019; Weinstein, 2000). Not infrequently, it seems the relevance is restricted to the researchers themselves boosting their CVs. Richardson (2000), for example, confesses that even when encountering texts on topics that she is very interested in, it is often difficult to keep on reading and she leaves many academic texts half-read. Her colleagues concur, and we share that experience too. Boredom is a common and often dominant experience when reading many contemporary research texts. The experience of boredom or even frustration is partly due to writing conventions, which give many research texts an impersonal, seemingly neutral flavour, with passivity and rule-following as salient characteristics. Journal articles are, for example, often standardized in terms of structure and the content does not necessarily differ much from other writings in the same domain. Many articles also use an abstract and high-sounding language, such as 'discourse', 'sociomateriality' or 'intersectionality' (often to camouflage a trivial content), making it unnecessarily hard to read and comprehend (Pinker, 2015; Sword, 2017; Tourish, 2019).

The experience of boredom, or at least very low enthusiasm, about much published research is also, and perhaps first and foremost, a matter of most texts having not that much to say in terms of novel ideas or rich empirical material. When one has read a few dozen articles or other publications within an area, it is often difficult to find something clearly memorable – a surprising insight or something else – that is worth passing on to other well-educated people who are broadly familiar with the field. In fact, many studies rather come across as trivial and without much value. Large numbers of publications seem to have been accepted because they tick the right boxes rather than offer an original contribution or empirical findings that are clearly non-trivial or non-predicted. This is not only an idiosyncratic opinion from the perhaps somewhat cynical authors of this book, who each have spent over three decades in our core field(s) and have tried to read relatively broadly across the social sciences. The first author of this book gave a plenary speech during a large conference and spontaneously paraphrased Churchill, saying to the 400 people or so in the audience: 'Never before in human history have so many had so little to say to so few.' This rather depressing and insulting message was met by a large spontaneous applause – the apparently broadly shared perception that despite there being massive efforts to produce research in social science, rather little of interest comes out of all of this.

Several editors and scholars have increasingly expressed concerns and frustrations about the lack of more novel, influential and relevant ideas published in journals in many areas within social science, including our own, organization studies. Gap-spotting, formulaic, pedantic, parochial and boring are frequent pejorative characterizations of current social research (Alvesson & Sandberg, 2013a; Gabriel, 2010; Grey, 2010; Starbuck, 2006). In many fields, isomorphism and parochialism rule, in the sense that research tends to be more similar-looking in form and more and more people eager to publish concentrate on their subspecialized subfields. These developments have resulted in highly constricted ways of conducting and writing research. Many follow templates and offer more of the same as others and as their previous work. This is most salient in quantitative studies, but also for many (most?) qualitative research studies, particularly those published in highly ranked journals. In the words of a previous editor of a top-tier journal: 'Like black cats in coal cellars, published studies are increasingly indistinguishable from previous ones, and the contexts in which these theories are tested or developed tend to fade into irrelevance' (George, 2014: 1). At the same, we need to acknowledge the huge variation in social science research on display in many leading methodology textbooks, such as in Denzin and Lincoln's *The Sage handbook of qualitative research* (1994, 5th edn 2018). However, much of the more varied work, and dissimilar to black cats in coal cellars, tends to be in somewhat esoteric areas and not published in leading journals or is viewed as offering a limited contribution, and therefore seen as peripheral, with limited readership and impact.

The main reasons behind the rather disappointing state of the art of much research produced within social science today can be debated. But the massification of research, an ongoing push for specialization, and the 'neoliberalization' of our universities (at least in the Western world) with its often strict and narrow performance management metrics, probably play significant roles (e.g. Fleming, 2020). We also need to consider the increased problem of saying something new as so much has been said before. It is simply difficult to add something valuable to areas in which there are already many thousands of publications. Perhaps the golden age of social science is over and what remains are footnote-adding studies, where research becomes mainly symbolic – demonstrating that the higher education institution is good and credible, as it produces research published in good journals, feeding the university ranking machines. Or, alternatively, perhaps research to a large extent has become an escape mechanism from teaching and/or a vehicle for promotion and the gaining of status and respect, and as a way of maintaining intellectual abilities and getting some inspiration for teaching – or justifying not doing so much of it. At least sometimes research and publications seem to be more driven by employability and promotability concerns than a strong wish to develop intellectually and socially valuable knowledge. With increased pressure – from others but also from the individual academic's wish to be in line with, or ahead of, others and show capacity and worthiness – research easily becomes guided by narrow instrumental concerns (Alvesson & Sandberg, 2013b).

Although the situation is a bit gloomy, we should add that we sometimes see interesting contributions that clearly make a difference and there are no reasons to give up doing research. On the contrary, we see the increasing complaints about contemporary research as motivating renewed efforts and rethinking the way we conduct and communicate our research. Without denying the need for university reforms. In this book we concentrate on what we, as academics, can do when we do social science, particularly qualitative research. Surely, we should be able to do much better than we currently do.

Many suggestions for encouraging researchers to develop more interesting and influential research have been made, such as problematizing implicit assumptions for generating research questions (Alvesson & Sandberg, 2013a); applying counterfactual thinking (Cornelissen & Durand, 2014); focusing on problem-oriented rather than theory-driven research (Corley & Gioia, 2011); using heuristics (Abbott, 2004); tricks of the trade (Becker, 1998); loosening up the formulaic writing style (Alvesson & Gabriel, 2013) or engaging in experimental writing (Richardson, 2000); changing the evaluation criteria for journal publications (George, 2014); reconsidering the institutional and professional norms governing research (Alvesson, Gabriel & Paulsen, 2017; Willmott, 2011); and opening up, and acknowledging, multiple meanings of theory (Abend, 2008; Sandberg & Alvesson, 2021). Although this book partly builds on, but mainly supplements these suggestions, we concentrate on another possible way forward.

PROBLEMATIZING DOMINANT CONVENTIONS AND TEMPLATES FOR QUALITATIVE RESEARCH

In this book we propose and elaborate a metaphorical framework that enables researchers to *problematize* and *broaden* the ways they think about the main elements of the research process. Our idea is that we need to be more open and mind-stretching in how we consider the elements of the research process: everything from research questions, literature reviews, interacting with data (empirical material), to how we write and formulate our contributions. We think there is a strong case for counteracting the closing of the academic mind following from standardized requirements for how to do and report research.

Specifically, we make the case that the dominant conventions and templates for conducting and reporting research are often constraining for researchers' imagination, creativity and innovative abilities for developing more interesting and impactful knowledge. As Weick (1989: 516) noted, researchers 'often write trivial theories because their process of theory construction is hemmed in by methodological strictures ... [which] weaken theorizing because they de-emphasize the contribution that imagination, representation, and selection make to the process, and they diminish the importance of alternative theorizing activities'. The constraining strictures Weick alludes to are the dominant conventions and templates that shape the way we conduct and communicate our research. As we will show, these conventions and templates create habits of thoughts about ways of doing research which we want to challenge in this book.

Some (e.g. Bluhm et al., 2011) claim that, in contrast to quantitative research, there are really no established templates, or 'boilerplate', as Pratt (2008: 856) expressed it, for how to conduct and report qualitative research. However, reading leading methodology textbooks within social science and the conformist nature of most journals suggests otherwise. Reviewing dominant textbooks on qualitative research across several disciplines, such as management and organization studies (Symon & Cassell, 2012), psychology (Willig, 2011), sociology (Hesse-Biber & Leavy, 2011), education (Hatch, 2002), as well as more cross-disciplinary approaches (Flick, 2018; Miles & Huberman 1994), it becomes clear that there are indeed well-established conventions and templates for how to conduct and report qualitative research. These textbooks portray almost in unison the process of qualitative research as being made up of a linear set of elements, such as 'theoretical framework', 'method', 'research design', 'data collection' and 'data analysis', suggesting the existence of well-established conventions and templates for how to conduct and report studies.

The existence of well-established conventions and templates for qualitative research is further evidenced by the fact that several researchers have raised their concerns about an increased use of more or less fixed templates and constraints for conducting and reporting studies in leading journals (e.g. Harley & Cornelissen, 2020; Tourish, 2020). Reay et al. (2019: 202), for example, note that 'most management and organization theory journals today endorse a format for empirical papers that is reminiscent of the physical sciences'. Similarly, in an editorial piece, Pratt et al. (2020: 12) argue that 'there has recently been an outcry that journals are becoming too enamored with the use of such templates in qualitative research'. The templates of qualitative research are increasingly fashioned in the image of quantitative research in many journals (Abend et al., 2013; Cornelissen, 2017), which is likely to increase, rather than reduce, the already 'dull and uninspiring scholarship – the opposite of what we expect of qualitative research' (Reay et al., 2019: 202). Köhler et al. (2019: 3) worry about 'some form of convergence on a template for qualitative research. This means that there now seems to be an expectation of what qualitative research methods should look like, what they should entail, and how they should be written up. This greatly limits the power of qualitative research methods for discovery, exploration, and refinement.'

Conventions and templates are, of course, important and necessary in many ways. They provide shared understandings among researchers about what research is and clear guidelines for conducting, reporting and evaluating research (Barney, 2020; Becker, 1982). Effective writing and communication, for example, requires an understanding of academic conventions and an appreciation of how editors, reviewers and readers in general respond to what we write. But it is also these very same conventions that often make research texts boring, as well as the research produced unimaginative and uninteresting.

A central problem is that these conventions and templates almost per definition form a shared and often taken-for-granted understanding of how to conduct and report research. They subsequently influence our thinking and decisions about how to carry out our research and developing knowledge in all aspects of the research process. In fact, they are even likely to encourage researchers to stop thinking and instead rely on templates to demonstrate rigour and impartiality (Harley & Cornelissen, 2020). They represent a form of functional stupidity – the following of a narrow rationality that makes sense based on taken-for-granted assumptions and within its own logic but appears irrational from a broader perspective (Alvesson & Spicer, 2016). While researchers are not entirely constrained by these conventions and templates, they are likely to have a significant disciplinary and normalizing effect as editors, reviewers and readers (i.e. we, the authors and readers of this book) often tend to evaluate each other's research in the light of those conventions and templates. For example, if editors and reviewers do not see that you follow the established convention, they may think that you have not understood what good research looks like or are just sloppy. These conventions and templates thereby act like normalized and established standards for conducting, reporting and evaluating research. The researcher internalizes these standards and defines her- or himself as a good academic through living up to the normalized expectations, i.e. becomes subjectified through this form of disciplinary power (Foucault, 1980).

METAPHORS AND IMAGINATION IN RESEARCH

Our aim in this book is to encourage researchers to become more thoughtful and imaginative in their research and to develop some healthy, ironical distance to the normalized way of working, including one's own work (Rorty, 1989). We contend that many of the established and taken-for-granted assumptions and views about research form the basis for the dominant conventional and template-driven studies and results. Often, assumptions and templates represent received wisdom and are simply reproduced without much thought. In order to enable researchers to break out from the captivity of taken-for-granted assumptions, they need to be identified, articulated and challenged by a set of alternative views. A slogan here can be 'I only know what I think when I have been confronted by another kind of thinking'. As Khaire and Hall (2016: 846) note in regard to innovations more generally, significant innovations often occur because innovators challenge and violate established conventions and templates in a specific area, and, through that, open up new thinking and ways of doing things in that area.

In order to enable researchers to generate more interesting and imaginative research, we aim to disrupt and break with the dominant conventions and templates by *metaphorizing* the elements of the entire process of research. Such metaphorization means that we emphasize the underlying images that are either explicit or implicit in various ways of approaching the research process and its different elements, such as formulating research questions, methods and contributions. The discovery of grounded theory is a good example, where the metaphors of 'discovery' and 'grounded' are often and easily taken for granted. But it is not given that research aiming for new knowledge is a matter of discovery – in the same way as people discover the source of the Nile or that a researcher has cheated. Nor is it self-evident that even ambitious and 'down to earth' studies mean that these are 'grounded' – perhaps the empirical ground is more like a swamp than solid rock. Our approach implies that established metaphors are targeted for critical scrutiny, reflection and possible more or less radical rethinking.

Metaphors are a key part of language use, including in scientific settings. Well-written academic texts typically make plenty of use of metaphors, being employed in skilful, and sometimes in almost poetic ways. A text by Suddaby (2006: 634) illustrates this in addressing misconceptions of grounded theory:

> A common misconception is that grounded theory requires a researcher to enter the field without any knowledge of prior research. There are several variants of this myth, each based on the false premise that the researcher is a blank sheet devoid of experience or knowledge. ... [In forgoing examining existent literature] the researcher honestly hopes to gain fresh insights by keeping out of the ruts earlier travelers have worn.

Suddaby uses metaphors effectively and seductively to get his message across. (At least we think so.) It goes beyond pure ornament and adds some sharpness to the message. Other authors more often fail in doing so in an appealing and reader-friendly manner – or prefer to write in a more strict and seemingly rigorous way. A wealth of metaphors can be spotted in Suddaby's texts, such as in the references to a researcher entering the 'field' (as if s/he was a farmer), the 'blank sheet' (the mind as a sheet), 'fresh' insights (again a farming metaphor, combined with the metaphor of peeping, i.e. seeing from the outside in).

However, we, the authors of this book, don't think that this detailed view of Suddaby's text is as interesting as considering his broader viewpoint, about research as insight-generation. Although we do take seriously the use of metaphors in order to write appealing publications, we are less interested in the details and technicalities of language issues and rhetorical tactics *per se*. We do not see as our major task to support beefing up texts with more colorful language, even though we hope to a degree also to encourage and give ideas for more inspiring social science texts. Our main interest lies instead in developing broader ideas of how to think more creatively and critically about the elements of the research process more generally, as well as in specific projects and writings.

As said in the Introduction, our key point in this book is to encourage metaphor awareness and an interest in actively metaphorizing various parts of the research process. We do so by suggesting a variety of metaphors – some conventional, some alternative (less common or marginal) and some almost unheard of – for the entire spectrum of key elements of the research process. The ambition is to encourage the reader to think differently and more actively about several issues that are normally taken for granted or normalized in research. Even if the researcher decides to continue in a conventional mode, and we are convinced that there are often good reasons for doing so on many occasions, it may still be based on better grounding through having thought about alternatives.

We are mainly interested in cognitions and images rather than in details of discourse or language use. Our intention is therefore not to conduct research on metaphors *per se*, but to elaborate a metaphorical framework that can function as a heuristic device for unsettling taken-for-granted ways of conducting research. This opens up finding alternative ways of doing more imaginative and interesting research. Although there are no guarantees and all deviations from a well-trotted path may be risky and lead to disaster, we still assume and hope that occasional departures from conventions are likely to make at least parts of social research more readable and impactful. At present we face the problem of a reverse theatre: there are more people eager to be on the stage than in the audience. In academia, we have many authors, few readers. There are many reasons behind this, but conventionalism and predictability of much research is a major contributing factor to a limited audience. Knowing metaphors better is, thus, a means, not the end, of this book. We are therefore not very strict in how we define and use metaphors – what exactly is (productively seen as) a metaphor is sometimes difficult to tell and we here prefer a fairly broad approach. Metaphors are vehicles or reference points for 'better' thinking about modes of doing research, from start to end.

The idea is here to encourage an awareness of, and interest in, a broader set of images, indicating different ways of thinking and doing research. Seeing the researcher as a 'truth-teller', an 'explorer', a 'provocateur' or a 'narrator' point at different possibilities. Viewing data as 'building blocks', 'uncertain clues' or 'narrative material' also indicate different ways of doing research. Too often researchers do not see different possibilities of conducting research, perhaps due to being locked into specific metaphors that constrain their way of thinking about research. The conventional and often taken-for-granted metaphors act as an invisible straitjacket that needs to be challenged.

Good research is characterized by what Weick (1989) calls *disciplined imagination*. Both ingredients are, of course, necessary, but we see more discipline than imagination in most (published) research. Researchers often seem very eager to avoid doing things wrongly and are more conventional and risk-averse than bold and innovative. This may often be wise but they (we) are perhaps too strongly domesticated by journal publication regimes and the sometimes convention-bound criticality of contemporary research communities, particularly when acting as reviewers. The response is risk-minimization. We want to push for the imaginative side of social studies and hope that this will inspire more crea-tivity without too many wild-eyed and badly supported ideas. We realize, of course, that imagination in social science is not just a matter of free-floating associations or loose hunches, but something that always needs to be balanced against, and constrained by, empirical material, existing knowledge and the demand for careful reasoning and theo-retical backup. A convincing, well-argued case is always necessary. There is usually fiction in research and fiction is often based on some type of research, but research and fiction are far from the same.

Metaphorical frameworks that stimulate rethinking on broad and profound levels, like those proposed by Burrell and Morgan (1979) and Morgan (1980, 1997), are as valuable as they are rare. We want to encourage a broadening and a rethinking of how we conduct research rather than adding precision and systematization to specific parts or details of the conventional research process. Knowledge contributions are increasingly subspecial-ized and narrow in scope (Alvesson & Sandberg, 2014). This book aims at enhancing the capacity of researchers on a broad scale through disclosing a wealth of options, only partly indicated so far. In particular, our metaphorization of the key elements of the research process (RP) provides a *kaleidoscope* of RP-metaphors. This metaphorical kaleidoscope ena-bles researchers to combine different metaphors in different parts of the research pro-cess, in a similar way as the kaleidoscope user rattles with the instrument and then the combination of glass leads to various images and colour patterns. The kaleidoscope can be seen as a super metaphor for doing research in a less conventional and predictable way than is common: a metaphor guiding the use of metaphors. The kaleidoscope of RP-metaphors offers a heuristic toolbox that helps researchers both to become aware of taken-for-granted ways of conducting research and to create new opportunities for carry-ing out more imaginative and interesting research and writing.

This overall approach has broad potential in rejuvenating research, but it calls for the researcher to be willing to engage in openness and flexibility as well as to make an extra effort. These virtues are often most common within qualitative research, which is what interests us mostly in this book, but large parts of the text are also potentially of relevance across the social sciences (and partly outside these) and across various methodologies and various idiosyncrasies for conducting research.

CHAPTER SUMMARY

In this chapter we have tried to set the scene for the rest of the book. We began by providing a broad outline of the current development of higher education and social research. During the last decades we have witnessed a large expansion of the number of academics and the amount of research funding in many fields within social science, and thereby a huge increase in research publications. However, despite all the good and rigorous research being produced, there is a broadly shared sense of a troubling shortage of novel ideas and really significant contributions within most of the social sciences field. Although there are many reasons for this problematic situation, we argue that current conventions and templates for conducting social science research often constrain and discourage more imaginative and original research. As a way forward, in this book we propose and develop a metaphorical framework – a kaleidoscope of RP-metaphors – that enables researchers to break out from the straitjacket of metaphors underlying the dominant research conventions and consider a broader range of research possibilities and, based on that, to develop more – a higher proportion of – original and impactful knowledge. In the next three chapters we develop the reflexive-metaphorical basis for such a kaleidoscope of RP-metaphors.

2
METAPHORS

As a first step in elaborating a kaleidoscope of RP metaphors, we introduce in this chapter the idea of metaphors and their pros and cons in the research processes. We provide an overview of the meaning of metaphors and point out their significance not only in terms of adding spice and quality to language use, but also – and primarily – in terms of their value in organizing thought and for being a resource for imagination. We do so by addressing how metaphors can function as a reference point and trigger for imaginative and creative thinking, as well as for the critical scrutiny of other people's thinking and for self-critique. We also discuss the advantages and disadvantages of using metaphors, with an interest in metaphors trying to indicate assumptions and thinking about a topic. Hence, the aim of this chapter is to provide a general understanding of metaphors and their functions in texts and in our thinking, particularly how they tend to shape and frame our cognitions and attitudes (and doings) of research.

MEANING(S) OF METAPHOR

Since Lakoff and Johnson's (1980) classic book *Metaphors we live by,* and before that R. H. Brown's (1976) insightful article 'Social theory as metaphor', many social researchers acknowledge the centrality of metaphors in research. The conscious use of metaphors for analytical reasons has expanded within the social sciences and is now important in many disciplines (Cornelissen et al., 2008; Gibbs, 2008; Putnam & Boys, 2006; Steen et al., 2010; Swedberg, 2020).

In a narrow, traditional sense, a metaphor is simply an *illustrative device*: metaphors are words that make language richer or more felicitous (Brown, 1976). A well-written, appealing text is often full of metaphors. However, a central insight that spans across most disciplines and schools is that metaphors are not only ornamental aspects of language, but also frame and summarize our thinking and doings in important ways (Black, 1962; Brown, 1976; Lakoff & Johnson, 1980; Ortony, 1993; Weick, 1992). Metaphors are then *cognitive framing devices* that trigger different images of reality. In social science, we rarely, if ever, relate directly to reality, but commonly do so through forming metaphors or images of the phenomena we address. For example, organizations are seen as if they are 'machines', 'organisms', 'political arenas', 'theatres' or 'psychic prisons' (Morgan, 1980, 1997). Consumers can be understood through metaphors, such as 'hedonists', 'rebels', 'victims', 'explorers', 'identity-seekers', 'activists', etc. (Gabriel & Lang, 2015), while higher education institutions may be indicated by metaphors like 'sieve', 'incubator', 'temple' and 'hub' (Stevens et al., 2008). Common metaphors for society are 'machine', 'organism', 'ecology' and 'system' (Swedberg, 2020). As Morgan (1996: 228) writes, the use of metaphors is 'a primal, generative process that is fundamental to the creation of human understanding and meaning in all aspects of life'. Metaphors – in the sense of root or organizing images, rather than poetic language use – draw attention to implicit or hidden aspects of different perspectives and vocabularies and may function as powerful starting points for new ways of seeing phenomena – or end points when a novel and helpful metaphor is developed in a research process. In all these cases, the mentioned metaphors refer not to explicit language use but to underlying metaphorical meanings in terms of basic images of research phenomena.

Hence, in contrast to 'the metaphor as the illustrative-device view', it can be argued that all knowledge is basically metaphorical in that it emerges or is 'constructed' from some point of view. So, too, are our experiences, for 'our ordinary conceptual system, in terms of which we both think and act, is fundamentally metaphorical in nature' (Lakoff & Johnson, 1980: 3). Metaphorizing can thus be seen as *a crucial element in how people relate to reality*, including when they do research.

Lakoff and Johnson (1980) refer to a variety of different types of metaphor and provide many examples (e.g. that 'time is money') and point to the conduit metaphor for communication. On a more general level they refer to orientational (e.g. up and down, front-back, in-out, on-off, central-peripheral) and ontological metaphors (e.g. entity, substance and container, such as inflation as an entity, the mind as a machine). In many cases, their examples highlight details in the use of language and do not say much about how metaphors relate to overall images or modes of thinking about an issue. Instead, they focus mainly on metaphor use in single sentences, but rarely look at a longer text in a more holistic way and point at an overall, underlying metaphor, not necessarily being explicit in the text.

It may be tempting to follow a more 'precise' or detailed metaphor-spotting route and develop a rich understanding of how language works from this perspective. We are less interested in such a route, and feel that it is of limited value for our purpose as it may draw attention away from the more holistic way of metaphorically summarizing how we think about the way we do research. The latter calls for looking more holistically and hermeneutically at texts and addressing root metaphors, not primarily pinpointing individual metaphorical expressions. While metaphors in text are fairly easy to spot, root metaphors are sometimes more difficult to identify (or construct): they are rarely explicitly articulated and they may lack clear boundaries and do not necessarily form a distinct gestalt. Looking at the explicit uses of metaphors can here be central, as they often both trigger effects and provide important cues to the underlying root metaphors.

HOW METAPHORS WORK

A metaphor is created when a term (sometimes referred to as 'modifier') is transferred from one system or level of meaning to another (the principal object), thereby illuminating central aspects of the latter and shadowing others, like seeing the organization (the principal object) *as* a 'pyramid' (modifier), consumption *as* 'waste' or man *as* a 'beast'. A metaphor thus allows an object (society, family, organization, consumption) to be perceived and understood from the viewpoint of another object (pyramid, prison, waste). Using words as metaphors therefore means a departure from their literal meaning: 'A word receives a metaphorical meaning in specific contexts within which they are opposed to other words taken literally; this shift in meaning results mainly from a clash between literal meanings, which excludes literal use of the word in question' (Ricoeur, 1978: 138; see also Steen et al., 2010). It is thus the combination and the interactional effect that is of interest and produces the metaphor – and the metaphorical effect on the reader, who is capable of seeing something in a new light. As Lakoff and Johnson (1980: 5) note, '[t]he essence of metaphor is understanding and experiencing one kind of thing in terms of another'.

Brown (1976: 173) points to the following characteristics as being central for metaphors. Metaphors involve what Aristotle called 'giving the thing a name that belongs to something else'. If a metaphor is taken literally, it usually appears absurd. For example, when we say that society is a 'machine' or higher education institutions are 'sieves', we do not mean that they are actual machines or sieves. To think so would be both untrue and ludicrous. Instead, by saying that society is a machine we want to highlight some features of society that can be understood in terms of the machine image, such that society consists of a huge amount of interconnected mechanical parts, which can be manipulated to create efficiency and precision or lack thereof. In this regard, the machine metaphor may generate some important insights and extended meanings about how society sometimes works. The necessary ingredient of difference between society and a machine has a specific cognitive function: 'it makes us stop in our tracks and examine it. It offers us a new awareness.' Metaphors are intended to be understood: 'they are category errors with a purpose, linguistic madness with a method' (Brown, 1976: 173). Madness here indicates the element of surprise and departure from the conventional and taken for granted. Metaphors must be approached and understood as if they were true at the same time that we are aware that they are fictitious – created and artificial.

According to Max Black, who is often seen as the founder of the theory of metaphors:

> [a] memorable metaphor has the power to bring two separate domains into cognitive and emotional relation by using language directly appropriate to the one as a lens for seeing the other; the implications, suggestions, and supporting values entwined with the literal use of the metaphorical expression enable us to see a new subject matter in a new way. The extended meaning that results, the relations between initially disparate realms created, can neither be antecedently predicted nor subsequently paraphrased in prose.... Metaphorical thought is a distinctive mode of achieving insight, not to be construed as an ornamental substitute for plain thought. (Black, 1962: 236–237)

A good metaphor, therefore, depends on an appropriate mix of similarity and difference between the transferred word and the focal one. Where there is too much or too little similarity or difference, the point may not be understood. As a result, metaphor generation is a precarious enterprise. According to Cornelissen and Kafouros (2008: 365), impactful metaphors in research and knowledge development are those that are (i) seen to capture multiple salient features of phenomena, and (ii) easily understood. Cornelissen (2006) suggests a more developed set of criteria for assessing metaphors in terms of 'optimality', including the integration principle (where the blend of metaphors can lead to a single unit), the typology principle (suggesting that the blend should match the relationships of their counterparts in other domains), the distance principle (where the source and the target concepts should come from distant semantic domains) and the concreteness principle (where the source concept compared to the target should be sufficiently concrete – and not abstract – to be grasped and manipulated).

At the risk of being repetitive, our interest in metaphors is mainly with so-called root metaphors (Smircich, 1983) or organizing metaphors, that is, metaphors that are behind or working as an image for how one relates to something. These are often visible in explicit texts, but there is not necessarily a one-to-one relationship between explicit language use and underlying root or organizing metaphors. This means we are less interested in the details of language use, although, of course, explicit texts are important to consider, but more as an entrance to understanding a broader issue. For example, the language use in the previous sentence may indicate a spatial metaphor, where 'entrance' suggests a building and 'broader' use of a size metaphor. This does not necessarily mean that we, the authors, base our thinking on a large-scale construction work metaphor or that we are interested in volumes. Language may directly point in this direction but reading our section as a whole hopefully gives an impression other than a 'mechanical' or single-word focused reading of metaphors. Metaphorical expressions in text chunks may go in very different directions, and for our purpose it is more relevant to look beyond getting caught in, and exaggerating, text details. Grasping root metaphors often calls for reading between and behind the lines.

Here we differ from Lakoff and Johnson (1980), who take specific words very seriously and move from specific textual expressions into broader metaphorical categories. For example, they move from specific expressions about making an argument, such as 'your claims are indefensible', 'he attacked every point in my argument' and 'his argument was right on target' to the metaphor 'argument is war'. However, there are plenty of other ways of expressing the core phenomenon in question (i.e. making an argument) without referring to a war metaphor. 'Your claims are very weak', 'he raised a severe critique on every point in my argument' and 'his argument was directed against the key issue', lack any explicit reference to 'war' but basically express the same meaning as Lakoff and Johnson's war metaphor. For the latter to make sense as a way of pointing at someone's cognition or overall communication of the subject matter, the war image needs to be consistent across a set of sentences and underlie these.

The precise marking of the words or expressions used may not, therefore, necessarily say that much about a metaphor summarizing a way of relating to a phenomenon, that is, a root metaphor. The former are uncertain indicators of the latter. Lakoff and Johnson (1980: 19) claim that 'no metaphor can ever be comprehended or even adequately represented independently of its experiential bases'. We agree, but they seem to do this themselves, as they consistently link specific linguistic expressions to a metaphor, seemingly without considering context and experience. Of course, a text or talk where the writer or speaker repeatedly uses the expressions of the 'argument is war' type may be said to use a war metaphor as the basic understanding, but this is different from a mechanical or indexical way of going from text chunks to some broader metaphorical category. Our point is that understanding the meanings of metaphors call for some interpretative work and cannot easily be conducted by a computer program directly translating language use into an underlying metaphor, that is, a root metaphor.

Let us have a look at an example of a journal text addressing the development and situation of an academic discipline.

> The search for optimal distinctiveness may represent a compromise that leads to an incremental reproduction of existing knowledge and ultimately maintains the status quo. In order to stay alive and be revitalized, fields require a certain degree of risk taking, which is often reflected in the adoption of novel practices and styles. As it moves towards a stage of maturity, our own field is increasingly in need of conversation starters, new ways of envisioning model readers, and authors who are able to develop more imaginative text building strategies. (Patriotta, 2017: 758)

We can here see the prevalence of and quite varied use of metaphors in the text. 'Search for optimal distinctiveness' indicates an effort to find something, a quest or exploration project, perhaps a calibration exercise. 'Represent' suggests a stand in or acting on behalf of someone else. 'Compromise' indicates a struggle between interest and a peace-setting negotiation outcome, while 'reproduction', 'stay alive', 'revitalized' and 'maturity' indicate a biology or organism metaphor. 'Stage' and 'field' reflect a theatre, geography or spatial metaphor, while 'envisioning' indicates that it is about perception and/or imagination. 'Maintains' and 'building' indicate construction work, while 'strategies' may suggest war and 'conversation starters' stands for the need to use a motor to trigger and engage in a new form of chatting.

Taking a fairly indexical approach, as in the above, where we just look at individual expressions (single words or brief combinations of words) and point out the metaphors used by Patriotta in various sentences, may indicate mixed metaphors and confused reasoning, but we don't read the text in that way. Rather, we see his text as a well-crafted and coherent statement. If we look beyond the specific linguistic metaphors expressed (and a Lakoff and Johnson approach), we may see the text as mainly being based on a medicine root metaphor, which is clearly hinted at by all the words referring to biology and organism as well as negative health issues. The author seems worried about the health of the mature patient, suffering from age and stagnation. There is the search for the optimal cure, the need for improvement and change of the threatening current state (status quo). Revitalization is needed to 'stay alive'. But the cure is dangerous, involving 'risk-taking', calling for some creativity and boldness, although this is moderated by the conversation metaphor. Perhaps the talking cure, that is psychotherapy, is what is needed. Through this root or organizing metaphor, all the other expressions, outside this metaphor, get another meaning than their literal one would indicate.[1]

ADVANTAGES AND PROBLEMS IN USING METAPHORS

The most frequently expressed advantage of using metaphors is their ability to encourage creativity, generate new ideas and guide analysis in novel ways, as well as their capacity to communicate (Cornelissen & Durand, 2014; Grant & Oswick, 1996; Morgan, 1980; Schön, 1979). Metaphors can also enable critical scrutiny of social research and practice, through indicating the partiality and arbitrariness as well as taken-for-granted assumptions. For example, a focus on (root) metaphors may facilitate examination of our ingrained understandings and basic assumptions of phenomena. It can also aid understanding of how we, in research communities and as advocates of particular theories and schools, are caught in box-thinking (to use a perhaps worn-out metaphor well versed to show constraints and narrow-mindedness) (Alvesson & Sandberg, 2014).

There are of course also problems with using metaphors. One is that metaphors may have a strong rhetorical and even seductive appeal but score lower on precision and rigour (Pinder & Bourgeois, 1982). Researchers with a more conventional mindset, arguing for what they see as a more precise language, dislike more than modest use of metaphors. Another risk is the supermarket orientation to metaphors (Reed, 1990), leading to shallowness; metaphorical expressions are (seemingly) easy to use but may lead to a poor ability to master and use them productively in research. An additional problem is that sometimes a specific image or idea is difficult to capture through a distinct metaphorical formulation. Available metaphors (metaphorical language) are limited and finding the nice combination between something one wants to illuminate and a specific expression illuminating metaphorical qualities is sometimes hard or impossible. Moreover, as Swedberg (2020) argues, the heuristic powers of metaphors can sometimes lead to the opposite problem, namely through their often multiple and ambiguous meanings, metaphors may offer too many options, over-stimulating our imagination, which may paralyse and confuse our thinking rather than informing and expanding it.

Metaphors may also simplify things too much and lead to or express reductionism. The metaphor idea may be appealing but it is often difficult to shoe-horn in a lot of ideas and phenomena that are not well aligned with a clear metaphorical expression in a specific metaphor framework. The seductive ideal of working with metaphors may lead to researchers – including ourselves – pressing work into a 'metaphor box'. It is easy to become seduced by and try to overdo the use of metaphors. So sometimes, it may be wise to 'hold your horses'. Very few would reduce any idea or line of reasoning to be only about a metaphor. But sometimes a seductive metaphor may draw attention away from other aspects or elements in more complex reasoning or aspects of the target in question. A case in point is Searle's (1984: 44) demonstration of how we have used different technologies as models for better understanding the human brain, and thus the danger of metaphorical thinking:

> Because we do not understand the brain very well we are constantly tempted to use the latest technology as a model for trying to understand it. In my childhood we were always assured that the brain was a telephone switchboard. ('What else could it be?') I was amused to see that Sherrington, the great British neuroscientist, thought that the brain worked like a telegraph system. Freud often compared the brain to hydraulic and electro-magnetic systems. Leibniz compared it to a mill, and I am told that some of the ancient Greeks thought the brain functions like a catapult. At present, obviously, the metaphor is the digital computer.

Metaphors can thus be seen as a double-edged sword – as perhaps can most things. On the one hand, they have the potential to help us to transcend and see our daily practices as well as our modes of thinking and developing knowledge in a new and novel light. On the other hand, dominant (but also novel alternative) metaphors can easily become a prison, locking us into unquestioned forms of understanding and doing research. A good dosage of reflexivity therefore appears central in metaphor work (Alvesson et al., 2008). In this study (i.e. in elaborating a kaleidoscope of RP metaphors), reflexivity involves a preparedness to employ a range of 'seeing as' tactics in addressing various elements of the research process. We will attend to reflexivity in the next chapter.

CHAPTER SUMMARY

As a first step in developing a kaleidoscope of metaphors that can aid researchers to generate more interesting and imaginative research, we have in this chapter elaborated the idea of metaphors. Metaphors can be seen as linguistic devices as well as underlying images of a phenomenon we are trying to understand or say something about. The former – metaphor as a linguistic device – is explicit and can be grasped through careful attention to explicit textual elements. The latter – root metaphors – are underlying, basic images or gestalts of phenomena. Root metaphors may be explicitly addressed, but are often more implicit and difficult to grasp. For example, viewing research output as an employability and promotability assessment device may indicate a root metaphor, but this does not necessarily appear directly in texts and talk about the subject matter. The root metaphor may only occasionally be indicated in the text. Although our primary interest in this book is root metaphors, the level of text and talk, on the one hand, and root metaphors, on the other hand, cannot often be separated. Some attention to both is therefore necessary. Sometimes the explicit text reveals rather directly the root metaphor, such as when authors claim to 'build theory' even though there may be different meanings of the 'build' metaphor.

We have emphasized the need to consider both the advantages and disadvantages with metaphor work. While it is important to be aware of the shortcomings, including a risk for getting into metaphor mania – seeing and emphasizing metaphors everywhere – we find a metaphor focus to be highly valuable. It fuels imagination and points at the selectivity of ways of addressing subject matter, thus stimulating a recognition of the limits and a preparedness to consider alternatives, at least for people with a flexible and curious mindset. Important here is a capacity for, and interest in, reflexivity – the topic of the next chapter.

NOTE

1.   Alternative readings, pointing at other metaphors, are also possible, such as a farming metaphor. Research is like crop-farming, calling for novel but not risk-free practices.

3
REFLEXIVITY

Working with metaphors involves a high degree of reflexivity. Contemporary developments in social research have also brought reflexivity to the foreground. It is no longer sufficient just to demonstrate rigour or the close following of recipes for doing good research. Researchers also need to account for their own subjectivity, the role of their cultural context and how these affect studies. As reflexivity forms an integral part of our metaphor framework, and as awareness of metaphors offers strong support for reflexivity in research, we find it motivating to account for this elusive concept and show how we relate to it.

Reflexivity is defined quite differently by various authors and one can work with this in an endless number of ways, with or without taking metaphors seriously, that is formulating reflexivity issues in relation to the use of metaphors. We see reflexivity as partly about ambitious considerations of alternative ways of considering what the research process and its various parts are all about. This involves the critical scrutiny of one's assumptions and framework and efforts to challenge and rethink these, at times. Considering metaphors and the mobilization of a set of conventional and alternative metaphors supports, and even pushes for, reflexivity. The reflexive researcher is not imprisoned by a favoured way of thinking and has access to a set of alternative metaphors for relating to research ideals and the subject matter being studied.

The aim of this chapter is to address the meaning(s) of reflexivity and outline our take on this. By way of background, we first provide a brief overview of the historical development and contemporary situation of qualitative research and thus situate reflexivity. Understanding the historical development of qualitative research in the social sciences is important because although the ideals and norms for conducting qualitative research constantly change and evolve over time, their histories rarely disappear completely, and therefore are likely to play an active role in the conduct of qualitative research even today.

We thereafter discuss some general meanings of reflexivity, followed by a discussion of the five central domains of reflexivity.

A BRIEF OUTLINE OF THE HISTORICAL CONTEXT AND DEVELOPMENT OF QUALITATIVE RESEARCH

Qualitative research in social science has grown into an enormous and varied field comprising several scientific research traditions, including positivism, interpretivism, pragmatism, critical realism and postmodernism. There are also multiple methodological approaches, such as case study, ethnography, grounded theory, discourse analysis, ethnomethodology and phenomenology. These traditions and methodologies are in turn used in combination with a whole raft of different theoretical perspectives, such as institutional theory, sensemaking theory, practice theory, gender theory and critical theory (Brinkmann et al., 2014; Denzin & Lincoln, 2005; Hammersley, 2011). This huge variation in traditions, methodological approaches and theoretical perspectivs offers an almost endless number of choices, from how to view reality (ontology), to how to develop knowledge (epistemology) and how to do research in practice (method). All these create opportunities but also difficulties in making decisions and risk confusion and contradiction, and call for quite a lot of reflexivity. The large number of options available can fuel existential problems and decision anxiety, compared to situations where there are fewer available options and a broadly agreed upon set of norms for social research.

In comparison to natural science, social science has a much shorter pedigree. It was gradually established around 1900, using the natural sciences as the role model, particularly in terms of the 'scientific method' as the central principle for, and engine of, knowledge production (Gower, 1997). As Winch (1958: 1) remarks in his short but influential book *The idea of a social science and its relation to philosophy*, it was assumed that as social scientists 'we must follow the methods of natural science rather than those of philosophy if we are to make any significant progress'. However, as Hammersley (2011: 19) notes, there were from the beginning 'important differences in views among social scientists about the nature of scientific method; as well as conflicting ideas about whether social science is distinctive in its goal or in the nature of the phenomena with which it deals; and, if so, about whether and how scientific method should be adapted to take account of this'. Dilthey ([1894] 1977), for example, made the important distinction between *Naturwissenschaften* (the natural sciences) and *Geisteswissenschaften* (the social/human sciences). While the former focuses on *erklären*, that is, to causally explain natural phenomena, the latter focuses on *verstehen*, that is, to understand the meaning of (social) phenomena (see also Giddens, 1984: 219).

Broadly speaking, it could be argued that the natural sciences were supposed to address 'natural problems', and the social sciences were supposed to address 'social problems', such as immigration, education, inequality, racism, etc., but also problems related to the management and functioning of organizations like businesses, hospitals, the police, and so on, and to provide a scientific solution to them. But as Manicas (1998: 45) observes, 'if social scientists were to be professional with legitimate claims to authority and autonomy, they must mark out their scientific territories, clear away all that was nonscientific, and establish their own system of credentialing. … It meant establishing distinct disciplines exactly in terms in which they believed any true science must be constituted', which they gradually did over the years.

Given its different philosophical roots and long and varied trajectory, it is not possible to do full justice to all the twists and turns of the historical development of the conduct of qualitative social science in the one brief account aimed at in this chapter. It is quite obvious that its history is not singular but multiple (Brinkmann et al., 2014). Nevertheless, according to Denzin and Lincoln's well-established (and often cited) historical account in their many editions of *The Sage handbook of qualitive research* (1994, 2000, 2005, 2011, 2018), it is possible to distinguish a set of critical moments or phases in the development of qualitative research within social science.

In the *first* traditional period (1900–1950), positivism dominates, and the social sciences disciplines are mainly preoccupied with appropriating the scientific method from the natural sciences in their studies as a way to generate valid and objective knowledge of social phenomena.

In the *second* modernist phase (1950–1970), more social constructionist/interpretative methodological approaches (Holt & Sandberg, 2011) emerged. Phenomenological, ethnomethodological and symbolic interactionist approaches made some inroads and more researchers were trying to formalize and further establish qualitative research method as distinct from quantitative research methods. The perhaps most famous example of such an establishment was Glaser and Strauss's (1967) book *The discovery of grounded theory: Strategies for qualitative research*. In that book they argued that qualitative research is mainly inductive in contrast to quantitative research, which is predominantly deductive in character.

In the *third* moment (1970–1986), which Denzin and Lincoln call the moment of blurred genres, qualitative research had made significant inroads and gained acknowledgement as a method in its own right within the social sciences. Through leading researchers and thinkers, such as Geertz, Bourdieu, Giddens, Habermas and Derrida, some researchers were now starting to draw more on ideas in the humanities rather than in natural science for further elaborating qualitative research methods in their own right. One reason for this shift away from using the scientific method in natural science as the role model and main inspiration was an increased awareness (and concern) among 'many social scientists that their disciplines had not achieved the demonstrable progress characteristic of natural science in the nineteenth century, nor the same practical payoff' (Hammersley, 2011: 19).

In the *fourth* and *fifth* (postmodern) phases (1986–2000), the social constructionist/ interpretative methodological approaches started to gain a firmer foothold in qualitative research. In particular, through the emergence of postmodernism and poststructuralism, together with an increase in gender, race and class studies, several qualitative researchers became more reflexive and started to more seriously question both the dominant models of truth and the idea of the researcher as a neutral observer. Through these shifts, qualitative research became entangled in a 'crisis of representation', which it is still trying to untangle (Sandberg, 2005). Smith and Deemer (2000: 878) neatly summarized this crisis in the following way: 'With the end of the possibility that we could think of ourselves as neutral spectators at the game of knowledge, the central problem that has preoccupied the thought of numerous researchers for the past few decades is that of "Now what are we going to do with us."' A key issue, even a 'must' in terms of reflexivity for many qualitative researchers, has been an increased awareness of gender, class, ethnicity, sexual orientation, etc. In a society 'marked by class, racial, and sexual conflict, no producers of knowledge are innocent or politically neutral' (Foley & Valenzuela, 2005: 219). The reader is hereby encouraged to consider to what extent the present volume expresses middle-class, white, male, heterosexual guilt and political partisanship.

In the most recent set of historical moments (2000 to present), qualitative research has been increasingly (at least in some quarters) fractured and politicized, such as the growing conflict between different qualitative research methods and different types of social positions and categorizations, at the same time as the longstanding conflict between qualitative and quantitative methods has been accentuated (Denzin & Lincoln, 2018). Denzin and Lincoln (2005: 26) suggest that 'we are in a new age where messy, uncertain, multi-voiced texts, cultural criticism, and new experimental work will be more common, as will be more reflexive forms of fieldwork, analysis and intertextual representation'. Here we see a situation of escalating pluralism and variation and a multitude of options for the well-read and informed researcher to choose from.

However, Denzin and Lincoln's account of the historical development of social science in terms of a set of consecutive moments can be questioned, particularly as their description is unlikely to reflect the historical trajectory of the great majority of qualitative research within the social sciences. Much of what they describe are rather esoteric parts of the broad domain of qualitative research. First, a large majority of contemporary qualitative research is likely to be less 'advanced' or trendy than what Denzin and Lincoln's historical moments suggest. A case in point is current qualitative research in tourism. In their study, Wilson et al. (2020) used Denzin and Lincoln's different moments of qualitative research as a framework to investigate what historical moment(s) qualitative research in tourism is currently at. In order to answer that question, they reviewed qualitative tourism research during the past decade (2007–2017), consisting of 1,541 qualitative papers across 51 journals. Their findings suggest that a large majority of contemporary qualitative tourism research is still at the early moments of qualitative research, that is, in the first three moments of qualitative research, and thereby 'still largely dominated by a positivist and postpositivist worldview' (Wilson et al., 2020: 800). Although the maturity and advancement of qualitative research in social science vary, most qualitative research is likely to reflect the early moments of its history in a similar way as tourism. (Of course, not all agree on characterizations such as 'maturity and advancement'. As most stick to the 'less mature and advanced' moments, they probably see much in the later moments as unscientific, fashion-oriented or in other ways expressing a problematic development.)

Second, although qualitative research certainly has become more diverse over the years, it appears (as noted in Chapter 1) that, at the same time, it has become more homogenous in the sense of an increased use of conventions and templates for how to conduct and report qualitative research (e.g. Abend et al., 2013; Hammersley, 2011; Langley & Abdallah, 2011; Reay et al., 2019). Hammersley (2011: 21), for example, notes that there has been an increased use of 'proceduralism' in qualitative research within the social sciences, which is based on the idea that 'good [qualitative research] practice amounts to following a set of rules that can be made explicit as a set of prescriptive dos and don'ts, or even in the form of recipes'. This is very much a matter of the increasingly dominant focus on journal article writing. The journal format varies, but dominant versions tend to drive researchers to a fairly homogenous format, counteracting the proliferation of the 'messy, uncertain, multivoiced texts' that Denzin and Lincoln (cited above) claim to be common. These are, and might be in the near future, rare, at least in the leading journals defining most of the social science fields.

An example of this homogenization is that the qualitative research process is mostly portrayed as linear within the reviewed methodology textbooks. As Knapp (2016) notes in his review, although the qualitative research process may vary quite a bit in practice, such as whether it is linear, iterative, structured or unstructured, it is predominantly portrayed as a more or less linear progression of steps that the researcher moves through until the desired knowledge is developed. This linear view becomes even more prominent in the reporting of qualitative studies in journal articles within the four different disciplines reviewed (sociology, psychology, management, education), in the following familiar linear fashion: introduction, literature review, conceptual framework, method, design, data collection and data analysis, results, and discussion. As Tourish (2020: 102) notes in regard to research texts in management journals, 'most papers follow this by now a very tired formula'. The anthropologists Foley and Valenzuela (2005: 224) write that dissertation committees, journal editors and others 'will press a young scholar to retain a pedantic, technical, academic, story-telling style. One's personal identity and professional success seem to depend upon mastering this peculiar form of self-expression.'

In other words, even though the actual practice of conducting (and reporting) qualitative research may be far more emergent, unstructured and iterative, which several researchers have pointed out (e.g. Knapp, 2016; Maxwell, 2012), the dominant convention seems to be that good (qualitative) research should be/is carried out (and reported) in a stepwise and recipe-like manner, largely mimicking the process of conducting (and reporting) quantitative research. Data tend to be addressed as robust and reliable, and most empirical studies we encounter show few indications of crises of representation. Instead, most report data such as interview statements as if these reflected the attitudes, perceptions and experiences of the subjects. There are few signs of the later moments suggested by Denzin and Lincoln in most research published in journals, according to our experience.

What this brief exposé of the historical context suggests is that the evolution of (qualitative) research in the social sciences is somewhat paradoxical. On the one hand, it is a highly varied and diverse field comprised by many different research orientations. On the other hand, we can witness an increased standardization of the (qualitative) research process in the social sciences, in terms of conventions and templates for how to conduct research. Certain metaphors for doing research thus seem to be dominant, while alternative, novel views are only present in the periphery. Also, many authors, perhaps preferring what Denzin and Lincoln refer to as moments three to five, appear to (be forced to) fall into research reporting styles of a more conventional type (Wray-Bliss, 2002). More broadly, one cannot stop wondering if the root problem to the increased homogenization of the (qualitative) research process is a never-ending confusion of the conventions and templates for social science with those of the natural sciences. Despite all the various moments and movements, there is a background norm of imitating the natural sciences that, at the end of the day, most researchers and champions of good science, in the form of journal editors and reviewers, try to live up to. Inspiration from the humanities or more free, independent thinking carry less weight by comparison.

ON REFLEXIVITY

Judging from the brief outline of the historical context and development of qualitative research, we seem to be in the contradictory situation of a rich and diverse wealth of options in terms of ontology, epistemology and method combined with a stronger grip of a template for doing and, in particular, publishing research. This invites reflexivity, on an individual as well as collective level. What do researchers do? What is really governing them (us)? How can this paradox of propagated variety and homogeneity co-exist? How do researchers try to navigate in this muddled and contradictory terrain, with mixed messages about research ideals?

Reflexivity is a buzzword and is used in many different ways. Authors have given different meanings to what reflexivity is in the context of research. It is commonly portrayed as a *source of awareness-raising for the researcher* (e.g. Finlay, 2002; Rivera, 2018), such as efforts to take into consideration how language is implicated in the construction of social reality (e.g. Gergen & Gergen, 1991; von Glasersfeld, 1991) and to find ways to deal with problematic issues of representation and writing (Richardson, 2000). Reflexivity can also involve attention to how one thinks about thinking in a broad sense (Maranhao, 1991), or be considered as a multidimensional interpretation of interpretations, where the researcher takes a step back and looks at his/her interpretations from another angle, based on an alternative perspective, challenging the one that the first interpretation is based on (Alvesson & Sköldberg, 2018). Dealings with contradictions, from diverse demands of sticking to the traditional formula and at the same time demonstrating creativity, novelty and showing an awareness of 'post-formulaic' views, trigger reflexivity.

However, reflexivity is perhaps most commonly regarded as a confessional account of one's own personal, possibly unconscious, reactions, reflecting the idea that the knower and knowledge cannot be separated and the relation between the two needs to be constantly assessed (Calás & Smircich, 1992). This is important, but also a rather narrow view of reflexivity. Our take on reflexivity focuses on the critical understanding of the roles of metaphors guiding the researcher in a number of respects during the research process. Below, we further unpack the notion of reflexivity by distinguishing five basic domains of reflexivity.

DOMAINS OF REFLEXIVITY: FIVE 'ISMS'

We identify five different domains on (self)reflexive examination of research in the literature: (i) researcher-knower focus and introspection; (ii) fieldwork experiences and mutual collaboration with research participants; (iii) emphasis on academics' paradigms, social conventions and politics; (iv) social critique; and (v) discursive deconstruction. These domains could be referred to as various 'isms' in reflexivity: me-ism (the researcher I), interaction-ism (encounters with the field/people being studied), we-ism (research community), criticism (societal problems) and discursivism (text work) (Alvesson et al., 2021; Finlay, 2002). All have a strong bearing on the doings and non-doings of specific forms of research. After this rush through various 'isms' signalling various versions of reflexivity ('reflexivisms'), let us go through each of them more carefully.

It appears that domain (i) *researcher-knower focus and introspection* (me-ism) is the most common preoccupation of reflexivist 'experts' and practitioners. In this domain, the researcher him- or herself becomes the focus of attention, often resulting in soul-searching and/or a confessional tale (Van Maanen, 1988). This kind of reflexivity is frequently regarded as motivating a confessional account of one's own personal, possibly non-conscious influences on research (Calás & Smircich, 1992). Key here is an interest in the researcher-knower him- or herself, his/her background, mood and various aspects of subjectivity. Many understand reflexivity, for example, 'as a strategy of using subjectivity to examine social and psychosocial phenomena, assuming that social discourses are inscribed in, and social practices are embodied by, the researcher'

(Kuehner et al., 2016: 699–700). Lather (1991: 129) means by reflexivity 'stories which bring the teller of the tale back into the narrative, embodied, desiring, invested in a variety of often contradictory privileges and struggles'. Sometimes reflexivity is discussed in the context of emotions (Rivera, 2018). How the researcher emotionally responds to issues, people, settings and dilemmas is highlighted and how s/he deals with various themes and concerns becomes the key thing in reflexivity. For some, 'strong reflexivity' 'pushes the idea of reflecting on the positionality, perspectivity and subjectivity of the researcher toward the extreme, as the researcher becomes not merely an *additional* subject of research, but its primary focus' (Ploder & Stadlbauer, 2016: 753). Sometimes this almost leads to a neglect of the world out there, which can't be separated from the researcher-knower becoming the chief subject and the main character of the story.

We, of course, recognize the relevance and significance of a researcher-subject focus view on reflexivity. No research is conducted without a human subject. This is crucial for the individual researcher in his/her work. Research is in many ways an individualistic (or small group) enterprise in terms of everything from asking research questions and selecting literature, carrying out interviews and making observations to doing analysis and the writing of research texts. But even though the individual is central and a self-evident focus for reflexivity, we see this as only one of several possible loci for the thinking through and challenging of what a research project is about. The term me-ism gives a warning about the risk for narcissistic self-indulgence, easily leading to a rather narrow and limiting form of reflexivity. It may blind or at least discourage the researcher from considering taken-for-granted, broader social forces impacting the research, making the unique, subjective researcher less as a theme or vehicle for reflexivity.

Sometimes the reflexivity domain (ii) *fieldwork experiences and mutual collaboration with research participants* (interaction-ism) is seen as a source of awareness-raising or facilitator in navigations and interactions in the field (e.g. Finlay, 2002; Rivera, 2018). Here the researcher-me may be downplayed as much of the attention is directed to what goes on in the field, involving many others, and therefore not reducible to the individual researcher. The acts and responses of those the researcher interacts with are central here, but of course the researcher is part of this. Qualitative research is very much a matter of interaction between researchers and participants, particularly in cases where the research aims for richer and deeper accounts of research phenomena, which require close contact with participants. Some researchers talk about the co-construction of research, emphasizing participants as much or more than suppliers of data.

That participants may have their own ideas and expectations as well as an interest in affecting the research outcome calls for careful consideration. The same also applies to the assumptions and sensemaking of the people being studied. Parker (2000) discovered that some of his interviewees saw him as a student, others as an expert and a third group as a management spy. This source of uncertainty and sometimes very selective answers are not well considered by the researcher focusing on his/her way of doing the research.

Jorgenson (1991) reports that her interviews about how interviewees saw 'family' changed when she became visibly pregnant later in the research process. The solution is not just to appear neutral and ask clearly structured questions or engage in extensive 'me-ism'. In other words, the researcher should not only pay attention to the data that interviewees or observed participants deliver, but also to what is beyond their situated responses. The latter is partly a matter of the researcher–participant interactions and how research results may be an effect of these more than simply participants' reports about reality (experiences, orientations, identities, etc.).

Some researchers are very concerned about how the researcher views and treats the participants as well as how their voices are being represented (Rhodes & Carlsen, 2018). These researcher–participant interactions and relations are a crucial domain for reflexivity, particularly regarding the politics and ethics of the realities of the groups being studied. It is something that has been a central topic for studies of ethnic groups and women and how they may have a voice in the representation of them and their interests (e.g. Bishop, 2005; Olesen, 2000).

Behind the individual researcher – being visible, self-aware and inclined to tell stories from his/her perspective – and local interactions with participants we find strong social, cultural and political forces associated with the research school and tradition s/he is part of and typically forms the researcher and guides thinking and acting. This is addressed by the reflexivity domain (iii) *emphasis on academics' paradigms, social conventions and politics* (we-ism). As Bernstein (1983) pointed out, the core of relativism – knowledge being an outcome of a selective viewpoint, constructed within a particular framing – is less a matter of the individual researcher's 'subjectivity' and more a matter of the paradigmatic convictions of a specific research group or community, agreeing within themselves about a particular set of 'truths'. 'Objectivity' is often simply a matter of shared beliefs and conventions within a specific group. Much research in an area looks more or less the same, particularly within a specific research stream, with its institutionalized and mainstream-affecting worldview, key references, vocabularies, methods and conventions for writing. We all belong to specific communities, often demanding adaptations and a high degree of conformism. We have referred to this as research boxes and academic tribes (Alvesson & Sandberg, 2014) and will come back to this in Chapter 5. As shown above, and also across specific research groups, there are several dominant institutionalized forces that lead much research to look the same in terms of overall templates for writing, but also in the doing of research. The key point for reflexivity, then, is not the individual researcher, the me, or even the field experience with relations to research objects or participants, but the social, political and cognitive aspects of the *we* that the researcher is part of and that often drive us into conformism.

The reflexivity domain (iv) *social critique* (societal problems) moves beyond the researcher, his/her interaction with those studied and the academic group and considers the larger societal and cultural setting. Such reflexivity then addresses not so much the 'we-ism' academic subtribe as broader, societal culturally and politically carried truths. As social scientists we are part of society and constrained by it. We also can't avoid either accepting and reproducing or questioning and disrupting those part of society or people in it that we study. The gendered nature of certain truths and methods, the ongoing identity politics, the domination of neo-colonial thinking, the link between power and knowledge – where knowledge involves the ordering and normalization of the world – are examples of key themes for social critical reflexivity. So is the pressure to be politically correct, to use the prescribed language and to embrace the social standard solution for societal improvement: for example, more education, diversity, innovation, leadership.

Some of the mentioned themes are part of the academic field, including paradigms, social conventions and research politics, associated with groups and coalitions. Others are of a broader, societal nature, where the research projects tend to bear heavy imprints on the preferred social myths of our time. A career in gender studies can, for example, risk not being successful without the researcher being strongly guided by and adapting to social norms for how to address gender at a specific time.

Timely topics like sustainability, innovation, entrepreneurship, ethnicity, globalization, digitalization and sexual orientation tend also to be studied in ways that rarely go against what institutionalized or trend-changing truths and recipes indicate. Reflexivity is then less about the adventures of the individual researcher, the school or other social groups of which the researcher is a member, or the specifics of fieldwork interactions and other 'local' issues than about responses (or resistance) to the broader, mainly 'extra-academic' societal issues and discourses constituting the institutions, ideologies, interests and identities in which knowledge work is immersed. Research may sometimes study the *Zeitgeist* with critical distance, but this calls for a struggle, as the researcher is often heavily influenced by it, and may express and reinforce it rather than studying it. Reflexivity then moves beyond the local ('we') version of the research community and addresses how the researcher and project are constituted within a forcefield of dominant and alternative social logics, including macro-cultural and political patterns.

The final reflexivity domain is (v) *discursive deconstruction* (deconstructivism). Much of reflexivity literature is, however, less about the researcher subjectivity and more about the general awareness of discourse, how we work with language, and produce texts through which we construct reality (e.g. Gergen & Gergen, 1991; von Glasersfeld, 1991). The specifics of metaphors in textwork are of interest here and are more of an exclusive concern than in the other reflexive domains. Issues of representation and writing become central (Richardson, 2000). How is reality being represented? The ideal of research mapping the social world or the research process is seen as naïve, and any kind of trying to tell it as it is – or even people's experiences, motives, narrations, etc. – becomes problematic and a key issue for reflexivity. Discourse analysis emphasizes that through language people – researchers as well as mortals – engage in constructing the social world, making any representation a matter of researcher's choice more than a reflection of the phenomenon 'out there'. Language is performative: it creates an effect. At least sometimes.

There are three important aspects to this (Potter & Wetherell, 1987). First, people – participants in studies as well as researchers – are producing texts, that is, actively creating accounts on the basis of previously existing linguistic resources. Second, they are continually and actively involved in selecting some of the infinite numbers of words and meaning constructions available, and in rejecting others. Third, the chosen construction has its consequences: the mode of expression has an effect, it influences ideas, generates responses, and so on. The performative nature of language leads to a greater reflexive interest in the crafting of research publications and the sociopolitics of getting work into a state such that it becomes accepted and published.

These domains or 'isms' can, of course, not be strictly separated, nor do they represent fixed states but rather dynamic situation-specific reflexivity considerations. Many scholars working actively with reflexivity also pay attention to more than one or even several of these versions. Reflexivity in research calls for reasonable attention to at least some of the isms, and at least some occasional consideration of all the 'isms' (and perhaps others). The way a researcher engages in his/her reflexive enterprise – irrespective of a more precise focus or 'mixed' attention – requires careful consideration and often implies privileging one domain over the other without losing sight of the bigger picture. It is often hard to be reflexive on all fronts at the same time, and often there is one overall key theme, leading to other aspects entering more indirectly or modestly. Sometimes the researcher may focus on criticism and then consider how societal ideologies and interests also affect the researcher me and we. On other occasions a focus on we-reflexivity may involve careful consideration about norms and conventions for researcher–participant interactions and/or how one adheres to dominant formulas for using language and producing socially compliant research results and text.

DE-FAMILIARIZATION

A central way of working with reflexivity is through the principle or method of 'de-familiarization'. The concept signals an effort to detach oneself from one's self, one's own culture, research tradition, favourite theory and normalized way of thinking and relating (Alvesson & Deetz, 2021). Müller (2016: 706) refers to this as 'strong reflexivity': 'The researcher-subject is transgressed in the sense that the researcher deliberately tries to break with her own life-world reality as a member of the field.' The researcher's preferred discourse or social theory as well as group membership are also themes that one could try to turn into something strange, foreign and exotic. For example, if one belongs to a research field that celebrates 'leadership' or is obsessed by 'gender', one can de-familiarize oneself from these fields by viewing them as something partly odd and foreign. Why all this leadership? What does it really mean? Can't people be self-motivated, perhaps with some support from administration? Or why is gender highlighted all the time? Are all people consistently busy placing themselves and others into gender categories, perhaps over-doing gender? Perhaps most people are relaxed about gender, while gender research-ers see and highlight gender everywhere? And, typically, with a persistent assumption about females being disadvantaged all the time?

Self-estrangement is difficult but possible. One may engage in role-playing and posi-tioning, or reading literature or talking with people who are outside one's usual habitat and, through that, generate some self-distancing. The key element here is simply to try to avoid the habitual ways of experiencing, thinking about and referring to phenomena – and to one's self and group. This is of course not easy, but some success is not impossible for the skilled, reflexivity-minded researcher. (For ideas of how to do boxed-out research, see Alvesson & Sandberg, 2014.) With de-familiarization the researcher can take an impor-tant step in avoiding being caught in conventions and a constraining view of self, group, society, language use and ways of relating to participants in research.

De-familiarization as a way of doing reflexivity can be related to the individual researcher and how s/he is the central character in the reflexivity story, to broader para-digmatic, social and critical issues guiding and being imprinted in research, associated with the researcher-collective ('we'), as well as broader societal and cultural themes (and possible critique). For example, we-ism, the research community, may be the topic of de-familiarization through seeing one's friends, colleagues and network contacts as a for-eign tribe, clan, sect, chain-gang or whatever. (We address these metaphors in Chapter 5.) Through seeing one's research community not only as a positive social force but also as a source of social and intellectual constraint, an inclination to conformism and to think as others may be counteracted.

De-familiarization can also be applied on fieldwork experiences and how the researcher–participants interaction can be played out and understood. Rather than relating to partici-pants in habitual, familiar ways, it is possible to approach them differently and openly. Standard categories – decision, resistance, professional, woman, ethnic groups – can be avoided. One may see human subjects as acting more like robots or carriers of non-predictable or open social templates (discourses, roles, habitus) or cultural orientations (the culture of narcissism, the risk society), avoiding defining people prematurely as gendered, etc. In terms of the detailed issues around language and representation, the researcher-author may show how texts can be opened up through re-interpretations, try to engage in estrangement writing or simply select some linguistic, social, political and theoretical issues for reflexivity.

All this may sound very complicated and demanding, but a lot of this is already being done by many thoughtful researchers, not being religiously caught in their favourite boxes of methods, truths and conventions. Thinking more carefully about issues for concern and considering options may strengthen the work.

CHAPTER SUMMARY

Let us try to summarize reflexive research, as we have defined it in this chapter. As we see it, the overall point of reflexivity is attentive consideration and critical reflection of how assumptions and frameworks guide the construction and writing of empirical material and theoretical ideas in doing research. Researchers' interpretations often take the front-stage in research, but the trick for reflexivity is to (temporarily) break out of our habitual use of our favourite framework and tribe-guided way of interpreting phenomena. Re-interpretations or anti-interpretations are then significant, and not just another, similar feminist, Foucauldian, Frankfurt school or whatever mode of ordering and fixing the material. Working with alternative metaphors that encourage mind-stretching, comparisons and confrontations may be valuable here, as this book tries to demonstrate.

We suggest five domains for reflexivity: the researcher-me, the research collective-we, the interaction with research participants, the societal context and the discourses materialized in research language and text. These are obviously not completely separated, but still offer a fairly distinct alternative focus for reflexivity. Prioritizing one leads to the downplaying of the others. We can't address everything.

All this reflexivity does not, of course, prevent the doing of research that is qualified and rigorous with solid backup of credible empirical inquiry. On the contrary, the latter calls for more than careful data management and reflexivity may support a less mechanistic and more careful way of dealing with empirical material. A central element here is the utmost awareness of the theoretical assumptions, the importance of language and pre-understanding, all of which constitute major determinants of the interpretation. Being reflexive then means more than just trying to reflect. It 'means looking at one's own reflection on the mirror, but with a detached attitude, taking the reflection as potentially criticisable' (Müller, 2016: 710). It all calls for, and may lead to, at least an element of de-familiarization. There is an element of disruption of the social world as we know it, emerging from careful reflexivity. In the course of this book, we will indicate some reflexive levels and principles, which we hold can be integrated into and stimulate empirical research.

4

REFLEXIVITY AND METAPHORS IN COMBINATION

Having described the notions of metaphors and reflexivity in research more broadly, the aim of this chapter is to bring them together to form the basis for our metaphor framework of RP. Reflexivity is to a significant degree a matter of directing attention to the assumptions, frameworks and language that we work with and which guide our interpretations. Much of this goes beyond what specific metaphorical expressions in texts can capture, but the root metaphor level offers a reasonably clear, distinct and manageable way of dealing with these broader aspects. Working with metaphors may sharpen reflexivity at the same time as reflexive exercises may lead to the clarification of metaphors in use and trigger ideas for new metaphors. We thus see *metaphorical reflexivity* as a good combination of resources for generating 'better' and, in particular, more creative research.

Metaphors illuminate the partial and, in a sense, the arbitrary ways in which we approach phenomena and research ideas. The very idea of metaphor and the formulation of metaphors remind the researcher of the significance of perspectives and imagination. As Brown (1976: 173) writes, 'the logical, empirical or psychological absurdity of metaphor thus has a specifically cognitive function: it makes us stop in our tracks and examine it'. Through the active and conscious use of metaphors it becomes obvious that there are alternative ways of conceptualizing and relating to a phenomenon. This is often best indicated by other metaphors. Such awareness forces or, at least, encourages the researcher to be reflexive of this: to realize that the phenomenon under scrutiny is formulated in a specific way – not The Way – and that there are alternatives.

At the same time, reflexivity suggests a careful consideration of the social, cultural and theoretical forces that are in operation and direct attention to the images or metaphors that play key roles in these aforementioned forces. The ideal of reflexivity makes it difficult to stick to just one metaphor – or to avoid thinking about the existence and centrality of governing images. Reflexivity thus means – or at least in principle can mean – awareness and exploration of the researcher's metaphors, both for the phenomenon under study and for his/her self-understanding and the research community's role in forming this understanding. Such reflexivity may involve considerable effort, particularly if the metaphor is taken for granted, which is arguably often the case – as we will try to show in this book. Reflexivity thus includes awareness of the metaphor used and with this also a possible opening up for considerations of alternatives. The conscious efforts to find or develop metaphors (or images) that can supplement or challenge one's (the research community's) favourite metaphor(s) are key here.

This is not to say that metaphors are the only way to work with reflexivity and, similarly, you can develop insights about metaphors without being specifically reflexive (in the ways covered above). The creative person may more or less spontaneously come up with alternative metaphors – or ideas formulated in other ways than as metaphors. There are other ways of working with reflexivity than through framing the project explicitly through metaphors. In fact, few people who are into reflexivity directly or explicitly address metaphors. Many are implicit about metaphor use, as well as about the reflexivity metaphor(s) itself (themselves). However, as we have argued and will try to show in this book as a whole, metaphors and reflexivity are natural bedfellows and can support each other.

LIVE, ZOMBIE AND DEAD METAPHORS

Using metaphors for creating more imaginative and novel research does not mean we regard rigour as unimportant. Rigour, broadly speaking, is always critical in research, but it is not the only issue of importance. By metaphorizing RP (the research process), we want to loosen up and challenge some of the current forms of rigidity and standardization (i.e. conventions and templates) of carrying out research within social studies. Sometimes rigour is confused with conservatism and conventionalism. Rigour is then more 'pseudo-rigour' than careful and tight reasoning. One example of such confusion is careful inductive data management work that uncritically treats data as building blocks or reliable inputs for the research project (i.e. without considering the value and relevance of these data for particular knowledge claims). A key reason for this rigidity is that the current tunnel vision of the research process is underpinned by a huge set of 'dead' or 'frozen' metaphors, that is, metaphors that are no longer understood as metaphors but have been taken for granted and have assumed a self-evident, literal meaning. As Brown (1976: 175) describes it:

> Just because pungent and connotatively rich metaphors stick in our minds when first encountered, a process of sedimentation tends to occur, until the metaphor is no longer seen as a creation of the imagination. It becomes instead simply a name or description.

Common expressions for RP elements, such as 'theory-building', 'data collection', 'design' and 'codification', are often treated not as metaphors but as precise representations of specific research activities. Most people, if encouraged to think about it, probably realize that these are metaphors, so they are not totally taken for granted when people are in a reflective mood. But a lot of work seems still to be carried out without much concern for what is illuminated and what is lost by the use of these images. Richardson (2000: 524) emphasizes the task of avoiding the endless re-cycling of aged or dead metaphors:

> Using old, worn out metaphors, although easy and comfortable, after a while invites stodginess and stiffness. The stiffer you get, the less flexible you are. You invite being ignored. In less metaphoric terms, if your writing is clichéd, you will not stretch your imagination (ouch! Hear the cliché! Hear the cliché of me pointing out the cliché!) and you will bore people.

It is possible here to point out a spectrum of various ways of relating to the metaphors in use. Much is on a continuum between the alive and kicking and the stone-dead metaphors. In between live metaphors, feeding into thinking and imagination, and dead, being taken entirely as given as the metaphorical quality is lost, we have the zombies, the living dead or half-dead. Social research is perhaps even more populated by *zombie* metaphors than live or dead ones. In the latter case – and for people totally caught in a mindset where metaphorization is an alien project – this book is probably not of much interest. But we hope to reach the zombies: both academics and students with some potential interest in the subject matter and the metaphors that are typically addressed – also by otherwise metaphor-interested researchers – in a way where the literal and taken-for-granted nature of the metaphors tend to dominate their use. Gap-filling, data collection, saturation and story-telling are examples. (We will show this later.) We should add that most researchers, including ourselves, are sometimes zombies in relation to some metaphors, as it is difficult to be consistently sensitive to these. Often it is good to turn the metaphor-autopilot on and move along in a zombie-like way. But too much of auto-piloting work means a lack of reflexivity and boxed-in research. The trick is to have reflexive periods, moments or loops where the auto-pilot is switched off and selected versions of me-ism, interactionism, we-ism, criticism and discursivism, together with de-familiarization, are on the agenda.

By reminding ourselves of taken-for-granted metaphors, we can become more (self-) critical and receptive to alternatives and, thus, find new ways of doing research. The point here is of course not that dead or taken-for-granted metaphors always indicate 'bad' ways of doing research. In many cases we have to accept taken-for-granted metaphors and metaphorical expressions as given, as roughly reflecting reality, and/or as practical and useful. Instead, the problem is that they are 'too much' into operation or miss significant issues which means that the disregard of their metaphorical quality leads to the freezing of our understanding rather than stimulating imagination and reflexivity.

In order to selectively wake up and become aware of such 'dead' or 'half-dead' metaphors and loosen up their grip on the way we think about and do research, generating counter-metaphors is key; meaning that our task is not a conservative one of reproducing what is out there (in contemporary texts), but to stimulate imagination, creativity and rethinking. In order to accomplish this, we generate a range of tensions between common and alternative metaphors. Such a reflexive metaphorical approach can be formulated in dialectical terms: starting point, negation and transcendence. The starting point is the common (and often taken-for-granted) metaphorical views on elements of RP held by the researcher and/or his or her field. Thereafter, one or several more or less radically different metaphors (from the one embraced by the researcher and/or her community) are invoked, followed by a confrontation with a set of these metaphorical views of the targeted RP elements against each other. The set should offer mind-stretch and means a challenge. This then aims to generate new and imaginative ideas about the elements and how to work with them.

SUPPORTING REFLEXIVE METAPHOR WORK: A KALEIDOSCOPE OF RP METAPHORS

We address in Chapters 5–8 the following key elements which are usually seen as central characteristics of the RP (research process): overall point of research, researcher's role, literature review, research phenomenon, literature review, theory, design, method, data, analysis, writing and contributions. Using these elements as a basis, we point out dominant or at least common metaphors and less common ones underlying the meanings of those elements, generating a spectrum of imaginative options of what RP is basically about. We begin metaphorizing more conventional understandings and then add alternative views of the RP elements. The key point is not that the latter is 'better' than the former, as all kinds of metaphors are potentially useful (and at the same time problematic). Their usefulness is related to the research project and the individual researcher (as well as research group and the fieldwork/study site's characteristics). The idea is that a set of suggested alternative metaphors, as well as general inspiration for developing new ones, may encourage reflexivity and less predictable and convention-bound ways to conduct and report research studies. Our aim is therefore not to provide a recipe for an alternative way of conducting research but to work on a meta-level. We promote this meta-level work through suggesting a *kaleidoscope* of RP metaphors, which has the capacity to generate a variety of novel patterns and angles for carrying out more imaginative research and writing more stimulating research texts.

A kaleidoscope is a cylinder consisting of one section of mirrors attached together at specific angles, and then another section of objects such as coloured pieces of glass. When looking into it and rotating it, the kaleidoscope generates a large variety of new and shifting patterns and images due to the reflections off the mirrors. In a similar way as the real kaleidoscope, our kaleidoscope of RP metaphors consists of two interrelated sections: one section of interrelated metaphors and another section of elements of the research processes. (In other words, we equate/liken the RP metaphors to the kaleidoscope's coloured glass.) When looking into it, the kaleidoscope of metaphors has the potential to generate several new and novel patterns and images of RP, due to the interactions among the RP metaphors. As Gunning (1997: 32) noted, Brewster [the inventor of the kaleidoscope] praised his invention as a labour-saving, art-making machine which would 'create in an hour, what a thousand artists could not invent in the course of a year'. Of course, in research we do not accomplish much in an hour or sometimes even a year, but rethinking our projects in a distinct way may save some time and effort, although the main advantage is less predictable and repetitive research projects and outcomes.

ON WORKING WITH A SPECTRUM OF METAPHORS

In evaluating research, a clear framework, logic and structure are often asked for. The researcher is supposed to live up to expectations and deliver accordingly. This is reasonable but can easily be taken too far (Alvesson & Gabriel, 2013). Order and consistency are typically not the best way to support creativity and variation. The ideal that a new idea or image is 'built' from something or follows a more or less linear trajectory from a starting point (data, literature) to an end (contribution) is often misleading. This is because such linear thinking imposes or at least encourages an un-creative or un-imaginative logic on research (at least in the written text) and, thus, risks leading to un-interesting studies and research texts having little of novelty to offer. Creative work often calls for frictions and breakdowns, doubts and rethinking. It is seldom a smooth route where free-floating brainstorming effortlessly leads to novel ideas.

Avoiding standard categories

Therefore, in order to provide an alternative, we do not metaphorize the RP elements in terms of some standard categories showing an overview of traditions, such as neo-positivism, interpretivism, critical theory and poststructuralism (Alvesson & Sköldberg, 2018) or positivism, post-positivism, critical theory and constructivism (Guba & Lincoln, 1994). Nor do we systematically demonstrate where the metaphors come from or their existence (i.e. that existing texts in the social science literature provide a textual basis for claiming that just these metaphors represent/highlight dominant ideas). Some metaphors have a clear origin, others have not. Neither do we offer a recipe or formula for the design and use of a set of metaphors that fit together. Doing this would not only be time- and space-consuming, but also offer little in terms of insights about how to create more imaginative ways of rethinking key elements in the RP. Nor do we want to promote fit or alignment. The creative component calls for other qualities than systematics, rigour and coherence – even though these qualities are necessary to consider, not necessarily to pri- oritize, when it comes to actually working with or applying the metaphors. Working with creativity calls for some steering away from narrow and prescriptive research. Similarly, we do not describe or analyse in detail the meaning of a metaphor. Metaphors appeal to imagination and associations and should not be targeted for dissection.

The challenge for imagination-stimulating and innovative work with metaphors is twofold: to unmask metaphors that have become myths/dead/zombies and to create new metaphors.

> It not only demands that we say 'no' to the organization of experience as it is given to us in pre-ordained categories; it also requires us to rearrange cognition into new forms and associations. ... New metaphors, especially elaborated into models and theories, are not merely new ways of looking at the facts, nor are they revelations of what the facts really are. Rather, the metaphor in a fundamental way creates the facts, provides a definition of the essential quality of what an experience must be. (Brown, 1976: 176)

Qualitative research, then, can be seen very much as a matter of metaphor work. The skilful and reflexive use of metaphors in thinking and writing is the key to good research craftmanship. This is particular the case regarding qualitative research because, as Aspers and Corte (2019: 155) note, qualitative research is essentially about 'making new significant distinctions' that lead to 'improved understanding novel to the schol- arly community'. Making new distinctions often involves high mastery of metaphors: to think through them, learn their meaning and the repository of ideas that follows with them, as well as acknowledging their advantages and disadvantages – what they allow or encourage us to consider and what are being missed or disregarded. A metaphor is often difficult to use; it is not simply a matter of picking or producing one and then apply- ing it in research. Demolition work, to take an example of a radical problematization of research, is not just being an elephant in a china store or boarding a bulldozer and then ramming the target: it calls for the careful and skilled situation-sensitive application of the theoretical and methodological sledge-hammers at hand for (or to be produced by) the demolition researcher. Some level of brutalism may be called for, but demolition as a metaphor for research – in opposition to research as building knowledge – includes a degree of surgical precision.

Our main point in this book, however, is not to facilitate expertise in the use of a specific conception of research, as it is played out in various stages or operations of the research process. Instead, we are interested in pointing at the variation of possibilities and to encourage new metaphors. In this sense we are anti-expertise – eager to counter inclinations to go too deeply into a specific metaphor, irrespective of whether it is finding a gap in the literature or working with the text based on the conduit metaphor, where the author seeks to transport communication in a noise-minimizing way. (More about these views below.)

Dialectics vs. smorgasbord vs. supermarket

We now address how we, on an overall meta-level, can see the use of metaphors as proposed here. In this regard, the kaleidoscope can be seen as a *super-metaphor* in that it is our master metaphor for metaphor work. At the lowest level, we have the *metaphors of RP elements*, such as data as building blocks. But in between these two levels, we have *meta-metaphors*, which are metaphors for how we combine and work with metaphors of RP elements, within the overall framing of the kaleidoscope. Below we discuss three possible meta-metaphors for how we can combine a plurality of metaphors of RP elements, indicating that our encouragement of working with a spectrum of metaphors can take various forms.

One possibility is a *dialectical* view – the *play of antipodes*. Dialectics means work with negations. The logic means that some dominating understandings (metaphors) are identified and, if necessary, made explicit and then efforts to negate them lead to alternative, opposite metaphors. In the next step, there may be a synthesis, so that there is an interaction effect between the dominant or 'first' metaphor and the negation, leading to something new emerging. All according to the classical formula of dialectics: thesis, antithesis and synthesis. But dialectics can also be seen as a kind of ping-pong game, where every move is calling for a new and often different response, not necessarily to the great synthesis, but ending with a powerful smash or clever stop-ball, encouraged by the hits of the opposing position. One example could be to consider and confront the common image of research as knowledge building – aiming to produce positive knowledge (e.g. finding patterns) – with an opposite image, research as knowledge demolition – aiming to problematize existing knowledge (e.g. indicating false patterns, ambiguities behind claimed certainties). The result could be a robust, re-constructed building, withstanding the sledge-hammer, or a selective destruction of something that is shown to be incapable of withstanding critique and thus leading to radical rethinking.

Another possibility is the *smorgasbord* approach. Here the emphasis is on the variety and choice, not a dominant view and a counterview standing in oppositional relation.

The smorgasbord should offer a fairly rich variety of options, encouraging free choice. A smorgasbord is still restricted and thought through so that the variety forms a sort of integrated whole. There should be variety but not mess. There is also a limited selection of well-balanced possibilities: a spectrum or set of metaphors making a good combination of ideas that together encourage and facilitate reflexivity and informed choices.

One may also talk about a *supermarket* approach: here things are less restricted and ordered, everything is up for grabs (purchase) and a more complete set of options are there for the researcher to choose between. The supermarket version means less of a careful consideration of the whole and more of a free supply of a large variety of options. The greater supply the better, given of course a reasonably high level of relevance and value as well as restrictions, partly by available metaphors and the imagination of the metaphor producer, but also in terms of numbers and overview. Excess is to be avoided.

Underlying all this is a consumer metaphor for how to think about metaphors and metaphorical options. The book is not advocating a specific research style or set of instructions for how to deal with methodology, but offers a range of options, both in terms of how to generally relate to the use of metaphors or images in research – dialectics, smorgasbord or supermarket offer a range of mindsets and imaginaries – and in terms of specific metaphors to consider at various stages of research. If we advocate anything in this book it is reflexivity, pluralism and imagination. In other writings we have suggested distinct methodologies for doing research broadly in line with our suggested metaphor approach (Alvesson, 2002; Alvesson & Deetz, 2021; Alvesson & Kärreman, 2011; Alvesson & Sandberg, 2013a; Alvesson & Sköldberg, 2018).

The three options have various advantages and disadvantages. Dialectics offer more of thought structure and firm intellectual support but may limit the imagination of the person who is supposed to be inspired – as there is a specific order/logic and it is easy to be caught within this. The supermarket offers variety but also potential chaos and confusion, and calls for more work to get an overview and put something cognitively supportive together. Too much of a supermarket may encourage superficiality – and overconsumption of everything so freely offered (Reed, 1990). The smorgasbord offers something in between, providing a rich but also carefully chosen and constrained variety.

We have chosen something in between dialectics and smorgasbord meta-metaphor – the 'dialectical smorgasbord' (to use a really odd expression); but we also give some space for the supermarket option. The alternative metaphors typically offer some form of negation of, or counter-thinking to, the dominant ones. If we take data as an example, a dominant metaphor of data as 'mirrors' of reality is confronted with alternative metaphors of data as 'fairly free-floating representations'. Our expectation is that the structure and number of alternative metaphors means a requisite variety, where readers are encouraged to think of options and of variations without facing too many options, and thereby mess. In order to open up further for free and alternative thinking, we also briefly mention some additional metaphors or images in line with the supermarket ideal.

In this book, we will therefore work with all the meta-metaphors: dialectics, smorgasbord and supermarket, although with an emphasis on the 'dialectical smorgasbord'. Kaleidoscope is an overall image, a meta-meta category. We apologize for the complexity – and perhaps illustrate the problem with metaphor mania, that is, a tendency to be too fond of metaphors and the playing and overuse of these.

CHAPTER SUMMARY AND WAY FORWARD

We see reflexivity and metaphor work as bedfellows, giving rise to metaphorical reflexivity. In combination, metaphors support reflexivity and reflexivity encourages the use of a limited or broad spectrum of metaphorical options. The reflexivity ideal stimulates awareness of established metaphors and a willingness to consider and/or develop new ones. Considerations of how me, we, fieldwork interactions, societal pressures and discourse are handled in research may aid dealings with metaphors at the same time as access to a variety of metaphors may challenge frozen notions of me, we, etc. An interest in metaphors adds to reflexivity, among other things, through sharpened awareness of the partiality of a specific image of the phenomena being studied and how the various parts of the RP is being seen. At the same time, too much enthusiasm for metaphors – both the general idea of using metaphors for illuminating alternative ways of thinking and specific metaphors – may also counter reflexivity. It is easy to be seduced by appealing metaphors and then one forgets thinking about them critically.

Reflexivity should limit people being seduced by particular metaphors and see these as necessarily superior ones – although enthusiasm in a particular project where the researcher feels s/he has got a great idea may be laudable. There is obviously a grey area between enthusiasm and getting caught in one idea or way of imagining research. Getting too enthusiastic about and getting stuck in one metaphor as well as indecisively flipping around and superficially embracing a varied set of appealing metaphors may both obstruct good research.

We view the kaleidoscope as a super meta-metaphor for our approach. The idea is that through the use of alternative metaphors in different parts of the research process the researcher will be able to produce more interesting studies and texts as well as research results being perhaps less predictable and boring than what is common. To develop and consider a spectrum of metaphor possibilities is important here. The spectrum may be seen as the play of antipodes, as a smorgasbord or a supermarket. The researcher can combine the overall metaphor of kaleidoscope with any or a combination of these.

Needless to say, most researchers have ontological and epistemological commitments that constrain the possible range of what they find acceptable or useful metaphors. At the same time, most researchers are not religiously tied only to a narrow way of seeing the world, but can consider at least some alternative viewpoints. Different projects may also lead to somewhat different paradigmatic standpoints. Sometimes there may be good reasons to emphasize clear findings and results. In other cases, ambiguities and complexities in the empirical material may encourage a more constructionist positioning. Many, if not most, researchers are also interested in producing more imaginative, original and impactful research.

Perhaps you, as the reader, find all this (too) demanding and complicated? It may lead to mental overload and confusion. We would then like to remind you that the purpose of this book is to encourage imagination and choice, and this calls for some effort and for attaining a multitude of inspirations, and to encourage varied consideration. As a reader, you are not expected to learn and employ everything, but to carefully consider what seems to work for you. Metaphors always have a context and situational quality, and function in relationship to specific people, with their background, mindsets, associations and imaginations, and specific settings. The selective use of the concepts and ideas above may sometimes make full sense.

The next step: metaphorizing the research process

In Chapter 1 we made the case that the dominant conventions and templates for conducting and reporting (qualitative) research not only enable, but also constrain, researchers' imagination, creativity and innovative abilities for developing more interesting and impactful knowledge. With domination follows taken-for-grantedness, which often constrains our ability to conduct research. As said, a central aim in this book is therefore to unsettle these conventions and templates. We do so by identifying and challenging the metaphors underlying them, and based on that, generate a set of alternative metaphors that enables researchers to be more imaginative and creative in research. As a first step in achieving this aim, we outlined in Chapters 2–4 the basis of our metaphor framework. In the next four chapters (Chapters 5–8) we will apply this reflexive-metaphor basis to identify and articulate the often taken-for-granted metaphors underlying the key elements of the research process, and to propose alternative metaphors that can be used to guide various parts of the research.

Our metaphorization of the research process is based on a broad reading and more concentrated readings of predominantly qualitative research methods in the social sciences. Our broad reading consists of both having taught research methods for over 25 years, acted as reviewers for numerous research studies in the social sciences, and written extensively about research methods. Our more targeted readings consist predominantly of a review of six leading standard methodology textbooks across four disciplines within social science: management and organization studies (Symon & Cassell, 2012), psychology (Willig, 2011), sociology (Hesse-Biber & Leavy, 2011) and education (Hatch, 2002) as well as more general social science and- and textbooks on qualitative research

(Denzin & Lincoln, 1994; Flick, 2018; Miles & Huberman, 1994). We review them with a specific focus on how they portray the process of qualitative research and its main elements. Moreover, as a way to investigate in greater detail how (qualitative) researchers commonly report their research in journals, we reviewed 16 journal articles across the four disciplines above. In order to capture possible differences in reporting style, we selected articles from four US journals (*American Journal of Sociology*, *Journal of Applied Psychology*, *American Educational Research Journal* and *Academy of Management Journal*) and four European journals (*Sociology*, *British Journal of Social Psychology*, *Learning and Instruction* and *Organization Studies*). Given that the literature on research methods in social science is now very large and is still growing rapidly (e.g. Hammersley, 2011), we are aware that our broader reading and specific review only covers a tiny fraction of that literature. Still, we think it captures reasonably well the (dominant) conventions and templates that underlie the (qualitative) research process in social science.

Although the literature varies somewhat regarding what elements make up the qualitative research process, most include the following elements: point of research, role of researcher, research collective, phenomenon, literature review, theory, design, method, data collection and analysis, writing and contribution. These elements can in turn be categorized into four broader groups of elements, namely grounding, framing, processing and delivering elements.

Generally speaking, dividing up RP in clear stages or elements is always a bit arbitrary as most things tend to hang together. Such a dividing-up may also reinforce a specific, far from unproblematic formula for doing and reporting studies in journals. Even though strictly separating different elements may be problematic, we find it useful for our purpose in this book. Of course, this does not mean that we suggest that the reader should follow our conservative structure in this book. Our purpose is to identify options and to encourage mind-stretching regarding conventional views of the RP elements, although these views may be combined, addressed differently or sometimes even skipped by the creative researcher. A good idea, for example, may be to skip the literature review and bombardments of references, and instead mention relevant literatures more economically at various places in the paper, dissertation or other texts where it is motivated.

Nevertheless, the subsequent four chapters in Part II are structured as follows. We begin by providing a brief overview and definition of the RP element in question, followed by an identification of some established and *dominant* metaphors underlying it. We thereafter propose a set of less common but still established metaphors as an *alternative* to show how they enable us to see the RP elements in a different light. Finally, we briefly point out (without elaborating) a set of *additional* metaphors that suggest still other, but more esoteric views of the RP elements in question. We identify additional metaphors mainly (i) to give readers not entirely satisfied with more 'established' alternative metaphors (to use a somewhat paradoxical characterization) some further reference points, and (ii) to stimulate further thinking through indicating that there are almost endless possibilities for the prepared and creative mind. All in all, for each RP element, we discuss 2–5 metaphors for every metaphor type (dominant, alternative and additional). We thus offer a surplus of metaphors – the reader may want to concentrate on a few of these that s/he find generative and not try to remember and take all seriously. One piece of advice could be to note and use a few that provide a good combination of metaphors offering a mind-stretch and input to reflexivity. One or two metaphors can then be more familiar, while one or two others may be alien and (initially) painful to work with – thus possibly encouraging and supporting reflexivity, and often calling for a bit of a struggle.

II

RE-IMAGINING THE RESEARCH PROCESS

5
METAPHORIZING THE GROUNDING ELEMENTS OF THE RP

In this chapter we focus on metaphorizing the grounding elements of the research process. They include the overall point of research, researcher's role, research collective and research phenomenon. These elements broadly point at what Kuhn (1970) referred to as the paradigmatic underpinnings of research. Although the boundaries between intra- and extra-paradigmatic work are not always clear and considerable progress can be made within or through developing established frameworks, more significant and original contributions typically go beyond established assumptions and conventions. Here, encouraging frame-breaking and non-conformity are vital for increased imagination. Thinking through a range of options about how to relate to what one is basically doing, such as how one views the overall purpose of research, the role of the researcher and his/her research collective, and the phenomenon to be investigated, widen the span of entering points in studies and, thus, possibilities to frame the work in more imaginative and original ways.

THE OVERALL POINT OF RESEARCH

A basic issue in research is the overall purpose of doing research, that is, why do research at all? Although most methodology textbooks have a section or two about the overall purpose of research, much seems to be taken for granted, including the assumption that social science is inherently meaningful. A counterpoint could be that research is not always meaningful, as it rarely contributes to the development of more original and valuable knowledge. A lot of research is of questionable relevance and value to society (Alvesson, Gabriel & Paulsen, 2017).[1] If we listen to Foucault (1980), all knowledge, including research, may be dangerous, because it creates particular types of 'truths', which then lead to the normalization of people, for example, into acting as 'leaders' and 'followers'.

Nevertheless, the overall point of (qualitative) research is typically portrayed as 'theory development'. That is, to develop scientific knowledge (inductively) that 'contribute[s] to the knowledge base in the field' (Merriam & Tisdell, 2015: 90, see also Bluhm et al., 2011).

Looking more specifically, in defining the overall purpose of qualitative research, many scholars contrast it with quantitative research, which they claim aims to 'produce objective knowledge; that is, understanding that is impartial and unbiased, based on a view from 'the outside', without personal involvement or vested interests on the part of the researcher' (Willig, 2011: 3). In contrast, qualitative research is concerned with developing knowledge about how 'people make sense of the world and how they experience events' (Willig, 2011: 8) and act on that sense or meaning. In Van Maanen's (1979: 520) words, qualitative research is 'an umbrella term covering an array of interpretive techniques which seek to describe, decode, translate, and otherwise come to terms with the meaning, not the frequency of certain more or less naturally occurring phenomena in the social world'.

But why do we need all these theory developments, one may ask, thus opening up the field for broader reflexivity. A purpose of research may be theory development, but what is the purpose of theory development? There are often some specific answers, where the theory is supposed to illuminate some social concerns, like gender inequalities, changing cultural values among the youth, attitudes to mask wearing during the COVID-19 pandemic or the experiences of ethnic minorities in sport clubs. However, just because there are many worthy social phenomena to be concerned about does not necessarily mean that they should be made into topics of research.

A more basic, and perhaps more intellectually helpful way of thinking through what research we do and why we are doing it, is to think about the purpose of science in terms of what Habermas called knowledge (or cognitive) interests. Habermas (1972) developed a framework including three basic kinds of knowledge, corresponding to three fundamental human interests. First, there is a *technical* knowledge interest in gaining greater *prediction and control* over unruly natural and social forces. Guided by this interest, diverse kinds of scientific disciplines and associated technologies have been developed to calculate and master elements of the natural world, including the behaviour of human beings, e.g. effects of crime prevention policies.

The second type of knowledge arises from an interest in how humans *understand themselves and their cultural context*. The purpose of such knowledge interest, Habermas contends, is not simply to improve our capacities to predict and control the natural and social worlds (i.e. the knowledge prompted by the first cognitive interest), but to develop a fuller understanding of other people's lifeworlds. This, Habermas maintains, is a scientifically coherent and defensible project in itself: in the form of historical–hermeneutic sciences, whose knowledge interest is directed at enhancing *mutual understanding*. It seeks, for example, to enrich our appreciation of what education means to different groups of people, thereby improving our comprehension of their world and enabling and enriching our communications with them.

A third *emancipatory* knowledge interest goes beyond predication and understanding and contributes with *critically reflective* knowledge about the world. The distinguishing feature of this interest resides in a concern to expose domination and exploitation. The ambition is to provide knowledge input to liberation from constraining thinking about social structures, ideologies, identities and interests, e.g. gender patterns and victimization of groups.

According to Habermas, the natural sciences, including medicine and engineering, are dominated by a technical interest, the historical–hermeneutical interest in understanding is prevalent in the humanities while the social sciences should be guided primarily by an emancipatory interest in knowledge. However, few would argue against social science also sometimes being oriented to a technical or a general understanding knowledge interest.

These basic knowledge interests can also be combined with other, more specific ways of answering the question of what is the overall point of research. Options may be the development of theory for improved technical mastery of, for example, pedagogy, psychotherapy or management, or the conducting of in-depth empirical studies to document the lifeworld of transgendered people.

Dominant metaphors

A dominant metaphor that is either explicit or lurking in many, if not most, texts is that research is about *knowledge building*. Doing research then means that the individual project contributes to the overall human project of expanding the ever-growing knowledge building of reality by adding some missing piece in the building. Theory is, for example, often seen as something researchers build, and accomplish through systematic, hard labour, based on building block elements – less of creative inspiration. Construction language is prevalent in social studies, implying a building metaphor.

Interestingly, and as a parenthesis, many social constructionists using construction vocabulary actually disapprove of, or are uneasy about, the building metaphor. This is because the social construction of knowledge often stands for another meaning than the one indicated by research as a construction site metaphor. These different meanings of 'construction' illustrate that we cannot work with mechanical or indexical interpretations of language use in order to understand underlying metaphors.

The building metaphor typically indicates an engineering view on the subject matter. Pre-planning, step by step, earlier elements being followed by subsequent ones. The process is rational, linear, almost predictable, building knowledge according to a specific plan, and is not particularly imaginative or creative. A well carried out, specific project adds another knowledge block to the great project being a collective enterprise, leading to the accumulation of knowledge. With the expansion of research, the stock of available knowledge becomes larger and larger. Increases in size are regarded as a sign of progress and preconditions for improved human rationality. There is thus a double metaphor of knowledge as building. As a researcher, you 1) carve out and deliver a stone and this stone is 2) a reliable and valuable part of the overall collective building of the knowledge cathedral.

Grounded theory is an influential research approach that very much proceeds from a building metaphor. This is, for example, evident already in the titles of studies using the grounded theory approach, such as 'Indigenous music therapy theory building through grounded theory research: the developing indigenous theory framework' (Daveson et al., 2008). Although the building metaphor dominates, there are also other common metaphors in grounded theory research, such as journey and discovery, demonstrating a mixing of metaphors. This is common. But in grounded theory, as in many other approaches, there is a dominant one.

A somewhat different but equally, if not more, dominant (set of) metaphors, which comes from the visual domains, portrays research as being about *picture generation*, that is, knowledge as a picture (of reality). It suggests that the purpose of research is to piece together an enormous 'jigsaw puzzle' that is assumed to gradually lead us to the true picture of reality. Central in this picture view is to generate (knowledge) pictures that accurately represent how 'reality really is', or at least as realistic as possible. A realistic picture is like a useful map: it does not necessarily aim to reflect all the details and messiness of reality but to highlight important features that create order and clarity. The idea is to give an overview and aid a broad, comprehensive understanding at a suitable abstract level.

Research as picture generation, then, is very much about map-making, that is, generating a valid and accurate map that can be used to get by in life. Sometimes there are white spots on the (knowledge) map that need to be filled in, sometimes more details are required to make the map more reliable, and on other occasions an aspect of the existing map provides an inaccurate picture of reality. An example of this type of gap-filling and knowledge map-making study is Blithe and Wolfe's (2017: 726) study of the regulation of sex workers in legal brothels in Nevada, which investigates the work-life conditions surrounding workers in a stigmatized occupation. The purpose is to 'extend work–life theorizing to consider how laws, regulations and organizational policies governing work and life boundaries emerge from particular contexts to oppress workers in unfair ways'. The quote also partly reflects a more grandiose purpose to contribute to fairer workplaces.

The picture metaphor is broadly in line with the building metaphor, particularly when it comes to the idea of constantly accumulating more knowledge about reality by adding yet another piece to the knowledge building or filling another gap in the knowledge map. However, the imaginary of knowledge development differs between the building and the picture metaphors. The focus of the picture metaphor is primarily on developing knowledge that accurately represent the unknown terrain, until the map is complete. In contrast, the focus of the building metaphor is more about constantly adding specific pieces of knowledge in order to complete an enormous knowledge cathedral. In this regard, the building metaphor generates the image of research as a construction work project, whereas the image of the picture metaphor suggests that research is more of a geographical project.

Alternative metaphors

While most researchers emphasize the knowledge accumulation ideal, in terms of completing or adding to a building or a picture/knowledge map, it is not shared by all and some research proceeds from different metaphors, including oppositional ones. A counter-metaphor to knowledge building can be that research is about *knowledge demolition* in the sense of challenging received wisdom (Davis, 1971) or emphasizing that research is about deconstruction, as poststructuralists do by trying to reveal how knowledge claims are notoriously fragile and precarious (Alvesson, 2002; Rosenau, 1992). One can also talk about unmasking of existing knowledge buildings, with the aim of opening up – perhaps in a destructive but creative way – established truths and categories. The assumption here is that much existing knowledge is problematic and that the entire building project – including the very idea of steady and reliable knowledge accumulation – generally or at least frequently calls for critical inspection and possibly demolition. Such research introduces frictions and points at the arbitrariness of assumptions and language use, preventing the smooth following of a particular route on the map, or, alternatively, challenges the idea of knowledge building and picture (or map) generation more generally.

Another alternative metaphor is to regard the purpose of research as *story-telling*. The story-telling metaphor suggests that research is more about developing convincing stories about some aspects of reality than of mapping reality as exactly as possible – mirroring it. In research as story-telling, the focus is more on trying to make sense of phenomena by developing a compelling plot that brings together reported events into a coherent story. As the literary theorist Kenneth Burke (1969) noted, many theoretical representations are plotless because they do not make meaningful connections between events other than in terms of chronology. They (theories) 'have scene and act, agents and agency, but no purpose – and it is the presence of the whole pentad of scene, act, agents, agency, and purpose that permits the creation of a plot' (Czarniawska, 2013: 109). In other words, when research is regarded as story-telling, it is the plot rather than building or picture that takes the front-stage and focus. There needs to be some underlying logic, making things hang together, and some development in the study, offering – in addition to everything else – a good story.

A perhaps somewhat more radical alternative metaphor could be to regard research as *point-making*. Instead of seeing research as delivering new pieces of knowledge either in the form of a building block or a picture fragment, the purpose is to make a specific point that emphasizes an angle or meaning that is not already covered, and typically is in some opposition to what is broadly available. In this regard, research is about making a specific argument, proposing a thesis, offering a specific perspective or more precisely a specific knowledge claim about some phenomenon. It can also be about developing a counter-point that challenges or supplements previous knowledge claims about a phenomenon. Point-making calls for creativity but also some capacity to neglect available knowledge and existing stocks of evidence and truths, and sometimes even engaging in some reductionism to be able to make the unique point forcefully (without being 'clouded' by a wish to account for all empirical complexities and thus mess). Point-making is in some ways more an outcome of the researcher's creativity, and is in opposition to the dominant metaphors, often including an element of critique, and thus demolition. This is particularly the case with counter-point-making, which more directly proceeds from knowledge demolition as the root metaphor.

Perhaps an even more radical image would be to see the point of research as *reality creation*. Social research produces and reinforces discourses that are performative, that is, they create a version of reality that tends to have truth-creating effects (Butler, 1990; Gond et al., 2016; Thrift, 2008). Regarding research as reality creation challenges the assumption that we, through scientific research, can map reality as it is in itself. Instead, the reality creation metaphor suggests that we create realities through our research texts, sometimes in harmful ways (Foucault, 1980; Ghoshal, 2005). Power resides in discourse and discourse has a reality-creating effect. Of course, the reality-creating effect is presumably an outcome of theory being read and made performative (Gabriel, 2002). One example is economic theories that work as self-fulfilling prophecies (Ferraro et al., 1993). Assumptions of maximizing self-interest and opportunism may lead to people defining themselves accordingly and/or social policies and practices being built around that model of human behaviour, motivating extensive incentive and control systems. Another example is diversity, that orders reality in a particular way and indicates certain norms and triggers of thinking and action, including diversity policies and management (O'Leary & Sandberg, 2017). In psychiatry, diagnoses and labels create effects on identities and practices.

The point of research as reality creation can be seen as quite grandiose, the researcher-king/queen rules the world, but more modest understandings and uses of the research as reality creation metaphor are, of course, possible. Critical researchers may, for example, engage in 'partisanship in the struggle for a better world' (Kincheloe & McLaren, 2005: 305), such as through expressing and reinforcing the voices of disadvantaged groups.

Additional metaphors

There are, as we hinted at in the Introduction, signs that significant numbers of research publications are not leading to much in terms of valuable knowledge contributions. Other motives and drivers are instead taking the lead. The purpose of research then becomes a *cultural capital-investment* (Bourdieu, 1984) or a return on investment (ROI) project – a roi-search project rather than the creation of valuable knowledge, i.e. re-search (Alvesson, 2013b). Research is then about boosting the CV of the individual or improving the metrics and rankings of the employing institution. Another view is that social science research is simply an *institutionalized myth* (Meyer & Rowan, 1977). Science is seen as self-evident, valuable and good, and thus a practice to be imitated so that a range of areas are capable of demonstrating that they are real academic fields. Here, the overall purpose is less about generating valuable knowledge to society but rather to demonstrate academic excellence, and the driver is the imitation, status and legitimation forces being increasingly powerful. Research may also be about *game playing* – a rather common, informally used metaphor in academia (Butler & Spoelstra, 2012). People then see research as either theatre or sports – different sub-metaphors may put stronger or weaker marks on the game playing for different players. The game metaphor indicates that the rules and engagement of the game are crucial and there are no strong values outside this logic.

Summary

Table 5.1 Summary of metaphorizing the overall point of research

Metaphors	*Dominant*	*Alternative*	*Additional*
RP element			
Overall point of research	– Knowledge building – Picture generation	– Knowledge demolition – Story-telling – Point-making – Reality creation	– Cultural capital-investment – Institutionalized myth – Game playing

The dominant knowledge building and picture generation metaphors suggest that the prevalent view of the purpose of research is that of developing knowledge about the world in an accumulative fashion: either by continuously building more knowledge of social phenomena, or by generating a more complete picture of reality, thereby contributing to the collective enterprise to make the world known (and possibly predictable or at least manageable). Underlying this prevalent view is that (social) reality is 'out there' more or less as given, and it can be accurately represented through systematic and rigorous research procedures. Research is assumed to at least roughly mirror social reality, where there is a 'fit' between data and knowledge claims. Although most researchers accept some form of soft fit between research results and something 'out there', many find this 'fit' ideal and the building and photography metaphors problematic.

As a way to counter this common view of research, we proposed the following set of metaphors: knowledge demolition in the sense of actively questioning existing knowledge; point-making by offering a different or counterview/interpretation of a phenomenon; story-telling by offering a compelling story about some aspect of reality; and reality creation by enacting new realities. These alternative metaphors challenge, in various ways, the assumption of a reality 'out there' as something that we can mirror or about which we can develop robust, authoritative knowledge. The additional metaphors of research possibly worth considering include: cultural capital-investment, institutionalized myth and game playing. These suggest that the point of research may not always be about knowledge development but, rather, about improving researchers' career prospects or the rankings of universities.

Working reflexively with some of these metaphors could mean choosing two or more to form a good contrast, either as part of a dialogue or as a confrontation. The researcher could, for example, compare or confront a knowledge demolition metaphor with a building one. Even a critical view of the purpose of research – informed by, for example, a Foucauldian or some other poststructuralist approach – could then be challenged by an effort to build something on the remains of a demolition project. Perhaps some parts still are intact, being robust enough to stand the sledge-hammer. It could be worth trying to do something more positive with these parts, forming an alternative building project. An image for such an enterprise of new knowledge following a demolition exercise could be the bird phoenix, which dies but obtains new life by arising from its own ashes.

RESEARCHER'S ROLE

Another central grounding element of the research process is the researcher's role, which is probably the easiest and most popular element to metaphorize. The researcher's role implicates both how researchers understand themselves as researchers and what roles they see themselves play (or should play) in the research process. How researchers see themselves and their role in research is central as it often shapes what research they conduct and how. For example, it matters whether the researcher regards his or her role as being (i) disengaged from the research phenomenon, where the researcher is standing on the sideline watching and analysing the phenomenon in a neutral way – the researcher as a neutral spectator emphasizing objectivity, (ii) committed to but not actively engaged with the research phenomenon – researcher as participant, or (iii) someone deliberately intervening with the research phenomenon – researcher as activist, at least potentially a reality improver.

Researchers can also take on an outsider role (etic) or an insider role (emic) in the research process, that is, moving between being very close to or distant from those being studied. The outsider/insider division may overlap with (i) to (iii), but points at something different. Even if you do emic/close-up empirical studies, you may be disengaged and neutral in terms of politics and value commitments. Equally, a researcher that takes an etic/distanced role may be engaged. A close-up researcher doing ethnography, for example, may still emphasize neutrality and make every effort to be as objective and socially disengaged as possible (or simply feel indifferent about the value aspects of the phenomenon being studied, having only an intellectual interest in it). Even researchers doing quantitative studies, such as on gender issues or poverty, may be very engaged in the subject matter. How questionnaires are designed, what statistical tests are carried out and how results are reported may reflect social commitments. It is easy to formulate questionnaire items and deal with data so that the 'right' number of cases emerge, be that instances of poverty or the frequency of sexual harassment, or so that the findings, such as the prevalence of stress in working life or the significance of leadership, are in line with the researcher's personal and political orientations.

Dominant metaphors

One of the most common metaphors for the researcher's role in qualitative research is to regard the researcher as the chief *instrument* in the research process. This is (almost) the opposite to quantitative research, in which the researcher is seen (at least according to the ideal) as a neutral observer with 'a view from nowhere' (Nagel, 1986), and is not 'subjectively' engaged in the actual process of knowledge production. In other words, while quantitative research largely tries to exclude the researcher as much as possible from the research process, with the help of questionnaires, statistics and other gathering and measuring devices, many, if not most, qualitative research approaches regard the researcher as the primary instrument of the research. Having been there, being involved in in-depth interviews, using pre-understanding and imagination and engaging in interpretative work call for a clear sense of the importance of the researcher-self. As Hatch (2002: 7) claims, 'the logic behind the researcher-as-instrument approach is that the human capacities necessary to participate in social life are the same capacities that enable qualitative researchers to make sense of the actions, intentions, and understandings of those being studied'. In contrast to other methodological instruments, the human instrument is immediately responsive and adaptive to the emerging research situation (Merriam & Tisdell, 2015: 16). In order to use the self as a sensitive and precise instrument, the researcher needs to be aware of the self that is in operation in research settings. But equally important is being aware how the research collectivity forms the researcher and how the broader societal-cultural environment ensnares him/her into adopting certain ideologies, discourses and pressurizes them into addressing and representing the subject matter in particular ways. The researcher-instrument is performed in various ways and may see and reproduce truths (perspectives, stories) in accordance with these.

Another fairly common metaphor is to regard the researcher as a *bricoleur*, an eclectic craftsperson who 'uses the tools of his or her methodological trade, deploying whatever strategies, methods, or empirical methods are at hand to come up with solutions' (Denzin & Lincoln, 1994: 2). Here there is an element of the researcher as an instrument, but tools are a key part. The approach is quite different from the following of a strict method and the use of a specific tool or set of tools. Thus, the bricoleur is another and more pragmatic-artist type of person than a specialized tool-user or technician. Key elements here are the eclecticism and flexibility or a promiscuous approach to methods and techniques, down-playing the rigour that is often celebrated in research. This can lead to inconsistencies and confusion, but also facilitate creative empirical work.

However, the researcher as an instrument and as a bricoleur also has important short-comings, such as biases and problematic prejudices that can distort or quite signifi-cantly limit the knowledge developed (e.g. Miles & Huberman, 1994; Sandberg, 2005; Schmidt & Hunter, 2014). In order to keep their biases under control and to produce valid (truthful) knowledge, researchers typically try to follow some strict procedures in collecting and analysing data. A metaphor for this is to see the researcher not only as an instrument but also as a *technician*. Here the idea is that the researcher is not an instru-ment him- or herself, but operational in using available techniques and procedures in a specialist way. A researcher may, for example, adhere strictly to a specific method and rigorously follow the strategies, techniques and procedures of a particular qualitative research method, doing detailed coding and then continue in the production of theory. This would avoid or, more realistically, reduce the problems (and advantages) of the researcher as highly subjective.

Grounded theory (GT) exemplifies the researcher as technician. Here the idea is that the researcher is diligent, systematic, refrains from ideas outside what is 'inherent' in data (not much according to sceptics, emphasizing the need for interpretation) and arrives at valid research results through the highly detailed adherence to technical procedures, in particular codification (Glaser & Strauss, 1967). This view has been softened up some-what, and many allow some space for a less mechanical researcher role, employing a form of soft procedure, allowing some intuition to oil the process (Charmaz, 2008; Suddaby, 2006). Still, the qualitative researcher is much weaker on tool-use than the quantitative researcher, which means that even a strict, traditional GT person would be seen as a rather weak technician in comparison to a quantitative researcher. Yet, within the context of qualitative research, the researcher as technician makes sense.

Hence, three common, although rather unspecific and vague, metaphors are the researcher as a (self-)instrument, bricoleur and a technician. The competent researcher, well versed in qualitative methods, may navigate with skill as an outcome of having internalized the right orientations and competence. This allows the qualified researcher to be seen very much as a *truth-finder* in most research, although the exact meaning of this varies with different notions of truth (Alvesson & Sköldberg, 2018). The truth-finder metaphor tends go together with the technician metaphor, as the idea of strict use of tools and techniques is assumed to lead to robust research results, but other types of research ideals may be in line with the truth-finder metaphor as well. The view of the researcher as an instrument may also be compatible with truth-finding, although it is common that an emphasis on the researcher self leads to the downplaying of truth aspirations (or at less truth-telling language).

There are different types of truths and researchers are more or less authoritative or cautious in their claims (Sandberg, 2005). Sometimes objective hermeneutics (the use of interpretation to find the true meaning of a phenomenon) work with an idea of a truth, although the typical interpretative work needs to answer questions with no clear answer, which makes the notion of truth uncertain and preliminary. People in progressive, constructionist camps tend to avoid the truth term, in favour of softer or 'weaker' formulations. However, even in some qualitative work with a poststructuralist inclination, the empirical study is somehow often portrayed as delivering some form of 'truth', even though texts may demonstrate mixed discourses (Wray-Bliss, 2002). As Stake (2005: 453) remarks, 'however accuracy is construed, researchers do not want to be inaccurate, caught without confirmation'. Nevertheless, the truth-finder is not a central metaphor for the researcher, who is more inclined to downplay truth-claims or make modest such claims, for example, through referring to the trustworthiness rather than the truthfulness of the research.

Alternative metaphors

As alternative metaphors to the dominant building and picture metaphors for understanding the purpose of research, we suggested knowledge demolition, point-making and story-telling. If the overall purpose of research is seen as soft or moderate knowledge demolition, or in other ways to express a counter-position to a well-established stream, the researcher may take on the role as a *provocateur* (Silverman, 2006). Such a role displays a somewhat disrespectful attitude to established knowledge by emphasizing the often-arbitrary nature of the meaning of data and theoretical reasoning. The researcher may be sceptical or ironical and questions the assumptions, the vocabulary or claimed findings and results of other researchers. Claims made by interviewees, questionnaire fillers or informants in other capacities may be doubted, for example, interview accounts may be seen as expressions of stories of victimization or identity boosting.

In some cases, the researcher may also take up the role as a *destroyer* and perhaps even as an 'exterminator' of existing knowledge building or pictures of reality. Here the researcher goes beyond simple provocations and aims much further in the questioning of established knowledge. Instead of reinforcing and strengthening or modifying already established knowledge buildings or pictures of reality, the researcher sees his or her role as questioning and problematizing the established knowledge, breaking it down as a way of opening up new areas and lines of inquiry. Accordingly, the emphasis is on the researcher's 'capacity to disturb and threaten the stability of positive forms of' knowledge (Knights, 1992: 533), as a way to highlight what is 'wrong' (e.g. misleading or dangerous) with existing knowledge (Deetz, 1996). Hence, rather than work with construction, the focus is on deconstructing knowledge claims, identifying the internal contradictions and ambiguities in theory. Here the researcher 'demonstrates the internal tensions of the text, the dependence of the said on the unsaid, and the eternal aporia of the foundational or grounding text' placing 'all attempts by authorities to establish knowledge, to convey wisdom or establish values … under suspicion' (Gergen, 1994: 59).

If research is seen as point-making, it is likely that the researcher's role would be more like an *insight generator*. The researcher then sees him- or herself as less searching for an empirically optimal research contribution and more for original ideas and interpretations. For example, as an insight generator, the researcher regards empirical material as a central input to generating new insights about a phenomenon rather than as the final arbiter for deciding whether a knowledge claim is true or not. Similarly, existing theories are seen more as a reservoir from which to generate insights than as established truths. The insights generated can certainly not be any wild ideas. Instead, an insight is typically a compromise between good empirical backup and the generation of a somewhat bold and speculative idea, where the creative element to some extent transcends what follows closely from the data or established literature.

If the point of research is seen as story-telling, the researcher tends to take the role of a *story-teller*. As a story-teller, the researcher regards empirical material and existing theories as inputs for the creation of a plot that can produce a compelling story about a research phenomenon rather than as an exact representation of the phenomenon being studied. Here the story is perhaps careful, credible and honest, but may still be seen as a narration of reality, for example, a confessional or impressionistic tale (Van Maanen, 1988). The idea of social research, at least qualitative studies, being about telling good (possibly truthful) stories is fairly popular. Of course, everything can be seen as a story, but a typical academic text, written in a formulaic manner, scores rather badly as a story.

Additional metaphors

There is a wealth of less common metaphors for the researcher. Many emphasize aspects from art and literature, while others draw upon the spheres of politics and social activism.

In the various literatures we find that the researcher is often seen as a *puzzle-solver* or *artist* (Denzin & Lincoln, 2018), strongly emphasizing the creative, artistic aspects of the researcher. The puzzle-solver may express ingenuity in solving a difficult intellectual puzzle, whereas an artist exhibits creativity and, when successful, brings about a pleasurable experience for the audience. Perhaps these metaphors are more in use to point at ideals rather than successfully practised modes of doing research. A different set of metaphors points broadly at the idea of a researcher producing knowledge with some potential effects on reality. Some social science researchers see themselves as *reformers*, eager to address some of the inequalities and injustices in the world. A related metaphor is the researcher as a *partisan*, more committedly fighting for the good cause, or, less ambitiously, the researcher as *advisor* to public servants, NGOs or business leaders.

Summary

Table 5.2 Summary of metaphorizing the researcher's role

Metaphors	*Dominant*	*Alternative*	*Additional*
RP element			
Researcher's role	– Instrument – Bricoleur – Technician – Truth-finder	– Provocateur – Destroyer – Insight generator – Story-teller	– Puzzle-solver – Artist – Reformer – Partisan – Advisor

The dominant metaphors suggest that the (qualitative) researcher's main role is to function as the primary instrument in the research process, such as being actively involved in generating empirical material and making sense of that material. A related but different view is the researcher as technician, operating the various techniques available for conducting research. A similar but more flexible image is the researcher as a bricoleur, a craftsperson who applies his/her tools in a creative manner to develop the knowledge desired. Although these dominant metaphors vary in orientation, they all articulate an image of the researcher as a knowledge producer, either in a mechanical (instrument, technician) or more flexible (bricoleur) way (and in that way are connected to the dominant metaphors of the purpose of research as knowledge building and picture generation). As a set of alternatives, we proposed a number of counter-metaphors, namely researcher as a provocateur, destroyer, insight generator and story-teller, which all, in different ways, challenge the prevalent images of the researcher's role as basically a knowledge producer. The additional metaphors proposed point to a range of more or less possible roles or identities (artist, reformer, partisan, advisor) that researchers may embrace in the research process.

In terms of metaphorical reflexivity, considering the self-positioning of the researcher is motivated. What kind of existing and alternative researcher role is being embraced? Are alternative positionings possible? Perhaps the researcher is caught in a constraining view of him- or herself, whether as a technician, provocateur, insight generator or an artist? Sometimes the view may be unrealistic, the desired insight generation is hard to accomplish and the ambition for social good-doing may only reinforce the victimization of groups portrayed as vulnerable and suitable for the researcher's, and other likeminded people's, saving ambitions. This kind of reflexivity does not only involve 'me-ism', but also the societal and cultural conditions that tend to lead to the production of compliant researcher roles and ideologies, such as management consultancy versions in business schools or as social reformers in sociology or social work.

THE RESEARCH COLLECTIVE

Researchers often like to emphasize their individuality. As research is often lonely work, at least for qualitative researchers within social science, this appears natural, even self-evident. Much research, even collaborative research, involves an extraordinary amount of individual (or small group) choices, from what to study, what literature to consult and how to refer to it, how to conduct the study, how to compose a paper or book, and what words to use in the crafting of a text. But even though the lonesome cowboy metaphor may appear striking, there is always some collective behind a person, which is often partly hidden and pre-structures choices.

This is broadly acknowledged, and there is a large literature on the sociology of research, emphasizing the role of social factors in the production and acknowledgement of knowledge (e.g. Jarvie & Zamora-Bonilla, 2011; Mir et al., 2016; Ritzer, 1980). This literature is not used much in the methodology literature, as method authors commonly emphasize the individual research project and how it is technically handled by the individual researcher. But this downplays the social nature of research. Although there is a wealth of social, ideological, political and economic factors influencing research, here we just draw attention to one, perhaps the most significant: the research collective, the 'we' behind the researcher 'I' and his/her identity and role positioning. As we emphasized in Chapter 3, 'we-ism' is a key issue for reflexivity.

In fact, being with others, like being part of a research collective, can be seen as constitutive of all forms of human ways of being. '*Initially* "I" "am" not in the sense of my own self, but I am the others ... and for the most part it remains so' (Heidegger, [1927] 1996: 121, italics in original). In other words, what we do and are as researchers are for the most part defined by those with whom we are engaged in particular research collectives. It is by taking over their ways of doing research that we come to know what it means to be a researcher and what work activities are involved in research and how to carry them out.

Belonging to a community seems to be increasingly vital in an age of mass research, where few people stand out and the large majority of researchers need to be recognized through their affiliation to a specific, easily identifiable group. As individual researchers, they (we) want to be distinctive rather than seen as non-distinct. However, the pressure to adapt to the norms and conventions of the research community, controlling criteria for, and access to, publication possibilities, makes it difficult for many researchers to cultivate individuality and originality. Adaptions to the expectations of peer/reviewer requirements control much, as do responses to reviews in journal submission processes. Not only norms but also cognitive orientations bear clear collective imprints. Few people are original thinkers. Most researchers' thinking is based on intellectual traditions, together with the collective they belong to. In this sense, the particular research collective(s) that researchers are affiliated with become very important to consider – and often to reconsider. Academics write primarily for other academics.

Research on the social organization of science has in different ways highlighted and described the evolvement and establishment of specialized research groupings, giving them different labels, such as disciplines (Fabian, 2000), paradigms (Kuhn, 1970) and epistemic communities (Knorr-Cetina, 1981). The biggest and loosest grouping is paradigm, which in turn consists of a range of subgroupings. Paradigms are about worldviews, methodological ideals, but also – and this is of interest for us in this section – social communities or academic societies. But it is not easy to specify the boundaries of a particular paradigm, as boundaries are loose and the researchers who try to identify the paradigms in a social science discipline can come up with very different numbers and categories of paradigms (e.g. Brinkmann et al., 2014; Denzin & Lincoln, 2018; Hammersley, 2011).

Often, from a social point of view, what is most interesting is the more distinct and often smaller and narrow research groupings that can exist both within and sometimes also ambiguously in between and across paradigms. Groupings may be people in the same network, referring directly to each other and/or the same gurus, or people who go to the same conference sub-themes, work in the same field and publish in the same journal, etc. – which is typically crucial for publication and career progression (Alvesson & Sandberg, 2014). Such specific research groupings are therefore more immediately relevant when it comes to understanding how research communities pre-structure the individual researcher's way of conducting research as opposed to the abstract mass of people who are neo-positivists, Weberians, liberal feminists, symbolic interactionists or institutional change researchers.

The research collective, in terms of the specific research specialization group we belong to, is often non-conscious or invisible, as the researcher may not be aware of, or acknowledge, the deep impact of the values, priorities and modes of thinking his or her social group exercises. Much of the socialization is taken for granted – the young researcher thinks s/he learns how the world is or is best seen, not a specific, group-based view of how the world is. Of course, researchers need to relate to others and there are always social constraints, sometimes countering bad judgement and preventing bad decisions. The collective also stands for a considerable degree of rationality, but sometimes it is a source of conservatism and conformism and thus the enemy of creativity and originality.

Dominant metaphors

The research collective may work and be understood in very different ways. It can be viewed as a *community*, which is probably the most frequently used term to describe the social context of researchers. As March (2005: 5) notes, one of the most persistent aspirations of social science is to form research communities, that is, 'to create ... associations of scholars that profit from exchanges of ideas across disciplinary, national and linguistic boundaries. Proclamations of the need for such communities are part of the standard mantra of contemporary scholarly life, stimulated by perceived needs of both scholarship and public policy.' Research is therefore often seen as a collective rather than an individual enterprise, consisting of different communities of scholars with shared interests, a common identity and a general spirit of helpfulness and care. A community is a kind of home, a social anchor in reality, a cure against a possible existential anxiety associated with isolation.

The research collective can also be viewed as an arena for *conversation* or debates. The conversation arena (or discussion club) metaphor points broadly in the same direction as community, towards support, consensus and a soft rationality. However, in contrast to community, which is somewhat more into social bonding and emotional qualities, the conversation image emphasizes debate and the sharing of ideas, that is, the cognitive element of a research collective.

> Scholarly writing aims to join conversations within a particular field of interest in order to improve understanding of a particular phenomenon. Some conversations are well established and easier to join, but they tend to take place within a crowded space, and thereby constrain the scope of a contribution. Newer conversations offer greater scope for contribution, but authors will need to spend more time legitimizing their chosen focus. Starting new conversations is a challenging endeavor, but if it is successful, it can lead to ground-breaking contributions. (Patriotta, 2017: 753)

The research collective as a conversation arena thus exhibits various types of discussions, where established ones are smooth and consensual but do not add much new – people only marginally vary conversation themes. More novel conversations tend to disrupt the easy flow, involve uncertainty, and perhaps frustration and questioning, leading to demands for legitimation and defence. The conversations may have elements like arguments and quarrels, but the more positive and supportive side still reigns. The overall image is one of social support for the progress of science.

A related common metaphor (albeit less social) is to regard research collectives as specific *fields* of research. This metaphor points at boundaries and is perhaps somewhat less cosy in that it shifts the emphasis from the social to the specific domain of a research collective, such as the (research field) of higher education, social identity, leadership, adolescence and parenthood. Each research field tends to have its specific norms and conventions for how to conduct research and what matters to make an impact on the field. Fields may also signal a particular, limited geographical space or domain where people tend to operate. However, it is often used to point at a broad social territory, where organizations or actors tend to be connected, relate to each other and be characterized by field-specific pressures for conformism. Bourdieu (1984), for example, talks about social fields, while neo-institutional organizational theorists are interested in institutional fields (e.g. DiMaggio & Powell, 1983). The field metaphor(s) here in use may of course vary heavily, depending on whether 'field' is used to indicate something like the crop growing there or the terrain, where people or organizations show connectedness and an inclination to scrutinize and adapt to each together. Fields can also, as with Bourdieu, be viewed as social arenas where status and power are at stake, driving social positioning efforts. (As we have pointed out, all metaphor use and understanding call for considering how the source (e.g. field) works in relationship to focal objects to be understood (e.g. research collective), and here one and the same word may attain quite different meanings.)

Research collectives can also be seen as specific interest coalitions or as *trade associations*. The building and photography associations provide representation and service to members and customers in the specific research area, including conferences, networking, publication, training and career support, but also norms and conventions for how to conduct research. Trade associations, particularly if they are big and prestigious, offer significant political power in the competition for status and privilege within the broader academic field. For instance, a powerful trade association can negotiate with conference organizers to establish special research tracks or symposia and arrange the publication of special issues of prestigious journals. Through their political power and often-high specialization they put up high entry barriers against intruders, which help its members to pursue their knowledge production in peace, without too much critique and disturbance. Critics are typically outsiders and can be dismissed because of their 'imperfect' knowledge of the field. However, given that trade associations often produce norms and conventions for how to conduct research they can be quite constraining for researchers' ability to generate more original and frame-bending research.

Another influential metaphor for the collective is a *marketplace*. In contrast to the association metaphor, which offers protection and pursues common interests, the marketplace metaphor emphasizes that researchers – as individuals and collectives – are in open competition. Ideas, perspectives, research results and researchers compete for attention, recognition and impact. Not only the quality of the knowledge offered but also efforts to be persuasive and to attain a competitive advantage through research politics and marketing are key here. Various research orientations as well as researchers are directly or indirectly in competition. They start and work with journals and interest groups, organize conferences and run special issues. Of course, in some cases the market is outside academia, in particular for books aiming broadly, but for most researchers the marketplace is the research collective.

Alternative metaphors

Community, conversation, associations (and to a lesser extent fields) are images highlighting the positive, consensual and supportive side of the research collective, while the marketplace metaphor also indicates the eagerness to perform better than others. You increase market share at the expense of others. Some alternative metaphors point also, or mainly, at the repressive and primitive aspects of social groups. Collectives can, of course, work in different ways and what is often helpful can be constraining and what is repressive may prevent people from doing wrong things. Tight social relations and strong group affiliation is often a mixed blessing – support and constraint may go hand in hand, as Foucauldian notions of power teach us.

One option is to consider the research collective through the *tribe* metaphor. What appears to be civilized and sophisticated – an advanced epistemic community – may hide other qualities. Here the collective characteristics and the constraining habits and norms are highlighted. The researcher places him- or herself strictly within one specific research camp, such as leisure, trust, race, disability or power studies. Being a tribe member may not be the role or (social) identity that is most flattering, but compared to the individual hero and great developer of unique knowledge it may for most people be quite revealing and precise (Alvesson & Sandberg, 2014). Researchers are in one sense autonomous, but the peer control is quite high and the pressure to adapt to social conventions within specific research collectives is very strong. The tribe is not necessarily mainly negative, as it points at a rather tight group, a source of safety, collectivity, integration, but also to primitive orientations and closure in its outlook. Groups may hold on to truths that for outsiders appear more as myths, ideologies or fixed ideas. Shared assumptions are seldom challenged. Traditions tend to rule and there is some animosity to new ideas and radical questioning of habits and worldviews. Deviants are not treated well.

A *chain-gang* metaphor suggests something partly different, where the individual member is not allowed to move out of tune with the others. There are strong interdependencies between people in the group, there are demands of careful coordination in meanings, language use and practices. People in the group are marching to the same tune. The chain-gang is not hostile or oppressive, but there are prevailing institutional norms and/or feelings of tight togetherness, making everybody in the research collective tied to particular ways of being, where deviation creates problems as people are incapable of handling this. One of us talked with a senior editor of a leading academic journal about options to make it less conservative and formulaic and the editor agreed about the proposal and said that he had tried, but others felt 'bound by the obligation to maintain the integrity of the journal', which could be seen as illustrating the chain-gang metaphor. People are heavily constrained by convention.

But there are more sinister aspects of social collectives. Sometimes group interests or cherished ideas are threatened, and the collective reacts with anger. This is well known by whistle-blowers (Kenny, 2018), and there is no reason to expect that academics are very different. A colleague at a conference raised a critique against the research tradition he broadly adhered to and received very negative feedback. 'I felt like [I was] being thrown in front of a bus', he said. One of us had a similar experience of receiving very hostile feedback against an effort to raise ironic remarks about a perspective that at the time was very popular among the audience: 'You are supporting our enemies', was one comment. Here the collective appears more as a *lynch mob*. This may appear to be extremely rare, but clear deviations from the established routes do trigger primitive responses. The lynch mob may function as a political interest group or as a carrier of emotional structures. A colleague described his frustrations after several efforts to publish a paper challenging some powerful theoretical ideas: 'We are up against a conceptual cartel.' Another colleague described reviewers of a specific journal as 'vicious'.

It is common to suggest that researchers often write mainly for other academics, and in the worst case only for the micro tribe that they belong to. If the key is to be published, the influence of the reference group may lead to box thinking. The social aspects of research then lead to researchers being caught in *social boxes* (Alvesson & Sandberg, 2014), to use a somewhat unusual metaphor for the research collective and its impact on specific research projects. It is similar to the chain-gang but evokes a slightly different imaginary and points at broader cognitive as well as social dependencies and restrictions, while the chain-gang mainly indicates the latter.

The box metaphor implies that people are rigidly committed to the specific setup in their particular research specialization. The research box provides an intellectual habitat and a habitus for identity and competence formation, which guides as well as restricts ideas of what research can be done and how it can be done. The habitat (or field) is the 'natural' terrain in which one moves, and the habitus is the set of cultural dispositions that has been acquired for being able to navigate competently only within the habitat. Hence, what are commonly portrayed as key ingredients for good research and scholarship – specialization, incremental work, adding to a subset of literature – may actually be the cause of a shortage of good research leading to novel and influential ideas and theory.

Additional metaphors

Another metaphor can be to regard the research collectives as *societies for internal admiration*, in which researchers emphasize how their specific research domain has made great progress and contributes to our understanding of some aspects of reality. People working on transformational leadership may, for example, say that the research has 'generated an impressive cachet of findings and has made a great impact on the study of leadership' (Jackson & Parry, 2008: 31). Here the 'we' aspect is strong, and people are highly committed to supporting other people with the right orientation as themselves. Research collectives can also be understood as *political coalitions*, where a research collective mainly drives the sectional interest of the group against the interests of others, who are more or less clearly identified as competitors or the enemy. If the point of research is seen as storytelling, the research collective may be seen as a specific *genre*, such as tragedies, mystery and romance. With an emphasis on the collective, story-telling appears as mass-produced rather than original work, and tends to be copied, in terms of style and plot. But if the leading metaphor for research is reformation of reality, then the research collective may be seen as a *social movement* or a *think-tank* with a specific agenda for how to change (and improve) the world.

Summary

Table 5.3   Summary of metaphorizing the research collective

Metaphors	*Dominant*	*Alternative*	*Additional*
RP element			
Research collective	– Community – Conversation – Field – Trade association – Marketplace	– Tribe – Chain-gang – Lynch mob – Social box	– Societies for internal admiration – Political coalition – Genre – Social movements – Think-tank

The dominant metaphors portray the research collective as scholars forming specific communities, associations, and engaging in shared conversations or research fields in which they happily work together for the greater good, namely to continuously advance our knowledge about reality. A less communalist metaphor could be to see research collectives as specific marketplaces of research. While the actors operate in a specific market, they do not cooperate, but rather try to compete against each other, or at least to triumph over each other through various means, such as publishing in more prestigious journals or being a board member of such journals or reaching high metrics.

As counter-metaphors, we proposed tribe, chain-gang, lynch mob and social boxes. These alternative metaphors articulate in various ways the more problematic sides of the research collective, such as silo-mentality, narrow-mindedness, rigid norm-following and competitiveness, where the primary interest is the preservation of some group interest rather than contributing to the advancement of knowledge more generally. This more negative side of the research collective is further articulated through additional metaphors, such as societies for internal admiration, political coalitions, social movements and think-tanks.

The 'we' of the research community is a key topic for reflexivity, which can be referred to as 'we-ism'. Issues around researcher-collectivity, however, may also be targeted through the other domains of reflexivity. The researcher self as a tribe member may be one option. Another is the careful scrutiny of how language use – discursivism – bears imprints of collective forces, for example, researchers follow established genres and templates for writing and use the same vocabulary as others in the community (tribe). Yet another is criticism, where research collectives are seen as being heavily influenced by societal structures and cultural blinkers can be used as an entrance to reflexivity on researcher's collectives.

RESEARCH PHENOMENA

A key aspect of all research is the phenomenon being studied. At the most general level, a research phenomenon refers to what is being studied, which 'can be any problem, issue, or topic that is chosen as the subject of an investigation' (Van de Ven, 2016: 265). For example, management scholars may investigate phenomena like leadership, strategy and decision making, while sociologists may study suicide, segregation and terrorism.

The prevalent view is that research phenomena are something more or less given 'out there' and the task of the researcher is to catch this aspect of 'reality as it really is' (Mol, 2010: 255). Research phenomena are therefore commonly seen as separate from the researcher, but which the researcher can investigate (with scientific methods) and make known. For example, this view of phenomena is indicated by the popular discovery metaphor (Glaser & Strauss, 1967). Similarly, Swedberg (2014) argues that theorizing starts with the observation of a phenomenon in reality that can be of interest to investigate and theorize.

Many other scholars, particularly qualitative researchers, argue that most phenomena are rarely fixed and completely given, but rather are indeterminate and ambiguous. Standard categories or ways of identifying phenomena are then questioned. For example, more original research may lead to revisions of what was, from the outset, believed to be the case. If the researcher can show that what appears, at the start of the research project, to be (phenomenon) X is better viewed as Y instead, s/he may demonstrate learning, progress and perhaps theoretical development (Davis, 1971). The latter is often a matter of revision of a phenomenon or even the invention of a new phenomenon. For example, the emerging phenomenon in the famous Hawthorne studies (Roethlisberger & Dickson, 1939) was initially a variation in job performance (assumed to be in relationship to physical work conditions), but gradually shifted to people's sensitivity and responsiveness to social relations at work, that is, they 'discovered' or constructed another phenomenon than they anticipated.

Still others argue that phenomena are typically not just lying around (as given or indeterminate), ready to be investigated and theorized in the form of personalities, leadership styles, ethnicity, subcultures or institutions. Instead, phenomena need to be created initially, then further developed, and perhaps radically revised. As Van de Ven (2016: 265) declares, 'phenomena do not exist objectively "out there;" they are uniquely perceived and framed by different people'. For example, the phenomenon of gender as 'doing', that is, as an interactional accomplishment, did not simply reveal itself to West and Zimmerman (1987), who suggested that gender is neither – as commonly believed – a role nor a structural appendix, but something we accomplish in social interaction. Similarly, the phenomenon of disciplinary and normalizing power, as viewed by Foucault (1976), did not simply exist out there before he developed the ideas. In fact, even phenomena approached for measurement and explanation in an objectivistic way have largely been constructed by researchers (Bourdieu et al., 1991). The phenomenon of 'authentic leadership', for example, is not only, or mainly, a direct mirroring of reality, but has in significant ways been determined through researchers' choice and specification of constructs, such as self-awareness, relational transparency, balanced processing and internalized moral perspective, being arbitrarily combined and packaged as 'authentic leadership' (Alvesson & Einola, 2019; Nyberg & Sveningsson, 2014).

There is obviously considerable variation between different schools of thought, but also variation in terms of the phenomena of study. Different schools of thought tend to address different types of phenomena. Qualitative research often investigates phenomena that are not clearly given and are therefore very much a matter of researchers' projections or order-creating moves.

Dominant metaphors

The perhaps most dominant metaphor is to regard research phenomena as specific *pieces of social nature*, that is, something given, and fairly stable, which can be 'picked up' and investigated. As pieces of social nature, phenomena such as professions, diversity, leadership, corporate culture, class and marriage are seen as forming part of a broader social nature, from which they can be identified, described and categorized according to their specific properties, in a similar manner as Carl Linnaeus (1735) ordered nature into a gigantic taxonomy in his famous *Systema Naturae*.

A related dominant metaphor regards research phenomena as *social objects*, defined by some distinct inherent properties. Social science studies frequently talk about social phenomena as research objects, such as 'Tourism as a complex interdisciplinary research object' (Darbelley & Stock, 2011), or 'The future of the study of public administration: Embedding research object and methodology in epistemology and ontology' (Raad-schelders, 2011). When research phenomena are seen as pieces of social nature or objects 'out there', it often assumes a strict separation between the phenomena and the researcher. Given their independent status, it becomes critical for the researchers to mirror the features of the phenomena in their knowledge about them.

However, as noted above, many qualitative researchers do not regard research phenomena as given but as socially and historically produced in ongoing and shifting social interactions among people. The metaphorical expression, then, is of a social construction. But this expression is very broad and covers many different approaches, from objectivism to radical constructionism, which means that it needs to be unpackaged with different metaphors, if one – as we do – follows the metaphor logic line of reasoning. As said before, one term (modifier or source) may stand for a variety of metaphors, depending on the focal object (e.g. the research phenomenon) being addressed, but may also be contingent upon the meaning of the modifier (source).

Many social scientists see social constructions as objectified reality. This means that researchers also regard social phenomena as having a specific history, that is, they emerged at some point in time but are now established and 'out there'. Many (most) qualitative researchers thus seem to regard social phenomena as fairly bounded and fixed, albeit historically produced and socially defined, being there for the researcher at a particular time to fairly easily identify and theorize. However, they still often assume that these social phenomena (diversity, professions, adolescence) are separate from the researcher, whose aim is to represent them as they are (in themselves). The metaphor for the object of study can then be seen as a *thing-like social construction* (to use an expression that offers far from optimal metaphor qualities in terms of elegance).

In contrast to regarding phenomena as more or less given things, another less dominant view is to regard phenomena as *process*. This view signals that phenomena are not something fixed, but are dynamic; they are always in the making and in progress, largely open-ended, and unfolding in and over time. This view emphasizes how phenomena, such as leadership, innovation, race, bullying, equality, family and power, come into being, along with their ongoing-ness and transformations. Above, we mentioned gender as doing. As Latour (1986: 273) aptly remarks regarding viewing the phenomenon of society as a 'thing', '"society" is not a thing discovered and defined by social scientists, despite the ignorance of their informants. Rather it is performed through everyone's efforts to define it'.

As we can see, regarding phenomena as process shifts the scientific gaze from trying to articulate the specific thing-like characteristics of social phenomena, to articulate how phenomena are continuously produced and reproduced: that is, the processes through which they emerge, evolve, reoccur, change and decline over time. Jorgenson (1991), for example, interviewed people about the meaning of 'family' and found that the lack of stable meanings, referring to 'family' in different ways during and in between interview settings, indicated the fluctuating nature of the phenomenon ('meanings of family').

Metaphors for research phenomena are, of course, also much more *domain-specific*. We now move from general metaphors about research phenomena to more specific ones, in use by researchers within their specific fields of study. On this level there are various dominant metaphors for what researchers set out to study, be it society, the mind, learning, an occupation or healthcare. It would be going too far to cover various fields of study here, and we want in this book to emphasize general aspects of the research process and not field-specific aspects. We just remind the reader that dominant metaphors for societies or organizations may be to see them as machines or organisms – the former emphasize a stable and consistent production apparatus, the latter indicate the interchange with the environment, adaptation tendencies, societal or organizational life cycles (Morgan, 1997; Swedberg, 2020).

These metaphors (organism, machines) are sometimes paradigmatic in nature, significantly guiding the research. For example, regarding society as an organism means that researchers tend to look at it as a living unit made up of specific functions that grows and develops over time. In contrast, if society is regarded as a machine, the focus is more on its mechanisms, efficiency and precision. Similarly, regarding the brain as a computer has significantly shaped the development of cognitive science (Gardner, 1987). One can also, of course, talk about more middle-range domain-specific metaphors, such as Weber's iron cage or Bourdieu's (1984) image of the social and the cultural as a specific capital, which has had a significant impact on many disciplines in social science. The point here is that domain-specific metaphors significantly shape the focus of scientific inquiry and theorization.

Taken together, we have two levels of metaphors of research phenomena. First, general metaphors that see research phenomena in different ways, such as pieces of social nature or human artefacts. Second, more specific metaphors that researchers use to create or revise the more precise social phenomena they target (e.g. organization as a machine, the family as a neurosis, gender as an identity trap).

Alternative metaphors

Alternative metaphors for research phenomena typically emphasize the loose, ambiguous or even fleeting nature of what the researcher tries to say something about. If the overall purpose of research is seen as story-telling, social phenomena, such as professions or marriage, are not seen as pieces of nature but as researcher-produced artefacts. That is, as something humanely constructed, not only in the sense that they are consequences of social development and human action – in the Stone Age there were no dentists, teenagers, burnout syndromes or tourism – but that the precise meanings are an outcome of how researchers and others construct these phenomena. One could say that they are *researcher inventions* – to separate this understanding from the reified or cemented constructions addressed above and from co-produced artefacts, as discussed below. For example, different researchers may come up with very different numbers of professions – and see professionals as a small elite or as a major part of all working people in a country.

Researchers with this bent then argue that social phenomena do not simply arrive neatly in the form of specific and pre-established objects of study, such as class, power, institution, ethnicity and innovation, which are widely assumed in social science. Instead, the phenomena presenting themselves for us, as researchers, are always created and shaped by our pre-understanding in the sense of the specific culture, historical time and language in which we are situated, as well as by established theory and specific data (Alvesson & Sandberg, 2021). What we study reflects research conventions. Hence, truly new phenomena are typically creatively constructed, and then developed, and perhaps radically revised.

Phenomena are of course rarely entirely a matter of researchers' imagination or discursive moves constructing something from scratch. Reality 'delivers' raw material in terms of physical objects, people that talk and behave etc., but out of all this, researchers carve out, structure and actively construct phenomena to be studied. For example, it is seldom obvious what is a community, sexual harassment, resistance, drug abuse or strategic decision making. Clearly, researchers cannot start in the dark, but need to have some idea of what is to be studied, which is typically informed by societal and research conventions. In most cases, too, a revision of a phenomenon is heavily based on the original view of that phenomenon – it is rare that entirely new phenomena emerge.

A related image is to regard phenomena as *co-produced artefacts*. Here researchers are not separated from, but form a significant part of, the production of social phenomena in interaction with those studied. There is an interaction between researcher and participants and they tend to form objects of studies together. Gender researchers and their interviewees then accomplish gender in interactions. Business school academics interviewing managers may trigger and reinforce responses that managerial work is about strategic management, leadership, decision making, etc. Motives are also constructed in situations where motives are on the agenda, that is when there is an expectation that some kind of account of motivations can and should be produced (Mills, 1940). Research phenomena are then interactional accomplishments, and are not 'just there' before researcher and participants join forces in co-producing the phenomena.

As we pointed out before, in all or at least most research fields there are several *off-centre domain-specific* metaphors in addition to the dominant ones. Organizations are, for example, not only viewed as machines, organisms and super persons, but also, as discussed in the Introduction, as theatres, psychic prisons, cultures, etc. (Morgan, 1997). Educational institutions are not only seen as social arrangements for learning, but also as unemployment buffers, CV-boosting vehicles and sites for cuddling. Gender can similarly be viewed through different metaphors: not only conventionally as socialization or structural outcomes or roles, but also as traps, labyrinths, prisons, moves, role-playing, etc. Identity constructions may be viewed as surfing, shaking, strategizing, story-telling, as work, play or manoeuvring (Alvesson, 2010). Leaders may be viewed as prophets, pastors, psychotherapists, pedagogues and party hosts (Alvesson, Blom & Sveningsson, 2017) or as cyborgs, gardeners, commanders, artists (Alvesson & Spicer, 2011). All these off-centre, domain-specific metaphors may be seen as reflecting phenomena 'out there', pieces of social nature, as co-produced artefacts or as researcher inventions. However, more colourful or creative metaphors typically rely heavily on the researcher's imagination and thus are more informed by the general image of research phenomena as artefacts rather than pieces of social nature.

Additional metaphors

One could potentially see research phenomena as *discourses*, in the sense that there are no 'real' objective phenomena beyond or behind the discourse, viewed as the constitutive and decisive element. The interesting thing is then not gender, leisure activities, youth crime, COVID-19 death rates or racism 'as such', but discourses about the subject matter. Other metaphors for social phenomena are *appearances* or simulations (or simulacra, as Baudrillard (1994 [1981]) formulated it). Here the interest may be on the image or the spectacle (e.g. Alvesson, 2013). Research phenomena may also be viewed as *political acts* (a representation like class society indicates injustice whereas a reference to post-affluence claims excessive consumption and an encouragement to reduce consumption).

If we look at domain-specific phenomena of study, rarer, and perhaps imaginative but possibly also far-fetched metaphors can be considered. One could see organizations as circuses, leadership as dancing, gender as comedy, identity as wrestling, society as drama, etc. Generally, we see much scope for working with alternative metaphors for the phenomena being studied, but our major take in this book is metaphors for the research process, not for how to theoretically understand the aspects of reality being studied.

Summary

Table 5.4 Summary of metaphorizing the phenomenon

Metaphors	Dominant	Alternative	Additional
RP element			
Research phenomenon	– Piece of social nature – Social object – Thing-like social construction – Process – Domain-specific, e.g. gender as performance	– Researcher invention – Co-produced artefacts – Off-centre domain, e.g. gender as trap	– Discourses – Appearances – Political acts – Off-centre domain, e.g. gender as comedy

The dominant metaphors of research phenomena as pieces of (social) nature or objects as something discrete and fairly stable are closely connected to the assumption that reality is more or less given out there. This of course reflects ontological and epistemological commitments about the nature of reality and how our knowledge-developing practices relate to these. Research phenomena are very much seen in a thing-like way, as entities with particular properties. Sometimes phenomena are regarded more as process – which is almost in opposition to the 'thing' view of phenomena – but occasionally more as a matter of stable things in motion. (There are many views on 'process', some emphasizing its essential nature; e.g. Sandberg et al., 2015.)

As alternative metaphors, we proposed phenomena as artefacts and researcher invention, suggesting that research phenomena are largely something constructed by the researchers themselves, sometimes for good and sometimes for less good reasons. It is less good when researchers' constructions of phenomena reflect cultural taken-for-granted assumptions, which is arguably quite common. The additional metaphors further point to the constructed nature of research phenomena, as well as to the inseparability of researcher and research phenomena.

One could add that phenomena creation is a key aspect of imaginative research, that is, one 'sees' or shows something one could study that has not really been considered before, or at least not studied before. Sometimes the idea of objects of study being pieces of social nature means a premature fixing and re-fixing of something that may be better understood and approached in other ways, that is as an artefact leading to a 'bad' (worn out, highly selective) representation of phenomena. Reflexive exercises moving between different metaphors may, in the end, lead researchers to stick to the piece of social nature metaphor, but the actual pieces being studied may be quite different from those originally worked with.

CHAPTER SUMMARY

In this chapter we have metaphorized the following four grounding elements of the research process: overall point of research, researcher's role, research collective and research phenomena. Some of these elements often seem to go under the radar in many methodology textbooks and in research, and therefore escape critical or reflexive consideration. Careful consideration of the overall purpose is easily ignored, as researchers often concentrate on studying something specific, aiming to extend knowledge on the subject matter without seriously asking why or 'so what?'. Also, issues around the nature of research phenomena and the significance and meaning of the research collective and its strong role in predetermining important aspects of the research process may easily be taken for granted.

Through a combination of identifying and proposing some novel metaphors not directly in circulation, we identify a spectrum of possible reference points for thinking about and rethinking the aforementioned grounding elements of research. As said, all the reflexivity domains (e.g. me-ism, we-ism, interaction-ism) may be used in combination with the various metaphors covering parts of the research process. It is fully possible, for example, to see phenomenon construction through a me-ism or discursivism approach to reflexivity. How do I tend to construct phenomena to make them accessible for my knowledge claims? Can I approach them differently? Use another vocabulary?

One can also view the researcher's role from the angle of criticism. The idea of social research is not necessarily an expression of some superior rationality as much as an outcome of contemporary trends to celebrate the 'knowledge society' and the associated basic ideology of expert-led social engineering leading to optimized social institutions and people. The naïve researcher may unconsciously and unwillingly be part of a social engineering state, and contribute with technological or legitimizing knowledge, involuntary supporting social elites and reproducing social order through participation in dominant discourses.

During a specific research project, it may be worth going back to the reflexivity domain options to see if some of them may be more helpful, given the project and the researcher's general situation. The research collective may, at different times, for example, be experienced as more or less of a helpful community, a highly competitive marketplace or as a social box. The spontaneous experience of the collective being a community may then be counteracted through the consideration of a metaphor that may at first be experienced as alien but, upon reflection, stimulate creative rethinking and reconsideration of the researcher–collective relationship. The supporting community may be thought of as a blinker or even a padded cell for the conformist researcher. The collective is arguably a key driver behind most research projects, but is insufficiently acknowledged, as academics prefer to emphasize their individuality and free choice. Important here are exercises in de-familiarization, i.e. cultivating reflexivity through trying to see what appears to be normal, acceptable and self-evident as strange, exotic, arbitrary and an expression of normalizing power, creating a closed mindset.

NOTE

1.   Of course, research may be meaningful to the individual researcher, finding it interesting or personally developing, but in many cases, this can also be doubted. The PhD student may be occupied by the research in order to complete the PhD and then move on, or the postdoc may do research only in order to be employable or promotable, mainly having an instrumental or cynical approach, and not necessarily believing in the value of the research (Alvesson, Gabriel & Paulsen, 2017).

6
METAPHORIZING THE FRAMING ELEMENTS OF THE RP

In this chapter we will focus on the framing elements of the research process (RP). Although all elements in one sense or another frame the conduct of research, key framers are often the literature review, theory and design. It is worth noting that although the methodology textbooks we looked at all regarded the literature review and theory (e.g. more general theoretical frameworks or perspectives) as key elements, there are variations of views of how to define them, and if they are addressed as two separate elements or not. By the 'literature review' we mean an overview and summing up of work within the substantive (empirical) domain, while 'theory' refers to more general perspectives, which are typically more abstract and apply to a range of empirical domains. Boundaries are, of course, often floating.

LITERATURE REVIEW

Systematically going through at least a sample of existing studies within a specific area is a vital part of almost all research. Many researchers find ambitious and systematic literature reviews highly beneficial, indeed necessary, as they help them to get a better grasp of a specific domain of research. In journal publications this is often mandatory and many journals are filled with extensive reference lists, sometimes occupying 20% of the article space. The lists seem to have increased over time and reading journal articles frequently means facing many inserted references, often obstructing the flow of the reading.

According to the conventional view, the aim of the literature review is to identify and evaluate existing studies related to the topic in question (e.g. childrearing in Hispanic middle-class families in Nebraska, USA, sexual abuse victims' experiences of encounters with healthcare professionals, or moral narratives of marijuana smokers) to give the researcher 'a sense of what the field takes to be known, what is possible, and what needs further exploration' (Hatch, 2002: 41). The literature review also 'informs the reader how knowledgeable you are about your research problem; it is a summary of work related to your problem; a critical evaluation of what is seen as relevant to your problem, what is known and not known about it' (Hesse-Biber & Leary, 2011: 336). In other words, the literature review is supposed to provide a map-like overview of the existing knowledge domain within which you can position your study by highlighting some gaps in the existing knowledge map that need to be filled (Alvesson & Sandberg, 2013a). However, as Barney (2020: 2) points out, research is not about filling any gaps but 'important gaps' in the prior literature. What is an 'important gap' is sometimes not particularly clear. For example, it may be more important for the researcher and others in his/her academic micro-tribe than for other people. This literature review or mapping of existing knowledge in an area may include reference to a single, 'overarching theory or by several related theories' (Berg, 1998: 28), but it is essential to locate the study in relation to theory that has already been generated in the appropriate area (Hatch, 2002: 39).

Many researchers seem to assume that the review domain is more or less given. Often what is 'in' or 'out' of a specific area is presented as unproblematic. However, as we noted in our discussion about research phenomena in the previous chapter, most of what we study has no clear or absolute boundaries. For example, although established bodies of literature may use labels such as 'institution', 'leadership', 'ethnicity', 'conflict' and 'teaching skills' to describe their domain, these labels may not convey much meaning due to the endless variation in their usage. The literature that needs to be consulted about childrearing in Hispanic middle-class families in Nebraska may be open for different understandings about who is supposed to be involved in the rearing, who should be classified as a 'child', when is someone Hispanic, what exactly is middle class and a family, and how relevant is Nebraska? What about 16-year-old 'children', people who could in a sense be categorized as children but who do not see themselves as particularly Hispanic (even though three of four grandparents spoke Spanish as their primary language and had lived in Mexico)? What about divorced people and those with close ties to grandparents and cousins, and families with one working-class and possibly one middle-class parent? And are Hispanic studies from Kansas, Spain or even further afield relevant to review?

Literatures using contrasting labels to represent different research domains may appear to mirror how different parts of reality can be conveniently distinguished. However, a closer and more critical look at these literatures may reveal that the same or similar domains are actually represented in very different ways. For example, role and identity are sometimes used as contrast, sometimes as synonyms (Alvesson & Gjerde, 2020). Many researchers using 'institutional theory' in organization studies regard variation as an indicator of healthy pluralism and see its different versions as offering the promise of theory integration. However, some argue that 'for those who have attempted to scratch beneath the surface of this supposed promise, one experience would have to be very common: considerable confusion' (Lok, 2020: 733). How the literature review is composed is therefore seldom straightforward. Often, the simplest way out is to go for key words or titles in leading journals and then read and summarize these in a straightforward way. But this may be problematic as key words may not tell us that much, and there is a risk that conservative and unimaginative ways of addressing the literature are promoted (Alvesson & Sandberg, 2020). Despite such complications, there is close to consensus that the literature review offers a platform for being able to utilize existing ideas and empirical findings and then to go further in adding to earlier knowledge. There is an assumption of a more or less distinct, relevant literature that needs to be read, summarized and drawn upon – to build upon or have a dialogue with. For example, vom Brocke et al. (2009: 1) argue that:

> science is a cumulative endeavour as new knowledge is often created in the process of interpreting and combining existing knowledge. This is why literature reviews have long played a decisive role in scholarship. The quality of literature reviews is particularly determined by the literature search process. As Sir Isaac Newton eminently put it: 'If I can see further, it is because I am standing on the shoulders of giants.' Drawing on this metaphor, the goal of writing a literature review is to reconstruct the giant of accumulated knowledge in a specific domain.

A common way of reasoning is therefore to carry out a literature review to show what is known, what is problematic, what can be expected, and how a new study may relate to existing knowledge and advance and contribute to a field. Often the literature review is assumed to be part of the accumulation of research. Review sections tend to promise that earlier studies offer, on the whole, a robust ground for further work. But as with almost all established truths, at least in social research, there may be alternative modes of reasoning.

Dominant metaphors

There is a strong tendency in many review articles to address a set – or a mess (to use a different metaphor) – of complicated knowledge contributions in a short format, sometimes with the pretence of summarizing several studies in one sentence. Crossan and Apaydin (2009: 1170), for example, identify 'leaders' ability and motivation to innovate' as a theme and refer, in one sentence, to a set of studies emphasizing 'factors' like tolerance of ambiguity, self-confidence, openness to experience, unconventionality, independence, proactivity, attribution bias, determination to succeed, personal initiative and managerial tolerance for change. The impression conveyed is that these signifiers effectively inform the reader about what is behind innovation, but it is open to discussion whether knowledge about complex reality can be efficiently summarized and reported in such a simple way. The idea of a review is nevertheless captured through the metaphor *knowledge packaging*. The idea of the literature review is very much about surveying existing literature, that is, examining and describing the areas and features of it to construct a map of it and to identify what needs more work in order to provide a solid base for the building project. However, how literature is connected, divided up and packed in reviews is often arbitrary (Locke & Golden-Biddle, 1997).

Broadly in line with this knowledge packaging metaphor is that many review authors see existing studies within a research domain as pieces in a large *jigsaw puzzle*. Elsbach and Van Knippenberg (2020: 1277) argue that 'we advance knowledge through programs of research in which studies build on previous work and set the stage for future research'. In this view, the overall point of the review aiming to integrate earlier studies is to piece together a clearer image of the domain in question and, based on this, to identify what pieces are missing and what pieces need to be shifted around to make the puzzle more complete.

The accumulation norm suggests that advancement of scientific knowledge occurs through an ongoing expansion and positive adding of studies within a research domain, as emphasized by the knowledge building metaphor. Thus, Elsbach and Van Knippenberg (2020: x) argue that 'we build knowledge through programs of research in which studies help advance knowledge by building on previous work and setting the stage for future research'. The wealth of studies combined may offer strong and reliable parts of a large knowledge-building project. The literature review, then, is part of, and feeds into, an overall image of the purpose of research as building knowledge and the academic doing a literature review is very much a type of construction worker-researcher, producing new pieces and/or putting them together in the best way.

Although the accumulation norm overlaps with the jigsaw-puzzle view, it is not the same. You may work with a jigsaw puzzle while being sceptical of accumulation or being distrustful towards much of the work within a domain, and you can believe in the accumulation view without adapting the puzzle metaphor. However, combinations of the two are common: working with a complicated puzzle and being suspicious about the value of many of the pieces mean an overwhelmingly complicated project.

In the prevalent view of research as knowledge building or picture generation, the literature review may be portrayed as *gap-spotting* (Alvesson & Sandberg, 2013a). The point is to scan – or even more carefully review – existing literature to identify missing or blurred spots on the overall emerging (accumulated) picture of the field. Literature review as gap-spotting focuses on what (pieces) are 'lacking' or missing in the current picture (or knowledge) of the world, as a way to point out what needs to be added to make the picture more complete. One can, of course, and should not only ask what is lacking but also potentially criticize the existing picture of some aspects of reality, as the current picture may distort, ignore or even silence or leave out (deliberately) some aspects of reality for consideration. Existing studies may be flawed.

The gap-spotting metaphor often indicates similar modes of approaching the literature review as knowledge packaging and the jigsaw puzzle, but they are not the same. Knowledge packaging indicates that the literature can be effectively summarized, the jigsaw puzzle metaphor indicates the work of getting pieces of knowledge together, while gap-spotting emphasizes a search for white spots on the knowledge map. They can – and often are – combined but can also indicate different projects or parts of a literature review process. However, sometimes the literature review may be seen as a selective and creative *construction project* rather than as a vacuum-cleaning or knowledge-packaging job in the sense that the researcher selectively brings together different bodies of literature in order to legitimize a specific research study (Locke & Golden-Biddle, 1997). The idea is that the construction project is an outcome of the researcher's choices and an active way of doing something with the ambiguous and scattered books and articles that are candidates for consideration in the literature review. This is not a strongly mainstream version, but still a fairly common one, and thus part of what we refer to as dominant or conventional metaphors.

Alternative metaphors

The dominant metaphors broadly regard the literature review as thoroughly and methodically reviewing existing literature in order to identify missing pieces in the communal jigsaw puzzle or white spots in the knowledge map that need to be filled, and, based on that, indicating how one's study will contribute to existing literature by adding yet another piece to the jigsaw puzzle. All metaphors are based on an approach to existing literature and knowledge as, on the whole, credible and offering a reliable ground to build on. But there are alternative views, emphasizing paradigmatic variation and the need for more basic critique and/or the significance of approaching literature as more open, preliminary and uncertain in terms of valuable knowledge.

Since Kuhn's paradigm theory (1970) there has been much critique and questioning of the knowledge accumulation ideal (Abbott, 2004). Studies rely on different assumptions, use language differently and have a variety of idiosyncratic characteristics, including focus and questions asked, etc., all of which make comparisons difficult and thus undermine the idea of knowledge accumulation. Alternative metaphors often see existing work in an open or sceptical way, and do not assume that one should necessarily build 'positively' on this. Much in social science is contested.

Many critical review articles show that much published research has serious flaws, sometimes of a methodological nature, but often they are based on problematic assumptions.

Also, in many research areas where several hundred studies have been conducted, the studies have fundamental weaknesses and offer little of real value. A case in point is (parts of) the leadership field. According to a growing number of commentators, many, if not most, sub-areas of leadership studies suffer from questionable assumptions, design and theoretical reasoning (e.g. Fischer, 2018; Hunter et al., 2007). Van Knippenberg and Sitkin (2013: 45), for example, argue that 'the vast majority of transformational leadership studies have relied on a measurement approach for which there is overwhelming evidence of its invalidity'. Hence, the varied credibility of studies in the leadership field (as well as studies in other research domains) suggests that there is a need to more carefully assess the identified studies before including them in a review and using them as more or less robust points of departure for knowledge advancement, something which tends to be overlooked by advocating a (near) full stock inventory. Here the literature review works more as a *fault-finder* or a demolition device. Fault-finding is of value in itself – critique is vital – but it is also a key part in developing new and better research questions, designs and studies.

Even though most researchers acknowledge that some theoretical background and inspiration is unavoidable, and possibly also useful, there are authors who point at the risks of reading too much, at least within a narrowly defined core domain (Alvesson & Sköldberg, 2018). They fear that the review will lead researchers into a pre-defined track, obstructing openness and the ideal of the data showing the way, with some nudging from the researcher. Here the review appears to be a *blinker*, blocking the wide-angle view and encouraging tunnel vision, or box thinking, and missing the open-minded exploration of reality. Extensive readings within a specialized area easily means that the dominant or conventional assumptions are taken for granted and the well-read researcher tends to imitate others. Being specialized means the risk of becoming functionally stupid, i.e. being competent within a narrow domain but incapable of thinking and dealing with issues outside this domain. Functional stupidity thereby limits people's reflexive abilities and imagination in research (Alvesson & Spicer, 2016). For some, the ambitious literature review may lead to contamination and loss of intellectual ability to do a good study, while for others it may lead to an unproductive, even harmful, way as it encourages testing a limited set of hypotheses and discourages more open inquiry.

> The real danger of prior knowledge in grounded theory is not that it will contaminate a researcher's perspective, but rather it will force the researcher into testing hypothesis, either covertly or unconsciously, rather than directly observing. (Suddaby, 2006: 635)

As an alternative to dominant metaphors like gap-spotting or jigsaw puzzling, as well as blinker, the literature review can be seen as a *sparring partner* or *dialogue partner* for creating counter-thinking in a field. Here, there is a somewhat less trustful and benevolent attitude to existing studies, but still learning possibilities are emphasized. The view is more positive than in assumption-challenging. The ambition is to have productive variation and (dis-)agreement. Optimally, the researcher uses the literature to cultivate his or her intellect and allows the literature to have a 'knock-on' effect on him- or herself.

> This type of approach foreshadows a text-building strategy that unfolds according to the following 'moves': 1) identifying a 'good' conversation, 2) analyzing the conversation, and 3) adding to the conversation. Conversations provide the baseline for a contribution: that is, they fix a reference point for establishing what is known in a particular area of investigation. (Patriotta, 2017: 753–754)

But if the point of research is to be more independent of existing knowledge and aim for novel ideas, including a strong element of knowledge demolition, the literature review may be regarded as an *assumption digger* – an exercise in identifying and challenging assumptions (Alvesson & Sandberg, 2013a; Davis, 1971). Here, the researcher does not look for gaps but digs down under the literature and theory to lay bare its footing and, based on that, generate a new set of assumptions that form the foundation of an alternative theory. In contrast to the knowledge-building review, which regards reviews as a building exercise, the problematizing review regards reviews as an opening-up project that enables researchers to imagine how to rethink existing literature in ways that generate new and 'better' ways of thinking about specific phenomena.

A problematizing methodology for such a reading could include the following principles: (1) identifying a domain of literature; (2) identifying and articulating the assumptions underlying this domain; (3) evaluating them and focusing on more problematic or limiting elements; (4) developing alternative assumptions with the potential to become the start of a novel theoretical contribution; (5) considering the new assumptions in relation to its audience (what is seen as new, credible and interesting); and (6) evaluating the alternative set of assumptions (Alvesson & Sandberg, 2013a). The ambition is to come up with productive and interesting new assumptions that mean novel research questions and lines of theoretical reasoning.

Additional metaphors

An additional metaphor for the review, in particular the more ambitious one, is one of *insight producer*. As an insight producer, the literature review must move beyond what is already known and offer something that also re-signifies (Reed, 2011) or breaks with (Bourdieu et al., 1991) established truth and/or expectations (Suppe, 1979).

A related metaphor for connecting to the existing literature could be *idea-picking*. Rather than an authoritative, well-packaged summary of the state of the art in a subfield, the literature is reviewed broadly and unsystematically with the aim of getting some unexpected inputs to a study (Alvesson & Sandberg, 2020).[1] This calls for variation in readings, which is often assumed to facilitate the generation of ideas.

In cases when research is seen as story-telling, the literature review may be viewed as a *reservoir of narrative material* for producing new and powerful stories that help us to see our world and ourselves in a new light. The researcher may then read existing literature in a search for advice with plotting, for example an inviting vignette, and good quotes, backing up the account and filling text space.

Still another metaphor is *vacuum cleaning*, overlapping many of the more conventional ones mentioned. Here there is a strong emphasis of an inclusive literature review, where the researcher needs to mention everything that could be relevant. This is sometimes operationalized as a search of articles with the 'right' keywords or titles in a number of leading journals for the last 10–20 years. This metaphor points at efforts to be inclusive, to a systematic but fairly superficial activity with a focus on volume, for example covering as much as possible.

Summary

Table 6.1 Summary of metaphorizing the literature review

Metaphors	*Dominant*	*Alternative*	*Additional*
RP element			
Literature review	– Knowledge packaging – Jigsaw puzzle – Gap-spotting – Construction project	– Fault-finder – Blinker – Sparring partner – Dialogue partner – Assumption digger	– Insight producer – Idea-picking – Reservoir of narrative material – Vacuum cleaning

The dominant metaphors of knowledge packaging, jigsaw puzzle and gap-spotting portray the literature review very much as mapping existing knowledge about a specific research phenomenon and, based on that, identifying areas which need to be further developed to make the overall knowledge map more complete. Here the review is viewed as a solid foundation for further work.

The alternative and more critical metaphors point at more open, fragile or even problematic aspects of the existing literature, suggesting more or less critical readings. These metaphors also highlight the blinker problem of unquestioningly reviewing the existing literature, as well as suggest seeing the review as an exercise in fault-finding and providing options for radical rethinking.

As possible less critical alternatives we proposed that the literature review can be seen as a sparring or dialogue partner in knowledge development; as an assumption digger, with the aim of questioning the assumptions underlying the established literature; and similarly, to regard the review as an opening-up exercise, with the aim of creating new and different ways of understanding a specific research phenomenon. The additional metaphors point to yet other possible ways of viewing the literature review, such as insight generator, idea-picking, or, in more conventional terms, as a vacuum-cleaning job.

Having summarized part of the literature, the reflexive researcher may then take a step or two back and look at this as an object of inquiry. How has this literature review produced a particular type of knowledge on innovation, poverty, sexual minorities, social work, leisure, brand value, or whatever. This may inspire a re-consideration and efforts to avoid reproducing conventional ways of ordering the knowledge field. The researcher may be inclined to move between seeing the existing literature as, for example, a helpful foundation, a critical dialogue partner or a potential blinker for the study. After consideration of the options, the chosen major metaphor(s) may be based on what creative and productive possibilities the researcher imagines, and not necessarily on the most convenient one, allowing an easy way forward. Sometimes that may involve building upon and adding to a specific literature, sometimes seeing this as something to engage with in more or less critical, non-conformist ways.

THEORY

Another central RP element is the theories that are used to inform a specific study in various ways. This is of course also the topic for a literature review, but there is a difference between covering existing studies in a domain and to go through a selected theoretical perspective and perhaps review the main thinkers and their key works. Many seem to share the view that qualitative research is often modestly theoretically framed and governed. The idea of the discovery of grounded theory is that theory emerges from data and there are only fairly weak and, in the research process, late connections to established theory. The researcher should produce his or her theory, based firmly on data, and not be guided by other, 'un-grounded', theories, which are seen as speculative and unreliable compared to grounded theory. Quantitative studies are often based on the production of hypotheses derived from the literature and thus are theoretically framed. However, qualitative research is also fairly often guided by some specific theory, such as institutional theory or a Foucauldian perspective, which means that the theoretical framing significantly drives the study.

The common view is that theory 'is the underlying structure, the scaffolding or frame of your study, it consists of concepts that inform your study' (Merriam & Tisdell, 2015: 85). It is typically comprised of a set of concepts that are linked to each other, providing an explanation of, or perspective on, something. There are, however, a rich variety of different conceptualizations of theory (Abend, 2008; Sandberg & Alvesson, 2021). One way is to regard theory as a specific framework. Examples of theoretical frameworks are (various versions of) structuration theory, psychoanalysis, Vygotsky's learning theory, practice theory, performative theory or institutional theory. A theoretical framework is also quite commonly seen as the specific paradigm or research tradition within which researchers are situated, and which therefore 'frames' their studies significantly. Denzin and Lincoln (1994: 12–13) argue, for example, that 'all qualitative researchers … are guided by highly abstract principles', such as ontology, epistemology and methodology, that is, by a paradigm. Similarly, Symon and Cassell (2012: 15) state that these paradigmatic frameworks 'have practical consequences for the way we do research in terms of topic, focus of study, what we see as "data", how we collect and analyse data, how we theorize, and how we write up our research accounts'.

Besides these high-brow concerns, a theoretical framework is typically comprised of more specific theoretical ideas about the subject matter, whether this is the nature of contemporary society, social characters, roles, stress and burnout among bus drivers, consumer decision making, gender victimization in late capitalist welfare states, opinions about immigrants, or whatever.

An additional view is that a theoretical framework is mainly about 'methodological theory' or 'methodological approaches', such as case study, ethnomethodology, discourse analysis and grounded theory. Nevertheless, the overall view is that the theoretical framework, be it a specific theory (e.g. practice theory), a paradigm (e.g. interpretivism) or a methodological approach (e.g. grounded theory), in different ways conceptualizes and frames 'what is under study' (Knapp, 2016: 11) in significant ways.

Theory can be seen as an input, process or an output of the RP. When seen as an *input*, the researcher's commitment to a theory significantly controls the project. The purpose is to use theory to illuminate a phenomenon. A major ingredient here is typically the received theory: Marxism, Foucauldianism, psychoanalysis, etc. As a powerful input, it puts strong imprints on the entire enterprise, governing hypotheses, design and the framing of results, tied to the theory. It 'frames' the study. Sometimes the outcome of a study is more or less given, as the theory applied by a believer tends to be confirmed.

Moving to the other extreme, theory is an *outcome* of the RP. This is the idea of grounded theory and other inductive studies, where the systematic, comparative work with data leads to a theory. Input elements, such as earlier studies and existing theory, are best blanked, or minimized as a steering force, while diligent, rigorous empirical work is the key driver. Theory is not significant as an input element but is expected to gradually emerge during the RP, driven by careful attention to data, and expected to show the way. (More about this view on data later.)

Theory as *process* means there is an interplay between theoretical ideas and empirical work and perhaps the researcher's creativity and empirically-supported imagination. This idea is a key part of abduction, that is, the ability to see patterns, to reveal deep structures. The researcher uses his/her ability to go beyond 'pure data', typically informed by a sense of theory, but not 'applying theory' (Alvesson & Sköldberg, 2018; Swedberg, 2016). Here there is less of a given theoretical framework and the theoretical contribution is rarely seen as a direct outcome of data and data management. But theory can stand in a dialogical relationship with empirical material. In this book, we mainly treat theory as a process element. That is, we downplay purely theoretical or theory-refining studies and consider theory as involved in the earlier parts of the RP, and we don't see it as purely grounded, but we do consider these views and address metaphors of the theoretical framework as a *steering mechanism* as well as a process outcome or *product*.

Dominant metaphors

Theory is often understood as a kind of *mirror* of reality. The theory is seen as a concentrated summary reflecting the selected part of the social world and pointing at how it is connected. For example, in much deductive research, the idea is to test to what extent a specific theory adequately reflects or can account for reality. The same holds true for more traditional inductive research, where the theory generated from data should represent that data as exactly as possible (Glaser & Strauss, 1967). The ideal, for example, is expressed in the principle within grounded theory that 'the matching of theory against data must be rigorously carried out' (Strauss & Corbin, 1994: 273). Still, the need for abstraction and some perspective on a theme always makes a one-to-one relationship theory-data difficult or impossible.

This idea of theory as a mirror, map or match – different words for the same root metaphor (the image behind the thinking) is dominant, but we recognize the many problems and shortcomings of theory as mirroring. Many see theory as more abstract, in that it offers general explanations or modes of understandings rather than mirror and map ideas. In knowledge-building thinking, specific empirical studies may be guided by mirror and map images, but theory is something different. Theory is about explanations, and thus about patterns and tendencies standing 'above' all the variations on the level of reality or data being close to the observable.

When research is seen as picture generation, theory can be seen as a *lens*, which is a fairly common metaphor. Here the emerging picture of the world is framed or shaped in a particular way, guided by a specific lens or perspective. Sometimes the picture of the world is framed in a practice theoretical lens, sometimes by an institution theoretical lens, and so on. These lenses highlight (and suppress) certain features of the emerging picture of the world. While being a mirror of reality downplays the starting point and perspective involved in inquiry, a lens allows for a larger role for how and from where the picture is taken. Theory is important here, working as a lens to illuminate a phenomenon in a truthful but somewhat selective way, depending on which lens is being used.

Another dominant understanding of theory is theory as a 'logically-connected system of general propositions, which establishes a relationship between two or more variables' (Abend, 2008: 177). Here theory can be seen as a general explanation device through functioning as a *variable connector*. Theory is then the work with independent, mediating and dependent variables, leading to an explanation of a specific phenomenon, typically through establishing causal relations. This idea of theory is often expressed in boxes-and-arrows thinking. Here reality tends to be downplayed somewhat as much energy is devoted to data and how they can be accounted for by theoretical work with variables. This is more pronounced in quantitative than qualitative studies, but sometimes also characterizes the latter, such as in several ethnographic studies within sociology (e.g. Abend et al., 2013).

Another common version of theory is theory as something that makes us understand a specific phenomenon in a richer way, offering 'an original "interpretation", "reading", or "way of making sense" of a certain slice of the empirical world' (Abend, 2008: 178). Here theory is more of an interpretation-support or *reading device*. (Reading is about interpretation and creative meaning-making.) Theory, then, is to offer a qualified understanding of social phenomena by determining their meaning: that is, what phenomena such as decision, diversity and identity are about. As Blumer (1954: 3) puts it, the purpose of theory is 'to develop a meaningful interpretation of the social world, or some significant part of it ... so that people may have a clearer understanding of their world, its possibilities of development, and the directions along which it may move'. Many researchers locate themselves very close to the subjects being studied to produce descriptive accounts of subjects' direct experiences of their world. However, developing theories that enrich understanding typically involves identifying and articulating a 'hidden' meaning or a deeper meaning than is directly experienced.

Another fairly common metaphor is theory as *Weltanschauung*, a *worldview* or philosophy that is used as an a priori and superior-ground perspective, being more or less independent of experience and the details of empirical work, 'logically prior to any contact with the social world' (Abend, 2008: 180). Examples could be Marxist, poststructuralist or feminist theory. These types of theories then become strong, reality-defining perspectives with paradigm qualities. A worldview tends to dominate the ways in which researchers understand social reality. The theory is so strong and definite that social reality and specific data referring to it are fairly weak in its capacity to kick back at the assumptions and ordering of the world suggested by the worldview theory.

These various views of theory form a spectrum in terms of the theory/data being central and driving the inquiries. Some theory metaphors indicate data-driven theory, others put theory into the driver's seat. Viewing theory as mirroring indicates an outcome of empirical inquiry. Lens and variable-connecting theory guide empirical study but are supposedly revised by outcomes. Reading-device theory is subordinated to efforts to produce interpretations of an empirical phenomenon. And in worldview theory, the idea is that theory is in control of empirical material, data being heavily guided, if not domesticated, by the theory being applied, although there is some space for internal critique or revisions.

Alternative metaphors

An alternative metaphor could be to see theory as a *performative force* shaping social reality. Social reality is strongly influenced by discourse and through the use of discourse researchers produce or reproduce, at least to some extent and as part of a collective force affecting how people think and relate to themselves and their world. Gender discrimination, sex roles, burnout, authentic leadership, strategic management, personality type, or learning style are parts of discourses that have a reality-defining effect, both through being part of general culture and through specific practices where policy makers and practitioners are guided by the knowledge and the normative control built into this (Foucault, 1980). Gender studies, for example, do not so much mirror as move gender relations in society, at least to the extent they are read and are taken seriously or influence public opinion, policy and practice.

In critical studies, theory is more a matter of provocation and aims to trigger emancipatory thinking. Theory is then understood as an *eye-opener* rather than as a mirror or a device for sorting impressions of the phenomenon being studied (Alvesson & Deetz, 2021). As an eye-opener, much of the theory's power is to make the person working with the theory more attentive to aspects that typically remain hidden from sight, such as cultural taken-for-granted assumptions. We may, for example, be caught by conventional categories and by thinking (only) of two genders and neglect the many possible forms and modes of doing gender. Theory, then, works against the spontaneous inclinations of the researcher. Eye-opening may work and, of course, also affects actions. It is, however, more cognitive in nature than pointing at performativity and is more open about possible impact, which may emerge in a later step rather than directly from the performative effect of research.

Theory may also be viewed as a *potentializer*, opening up new possibilities of thinking and acting. The theory is then a cognitive resource that empowers the person familiar with and capable of using the theory. The potentializer-theory means that sharper, more nuanced ways of thinking about (selected parts or aspects of) the world become possible. Theory functions – at least this is the intention – a bit like an IQ improver, but more clearly as a guide or inspiration to new ways of acting. Here the metaphor indicates something different from theory as eye-opener, which is more an intellectual input to liberation from constraint, a counter-force to cultural taken-for-granted ideas that function as blinkers or vision-blockers. The potentializer may indicate more 'technical' possibilities for better, more nuanced or rigorous thinking. Through valuable concepts and differentiations – possible elements of theory – we can think more cleverly, that is, make insightful distinctions.

However, there are no guarantees that functions like eye-opening or potentializing are realized. Theory, like other elements in research, may fail and lead to the opposite of what is hoped for. But the idea is that theory can work in positive ways – to help us to break out of established way of reasoning and thinking more sharply or at least differently about what is being studied. The two metaphors sometimes go together, but they can also encourage ideas of theory that point in different directions, as potentializing may not involve great new understandings and eye-opening insights may not be easily translated into possibilities for action or better analytical and precise thinking, but rather into thinking differently.

Theory as a *cage* (or box) is at some distance from what emerges in explicit texts, typically exhibiting a positive, if not celebratory, view of theory. It is the opposite of the potentializer. When theory is seen as a cage, the constraining impact is emphasized. Often researchers are caught in psychic prisons, such as commitments to theories or political ideologies, controlling and limiting their thinking or sight. Gender students may see patriarchy and oppression everywhere, post-colonialists may explain almost everything worth paying attention to as being related to colonialism, imperialism and racism, and leadership researchers may divide the world into leaders and followers without much thoughtfulness. This is, of course, not only potentially relevant for rigid, cause-and-effect types of theories, but also for seemingly cage-unlike theories. For example, process theory may be seen as a cage, when every aspect of reality is viewed in terms of fluidity, even though some more stable patterns and recurrent themes could potentially be better understood in terms of structures and functions. All theories can be understood as intellectual cages (or mental prisons), including poststructuralism, where a focus on internal contradictions, the unsaid and the indeterminacy of texts may mould researchers' interpretations in specific ways.

The cage may be seen as an entirely negative metaphor, as it draws attention to what a specific focus may mean in terms of constraints and missed opportunities. But cages may have advantages: it is a safe domain and it facilitates focus. Much research, even successful (or perhaps especially successful) traditions, may be firmly established and thus have considerable cage-qualities, keeping theory and its proponents in place. Many researchers seem to prefer to move within a small theoretical space, spending decades on, for example, psychoanalysis, studies of unions or education in physics, using a specific theory. This insight may sometimes lead to 'anti-theory', efforts to break out of a rigid and constraining theoretical grip. The reflexive researcher then tries (or should try) to investigate his or her own theoretical cages, which is often contingent upon the research collective's shared wisdoms and, more broadly, socially established truths and dominant discourses.

Additional metaphors

An additional metaphor could be to see theory as *reflexivity-stimulator*. This overlaps with theory as eye-opener, but while the latter is emphasizing the positive, liberating qualities, the reflexivity-stimulator metaphor leads to a call for a less smooth response. Theory then works not primarily in connection to empirical phenomena, but to the researcher's individual and collective ways of seeing the world, stimulating reflexivity at different levels – perhaps primarily in terms of discursivism, that is, what language is being used and how texts are set up by the researcher,[2] but also as me-ism and we-ism (Alvesson & Sköldberg, 2018). Raising (self-)critical questions is central here. Theory can also be seen as *religion* or *anti-religion* (or ideology). For many advocates of a specific theory, this may have an almost sacred meaning. Marx, Freud, Lacan, Foucault, Bourdieu, Heidegger, etc. may have a guru-status for many. Timmermans and Tavory (2012: 169) suggest that if we want to 'foster theory construction we must be neither theoretical atheists nor avowed monotheists, but informed theoretical agnostics'. Here also, theorists who are themselves agnostics may be canonized by others, for example Foucault by devoted Foucauldians.

Summary

Table 6.2 Summary of metaphorizing theory

Metaphors RP element	Dominant	Alternative	Additional
Theory	– Mirror – Lens – Variable connector – Reading device – Worldview	– Performative force – Eye-opener – Potentializer – Cage	– Reflexivity-stimulator – (Anti-)religion

By far the most dominant metaphor is theory as a mirror of reality, that theory somehow reflects or accurately represents some aspects of reality, something which is also inherent in theory as variable-connector. Common here is the ambition that through theory we are able to explain something. Often this is done with box-and-arrows thinking, where various variables are identified and connected, often in a causal way, and thus explain how things hang together. 'Mirror' may mean different things, and few would use the metaphor as indicating a straightforward replication of reality – that would be as pointless as a map as big or detailed as the part of the world it represents. So, there is always some 'twist' or mode of mirroring involved.

However, many, if not most, qualitative researchers have a less objectivistic outlook and regard theory more as a specific reading device or worldview, illuminating reality through a particular lens or perspective. As a way to counter these dominant metaphors, we proposed that theory can also be seen as a performative force, eye-opener, potential-izer or cage. While the last metaphor indicates the constraining effects of theory, the three former metaphors point to how theory can be used both to change reality and to liberate us from specific entrenched and taken-for-granted views of reality. The idea is that theory is not only or primarily used on phenomena that we try to understand, but is directed to our thinking about the phenomenon, that is, it directly serves reflexivity and may make the researcher better prepared to see other aspects than the conventional ones that so much research imposes and reproduces. The additional metaphors offer yet other possible ways of illuminating the many faces of theory.

Various metaphors for theory may be put into play – as dialectics or, more broadly, as a variety of smorgasbord or supermarket inputs – for the sake of considerations of both frozen paths and new ones. One interesting dimension is to see theory as an eye-opener or potentializer versus as a cage. Theory facilitates seeing, but may also cloud or block our vision, as we see what we are encouraged to see and easily miss what is outside a theory's range and focusing inclinations. One can make a parallel to a microscope. Working with theory as a combined eye-opener and blinker may be fruitful.

DESIGN

Design is another central framing element in the research process. In methodology text-books, design is typically seen as a plan or strategy for how to conduct research. Yin (2014: 28, italics in original), for example, proclaims that research design is a *'logical plan for getting from here to there*, where *here* may be defined as the initial set of questions to be answered, and *there* is some set of conclusions (answers) about the question'. Similarly, Hatch (2002: 38) contends that in order to conduct qualitative research, you need to work with a research design, a 'solid plan that includes attention to' key elements in the research process, such as 'the place of theory, research questions, contexts, participants, data collection strategies, data analysis procedures, and the nature of anticipated find-ings'. The design element is closely linked to the method element (as technology) in that the design is a blueprint or a looser plan that outlines a procedure for carrying out the research in a coherent, logical and systematic way. Put differently, in order to convince the readers of the soundness of a research study (or research proposal) the researcher needs to justify the research design, such as the choice of theoretical framework, sampling procedures, use of data collection techniques and strategies for analysing data that will enable him/her to answer the proposed research question in an adequate way.

Although design typically points at planning and a laid-out structure with steps that are supposed to be followed, the emergent and iterative nature of qualitative research is also highlighted in many texts on the topic. Maxwell (2012), for example, concep-tualizes the process of developing knowledge as an evolving system of interconnected design components.

> Qualitative research design, to a much greater extent than quantitative research, is a 'do-it-your-self' rather than 'off-the-shelf' process, one that involves 'tacking' back and forth between the different components of the design, assessing the implications of purposes, theory, research questions, methods, and validity threats for one another. (Maxwell, 2012: 3)

We could add that much qualitative research is rather loose and falls short of thinking through design issues. A random sample of people are interviewed once in semi-structured interviews. Bygnes (2020), for example, interviewed 25 people living near asylum centres about their views on the establishment of these, while Bristow, Robinson and Ratle (2017) interviewed early career academics about their resistance without much demonstrated thinking about how to structure the studies. The assumption is that the interviewees express their views during single encounters and the interview accounts offer sufficient material for further work. In many other studies there is no specific thought about how to conduct studies where social desirability bias, adaption to norms of talk about a certain topic, interviewer effects, interviewees' shortcomings – inability or unwillingness – to talk about certain issues are addressed. Source critique is often lacking (Schaefer & Alvesson, 2020). A soft design for dealing with the problems of getting good accounts and perhaps finding the right combination of interviewees or – in observation work – the informative situations or episodes to observe, could improve qualitative research, but often there is a lack of care in the thinking through of how to do studies.

The research plan in qualitative research needs to be balanced between being too fixed or cunning and laid back or thoughtless. It needs to consider what is possible in terms of constraints that are always present, including access problems and ethical questions. The question 'how can the research question be best investigated?' is a good starting point for a plan. Most qualitative studies are based on a sample of interviewees or observations – but who or which site or group of people to select? If the unit of analysis is a village, a political issue, an association, a healthcare clinic or social service clients, which actors, sites or moments are to be selected for interviews or observations, and why? Geertz (1973) argues that anthropologists do not study villages, they study in villages, but what parts and what aspects, and how to access and assess these? Observing some revealing events, following certain processes or interviewing a sample, many or a few in depth? And how can one make sure that interviews are more than interview talk following norms of how people talk with strangers, following social conventions, including political correctness or repetitions of what they have read in the media or remember from a textbook? Perhaps one should do re-interviews or try different angles in interviews to check for consistency? One key element is to be open about whether some of the preconceptions informing a study are possibly wrong or misleading. As an example, Goffman (referenced in Müller, 2016) suggests that we study not men and their moments but moments and their men. We can look at actors in a social scene or observe the scene and then consider who is acting or inhabiting it. An initial phase may include significant work helping the researcher to understand the setting and/or the people being studied. Of course, it is important to work with the dilemma of getting close and retaining distance. Here, too, reflexivity is very much about balancing these two ideals.

Dominant metaphors

Referring to parts of the research process as design is, of course, in itself quite heavily metaphorical, although it is typically not recognized as such, and thus is a dead metaphor. As is often the case with dead metaphors, they are seen as cut in stone and not recognized as metaphors. The research design can be conceptualized as a *blueprint* (or master plan) for how to conduct research. In the words of Abutabenjeh and Jaradat (2018: 238), 'a research design is a blueprint to guide the research process by laying out how a study will move from the research purpose/questions to the outcomes'. This is particularly the case when research is seen as knowledge building, where design becomes the master plan for the knowledge to be built, indicating something fixed and solid to be executed. As the editors of a leading journal, *Academy of Management Journal*, point out to their reader, 'choosing the appropriate design is critical to the success of a manuscript at *AMJ*, in part because the fundamental design of a study cannot be altered during the revision process' (Bono & McNamara, 2011: 657). The design is then the principal input and structuring principle for execution. Similarly, in his well-cited textbook on methodology, Creswell (2009: 5), states that 'research designs are plans and the procedures for research that span the decisions from broad assumptions to detailed methods of data collection and analysis'.

If research is about picture generation, then design can be seen as the *composition* of the picture to be generated. As in photography, composition refers to the elements to be included in the picture, particularly their specific arrangement in making up the picture, and how the subject matter is expressed in the picture. Design as composition is the setup for the optimal mapping of what is to be studied: how can the phenomenon be mirrored in as precise a way as possible, or rather in a way that is as precise as the research questions calls for? The design work is a matter of considering coverage as well as precision, of getting a good combination of being able to provide a valuable map that is fairly accurate and reliable, but that also covers more than tiny terrain. As always there is a tradeoff between precision and coverage, and design is partly a matter of handling this.

Often a design is not just a plan, but also (or rather) a credibility account or, more precisely, a *legitimizing account*. Research questions, theory invoked, the plan, the data collection process, the data management, analysis, the theory–data fit, the writing up and the contribution being a clear answer to the research question forms a united whole in the account for design. Ideally this appears as a water-tight and flawless research machinery, having been set in motion and found to be delivering. As such, design as legitimizing account comes fairly late in the project and can be seen as a construction project patching all the ingredients together. But it can also come early, such as in the planning stage in the form of a research proposal, demonstrating rationality to convince research funding authorities about the scientific soundness of the research in question. Whether this overlaps with the research that is actually carried out is another matter.

Instead of regarding design as a more or less fixed plan to be executed in a sequential manner, one can view it as a *pattern following*. In such a view, design changes from something closed and pre-planned to a demand for openness, receptiveness and sensitivity to the variation and complexity of the phenomenon under investigation. In this view, the design is the pattern of the phenomenon that gradually emerges in the research, and which guides the researcher's inquiry, helping the researcher to 'connect the emerging dots'. Design as pattern following is central to many forms of inductive research, where the idea is to let the phenomenon and related theory gradually emerge and take form through the study. For example, ethnographically inclined researchers may focus on cultural, economic or human social behaviour patterns, which require design decisions to be made based on the emergent pattern of data (e.g. Van Hulst et al., 2017). Similarly, design as pattern following often teams up with the view of phenomena as process, where the point is to articulate the patterns through which phenomena emerge, evolve, sustain and sometimes even disappear. Also, phenomenon-driven research (in contrast to more theory-driven research) commonly applies a pattern-following design and through it focuses on 'identifying, capturing, documenting, and conceptualizing a phenomenon of interest in order to facilitate knowledge creation and advancement...within a field rather than to specific theory' (Schwarz & Stensaker, 2014: 480).

Alternative metaphors

When research is regarded as story-telling, design can be seen as *plot plotting* of the story to be told. That is, an outline for how the story and its plot will be developed over time in terms of scenes, acts, agents, agency and purpose making up the plot. (There are other ideas of what makes up a story, but these are often seen as important elements.) The design of a study is therefore very much a matter of careful planning of how to produce material to say something about these key components of the research story. A story-telling metaphor would normally inspire something other than a highly formulaic research account, and perhaps include elements such as an inspiring vignette, some observations and/or interviews, including what an audience may find to be rich and interesting content.

In cases where research is seen as more open-minded, design seems to become a misleading term, but one may perhaps stretch the concept and still retain some elements of it. In such cases, possible alternative metaphors could be *journey*, exploration or even intellectual adventure. Design as journey would still indicate some structure and direction in the project – the journey is not unplanned or just wandering or floating around or jumping on any means of transport going in a random direction. The journey has a purpose and has some kind of notion of a direction, although the metaphor does not point at a straight journey from place A to B. Journey may have different meanings and stand for different metaphors, such as being more or less of an explorative or adventure type of journey than fairly predictable transport. Commuting, regular tourism or a jungle tour may signal different metaphors, but here we are satisfied merely with identifying the journey metaphor and only mention that there may be different versions of this that are of value for the reader.

Another view of design is to regard it as scanning a terrain in search for empirical material that may serve as golden nuggets and trigger ideas or valuable clues for developing something interesting. Gabriel (2015, 2018) suggests that qualitative research design could be seen as *beachcombing*, which surveys a beach looking for valuable objects and materials or at least for objects and materials which offer interesting possibilities. In this sense, Gabriel writes, a beachcomber is in a quest not for objects themselves but rather for the possibilities offered by different objects. To a beachcomber, a piece of driftwood may suggest things as diverse as a bonfire on the beach, an artistic installation or the existence of a nearby shipwreck. A seashell may suggest an addition to a child's mobile or may spark the inspiration for a collage or a painting. The key point of a design would then be to optimize possibilities for the creative and novel line of thinking. Design as beachcombing may mean strolling around and covering vast areas but only spending time and energy on what seems interesting and generative.

Yet another alternative metaphor of design is *mystery creation* – the researcher encounters or aims for an unexpected empirical observation to challenge dominant understandings (such as in the Hawthorne studies, mentioned in Chapter 5). This calls for a more flexible and open study than one informed by a strict design (Alvesson & Kärreman, 2011). The mystery creation metaphor highlights that research can be about confronting or preventing a particular logic or modes of thoughts from being outlined and thus creating a breakdown in existing assumptions and beliefs. Agar (1986) views some form of anthropological work as a matter of interaction between the researcher's home culture and a foreign one, leading to (potentially productive) confusions and misunderstandings calling for investigation and learning. The knowledge-creating process is one of encountering and learning to understand and thus 'solving' breakdowns in understanding. It is the unanticipated and the unexpected – the things that puzzle the researcher due to the deviation from what is expected – that are of particular interest to a reflexive researcher drawing upon the mystery (or breakdown of understanding) metaphor. Accordingly, theory development is stimulated and facilitated by a selective interest in what does *not* work in an existing theory, in the sense of encouraging interpretations that enable a productive, non-routine and non-commonsensical understanding of ambiguous social reality. The ideal research design then includes two key elements: (i) to create a mystery; and (ii) to solve it (Asplund, 1970). A surprise is triggered by empirical observations that deviate from what is expected and leads the researcher into a (temporary) stage of bewilderment and loss. A mystery appears when we cannot understand something, calling for a new set of ideas that deviate from established assumptions and wisdoms and are necessary to resolve the mystery (for an extensive description and exemplification of this methodology, see Alvesson & Kärreman, 2011).

Additional metaphors

We can also mention metaphors that are even further away from the research as a fixed design or blueprint metaphor. Design can be seen as a *dance routine*, as there is often a dynamic interaction between the different design components as 'the researcher moves back and forth in the steps of research, almost as if they are doing a dynamic dance routine' (Hesse-Biber & Leavy, 2011: 36). Following Martin (1981), qualitative research design can be seen in an even looser way, namely as a *garbage can* (after Cohen et al., 1972), in which the different design components are interactively swirling around without a clear starting or end point. Sometimes they come together and lead to a design, not necessarily being so much rational and predictable as randomly produced. More constructionist paradigms also generate other much less structured designs, following a *path of discovery* rather than a strict roadmap. An additional metaphor is to regard design as *grammar* (e.g. Johnson, 1992). Here the idea is that the research design is a language with a particular grammar. For example, the elements of the design (such as research questions, purpose of study, theory and method) are the visual grammar and expression of a particular research approach or inquiry.

Summary

Table 6.3 Summary of metaphorizing the design

Metaphors	Dominant	Alternative	Additional
RP element			
Design	– Blueprint	– Plot plotting	– Dance routine
	– Composition	– Journey	– Garbage can
	– Legitimizing account	– Beachcombing	– Path of discovery
	– Pattern following	– Mystery creation	– Grammar

The prevalent metaphors underlying design are master plan, blueprint, composition, and legitimizing account. Here there is a strong emphasis on planning and structure as key ingredients. These metaphors all in different ways portray design as a more or less fixed plan that the researchers should follow to conduct their research in a similar manner as builders have to follow the master plan for the specific building they are constructing. Advantages include the thinking through of issues in advance and accountability.

The set of alternative metaphors – plot plotting, journey, beachcombing and mystery creation – counters the prevailing views of design in significant ways. They all suggest that design can be (and is) far more loosely structured and iterative, as a way to be more sensitive to what is coming up in the research process. This more tentative or provisional view of design is further illuminated by the additional metaphors regarding design as dance, garbage can or path of discovery. Some of these alternative and additional metaphors stretch the notion of design quite far and may neither draw upon the design metaphor (as generally understood), nor really suggest alternative metaphors for design, but may be into something else. It can be debated how far one can use one's imaginaries here, and we just note that some authors claim to metaphorize design in unconventional and possibly highly stretched ways. There is, however, sometimes a point in raising anti-metaphors (as different from alternative ones) as part of the reflexivity-inspiring overall exercise. The researcher may seriously consider whether a master plan view is motivated *or* if a looser, journey-like idea of just interviewing 40 people or so without a clear idea for a good design can be justified.

In qualitative research there are typically planned, more loosely planned and unplanned moments. These may vary heavily in scope and significance. 'Go out there and see what the natives are up to' is one extreme. Thinking through carefully how to use time wisely, making sure in advance that you optimize possibilities for a strong study, is another. The reflexive researcher may think about both options – perhaps being careful of adopting either extreme without having thought about their pros and cons – and also be prepared to change guiding metaphors during a study. There may be reasons discovered during the journey (if that metaphor is used) for both tightening and loosening up the design. Sometimes a beachcombing stage may lead to a stricter design in order to explore the potential finding or idea more systematically and rigorously. Or a blueprint-governed study may, after some time, lead to a journey following the path of interesting observations and ideas, suggesting a change of direction.

CHAPTER SUMMARY

In this chapter we have discussed some common and some less common images underlying the main framing elements of the RP: the literature review, theory and design. These elements can be seen as distinct, as they each frame the conduct of research in particular ways. For example, when the literature review is regarded as gap-spotting, it takes aim at some overlooked area within existing literature that needs to be addressed. But when the literature review is seen as fault-finding, it takes aim at what is problematic and 'wrong' in the existing literature rather than what is missing. This means that the specific view of the literature review is also likely to frame the overall research. The same holds true for the other two framing elements, theory and design. However, although each framing element is distinct and frames research in particular ways, the elements also overlap to a large degree. This is particularly true regarding theory and design, where a particular theoretical perspective, like practice theory, significantly shapes the design of research.

Our conceptualization of the elements addressed in this chapter as framing does not indicate that they are in any way fixed in a study. Instead, there is often a reframing of these elements, such as the theory used or how design issues are considered in various stages of the research process. This means that these elements may look quite differently at the final stages of the process compared to when the research started.

NOTES

1. Although this point may seem to be a bit 'wild', our intention is not to neglect conventional academic concerns about relating to earlier work. Idea-picking literature reviews would differ from conventional, 'vacuum-cleaning' reviews, but include elements such as the covering of important works in the focal area and making sure there is an ongoing dialogue with existing studies, such as relating one's results to the existing literature.
2. Often what the researcher sets up in terms of texts and language use is of course already set up before him or her, and then s/he is reproducing and varying discourses in operation, forming the research project.

7

METAPHORIZING THE PROCESSING ELEMENTS OF THE RP

Although every element of RP is processual, in this chapter we address the more active elements involved in carrying out a specific empirical study, namely: method, data and analysis. These elements can also be seen as midstream parts of a study, being in between the researcher's paradigmatic and other grounding and framing elements, and the contribution and writing elements, which are more salient in the latter part of the research. Why methods, data and analysis can be seen as processing elements of the research process (RP) is because they are all directly related to the actual production phase of research, that is the execution of research, particularly in terms of collecting and analysing data, leading to the production of knowledge.

METHODS

Method is by far the most discussed element of the research process. Method commonly means to do something in a systematic and orderly way, from baking a cake to conducting a medical examination. As Shakespeare wrote in *Hamlet*: 'Though this be madness, yet there is method in it', meaning that there is a rational purpose in one's conduct even though it may come across as crazy, which even happens occasionally in the social sciences.

Method is typically seen as consisting of a specific set of rules and steps for attaining a specific end, like a tasty cake, a cured patient, a solved crime or, in the case of research, truthful knowledge about some phenomenon. In this regard, a research method is a specific way of carrying out an inquiry about something in a rational manner by following a set of logical steps. For example, in standard methodology books (e.g. Flick, 2018; Sekaran, 2000), deductive research methods stipulate that the researcher needs to adhere to the following sequential steps: theory formulation, hypothesizing, operationalization, sampling, data collection, analysis and validation. Inductive research methods are often depicted as more circular than linear, consisting of moving back and forth between data collection, analysis and case comparison until the theory is 'fully' developed.

Method can be defined more or less broadly. Often the term 'methodology' refers to an overall approach for conducting research, including philosophy, design and strategies for collecting and analysing data in the production of scientific knowledge. However, when talking about 'method' we aim for something more specific and want to avoid overlap with design and other elements in the research process. Method is frequently used in order to point at specific tactics or techniques for collecting and processing data. Hence, although method is portrayed in varied ways and with varying scope, in this chapter we limit the term 'method' to refer to the practical work of generating and processing empirical material (turning it into data).

Dominant metaphors

The overarching image of method is to regard it as a specific and rational technique for developing valid and reliable scientific knowledge of reality. As a technique, method is seen to be made up of specific tools (Hesse-Biber & Leavy, 2011: 5; Vannini, 2015: 10) and procedures (or recipes) (e.g. Willig, 2011: 2) for collecting and analysing data, leading to the development of new knowledge. Hammersley (2011: 5) aptly captures this conventional view of method as technique as follows: 'At its simplest, methodology-as-technique is an attempt to codify the methods social scientists use, specifying their character and proper application in relation to the different research tasks, indicating the grounds on which choices among methods should be made, and so on.' Although there are other meanings of methods, the view of method as a technique has come to dominate most disciplines within social sciences (Bell et al., 2017; Hammersley, 2011). We suggest that the metaphor of *instruction manual* captures this.

The view of (scientific) method as an instruction manual or technique is closely linked to the Enlightenment project to build a society based on rational knowledge, free from superstitions, religious dogma and other problematic prejudices. As Capaldi (1998: 17) explains: 'The Enlightenment Project is the attempt to define and explain the human predicament through science as well as to achieve mastery over it through the use of a social technology.' Although many different versions of method as technique have been developed within both natural science (Chalmers, 1999; Gower, 1997) and the social sciences

(Miles & Huberman, 1994; Smith, 1998) over the years, they have in common that they offer a set of principles, tools and procedures for how to avoid or keep researcher biases and prejudices away from contaminating formal data and theory in the process of knowledge development, that is, it is an instruction manual for knowledge production.

Research methods seen as an instruction manual consist of specific steps and procedures for the researcher to follow and obey in order to generate an accurate representation of reality. Here, methods involve choosing the right ingredients (a representative sample, a standardized measurement instrument, the appropriate statistical test or a reliable interview technique) and administering them in the right order (the 'procedure') (Willig, 2011: 2). Follow the manual and the result will be valid and reliable knowledge.

Method may also be seen as a *construction process*,[1] in the sense of how social reality is actively constructed on a more ongoing basis, that is, being invented and shaped by the researcher through his/her language use, interpretations and writing practices. Constructions are here 'researcher-produced', that is, there are constructions of constructions where the researcher is the central driver rather than the people studied. Method, then, would indicate the systematic, careful way in which researchers construct specific empirical material as well as its specific meanings. What others may refer to as codification would, given the construction metaphor, be less about reflecting data than the interpretative inclinations of the construction-engaged researcher, informed by pre-understandings, imagination, theoretical ideas, paradigms, societal culture and other construction-supporting (or determining, interfering) elements. In the words of Law (2004: 5, italics in original), 'it is that methods, their rules, and even more methods' practices, not only describe but also help to *produce* the reality that they understand'.

A related metaphor (or set of metaphors) highlighting the role and significance of the interviewee as well as emphasizing interactions, circle around the idea of the co-construction of knowledge. In this respect, a specific metaphor for interviewing is *collaborative knowledge production*. The ambition is to create a community of interest and construct interviews 'so that interviewers and respondents strive to arrive together at meanings that both can understand' (Bishop, 2005: 125). Here, those involved make attempts to co-construct a mutual understanding by means of sharing experiences and meanings. In interviews, the researcher's interventions transform the interview subject 'from a repository of opinions and reasons or a wellspring of emotions into a productive source of knowledge' (Holstein & Gubrium, 1997: 121), as 'the subject's interpretative capabilities must be activated, stimulated and cultivated' (p. 122). The interview subject has potentially much of value to say, but this calls for the researcher actively leading or supporting the subject into intelligent talk. The interviewer and the interviewee collaborate in the 'co-construction of knowledge'. The positions of 'interviewer' and 'interviewee' then become less distinct and the value of the terms may in some cases be questionable.

Another common metaphor of method is *triangulation*. The expression comes from navigation, where the use of three measurements allowed a reasonably precise establishment of the position of the ship. In research method, triangulation works as a metaphor. This is often seen as the use of multiple perceptions or measurements to clarify or establish meaning or truth, but there are also ideas about triangulation being about identifying ways in which a case is being seen (Stake, 2005: 454). Most see triangulation as a way of 'homing in' on an observation or a knowledge result, often with the use of different data sources and techniques for generating data. But some emphasize that the use of multiple data sources and techniques for generating data are likely to produce diverse views of phenomena and, thus, open up for different interpretations and results (Potter & Wetherell, 1987). Some view triangulation as a way of enriching a study through drawing on a multitude of empirical materials. The various meanings of triangulation indicate different metaphors – position or truth establishment is quite different from enriching a case, the former moving away from establishing 'how it really is'. Nevertheless, there is still some common ground, including recognition of uncertainty and ambiguity and the need for or benefit of using different types of data.

Another fairly common metaphor for method (particularly qualitative methods) is *voice recording*, which emphasizes the centrality of allowing the research subjects to express their experiences, opinions and interests regarding the phenomenon investigated. The concern for many feminists, for example, is 'to find and express women's voices' and the challenge is 'how to make women's voices heard without exploiting or distorting those voices' (Olesen, 2000: 231). To make the voices heard, the method for this could be seen as megaphone holding – a method is very much an instrument for amplifying the volume of these voices, which are often seen as repressed, weak, silenced or distorted. The key methodological challenge is to capture these voices in a fine-tuned and sensitive way. This would be partly in some opposition to method as an instrument for reality construction, as construction emphasizes researcher intervention in terms of definitions and shaping the discourse.

Alternative metaphors

If the point of research is seen as point-making or knowledge demolition that may shake conventional truths or ideas, method may be seen as *negation searching* (Alvesson & Deetz, 2021). Here the idea is to consistently try to consider a clearly alternative meaning of what appears to be an established one. This of course calls not for investigating the exact meaning of data, but of questioning conventional modes of seeing it. Of interest here would be to not just look at the explicit meaning, but also at what is not said, the repressed and non-imagined. When, for example, subjects present something on gender, for example, an interviewee saying 'as a woman…,' this may reveal something of the subject positions not being expressed. Another example could be to turn the dominant control view of leadership around and to see leadership not as being in control but as reflecting the disciplinary power of the leadership discourse that forces managers into something 'leader-like', which is difficult to live up to for managers typically busy doing administration (Alvesson & Sveningsson, 2003). In this scenario, leadership does not signal being in control but rather being controlled. Managers could then be asked about the burdens of living up to leadership ideals or the researcher could simply consider the viability of this interpretation, even if interview or observational material do not explicitly invite such an interpretation.[2] In terms of method, the idea here is not to impose any alternative meaning or aspect on a study, but to introduce negations or counter-thinking to those being studied or testing the alternative on an empirical material.

Another alternative metaphor could be *intellectual wandering*. Here the method is quite far from an instruction manual or recipe and is more about how to get empirical inspiration for thinking differently about established ideas and truths. Method may be more a matter of accessing variation than following a specific technique or instruction manual, as well as moving around theoretically and empirically rather than staying at a particular place. Its primary focus involves looking for interesting and inspirational clues rather than the systematic and focused inquiry of a more limited terrain, thus being closely in line with the beachcombing metaphor discussed in the section on design in Chapter 6 (Gabriel, 2015).

Another metaphor is *insight gathering*. Here the assumption is that method is very much about finding and mobilizing qualified people who can produce not only relevant information but also analysis. Most views on method assume that participants – mainly interviewees or diary writers – are valuable for offering data that can be used only or mainly for descriptions. Data collection is then the basis for the analytical work of the researcher. Method as insight gathering means that participants are assumed to be qualified thinkers who can support the turning of data into insights as a vital in-between step to the final research results. Kreiner and Mouritsen (2005) talk about the analytical interview, which is different from the descriptive interview. Holmes and Marcus (2005: 1104) address some informants as 'experts' to be treated 'not as collateral colleagues helping to inform fieldwork to occur elsewhere but instead as subjects fully within their own analytical ambit whose cognitive purview and social action range potentially over multiple, if not countless, sites and locales'. These subjects should be seen and worked with as collaborators or partners in research. Holmes and Marcus (2005) refer to these experts or knowledge workers as para-ethnographers. The metaphor may be used more broadly and then inform work with all participants as being analytically skilled on the subject matter of the study. But the metaphor could perhaps more typically inform efforts to find and work with people who are highly suitable for insight generation and communication.

Occasionally, researchers see the writing as the key element in qualitative research and even consider *writing as a method of inquiry*, as 'a way of finding out about yourself and your topic' (Richardson, 2000: 516). Method as writing then means active text work in terms of exploring, introducing, revising, fine-tuning ideas and representations. In particular, ethnographic work with observations is very much a matter of writing during empirical work periods. But writing may be a key part of everything, from reading texts, taking notes when reading, to portraying interviewees and rewriting drafts of a journal article or a book. Writing is here 'upgraded' and forms a major part of the method. Writing as a method is probably located more in the upstream part of the research. This means that writing enters the research process earlier than is typically the case. A key focus in the method is then the use of material that facilitates early writing and text production, allowing less final reporting and more the creation of a well-functioning story. This typically calls for rich data – perhaps ethnographic work involving observations of rich episodes or interviews with people providing inspiring accounts.

Additional metaphors

Some scholars, like Feyerabend, Gadamer and Foucault, also talk about *anti-methods* in the sense of the opposite of what methods usually mean, that is, chance, randomness, chaos, etc. Their talk about 'anti' is very much an effort to free us from the illusion that a method is producing objective knowledge (Gadamer) or that an apolitical method is possible (Foucault) (Shiner, 1982: 386). More radically, Feyerabend (1975) dismisses method completely by declaring that 'anything goes'. For many critical and progressive researchers, method is an ethical rather than a technical project. For example, they see the interview as a basically ethical endeavour and suggest that 'the new empathetic approach takes an ethical stance in favor of the individual or group being studied' (Fontana & Frey, 2005: 696). Here method functions as *morality elevation*. The researcher then tends to respect the voices of those being studied and brings out their experiences without censorship or privileging a research discourse, which may lead to interview accounts being taken at face value. An additional metaphor for method could be *scene-setting*. Holmes and Marcus (2005: 1100) talk about a dramaturgical regime of method, being about images and scenarios, suggesting that research, in particular ethnography, 'is able to set scenes that can be entered through concretely visualized and situated thought experiments'. If the point of research is story-telling, methods may be seen as *story generators*. Denzin and Lincoln (1994: 5) argue that although there are different research methods, such as positivist, postmodern and interpretativist, none is better or worse than the other, they only tell different stories about the social world.

Summary

Table 7.1   Summary of metaphorizing the method

Metaphors	Dominant	Alternative	Additional
RP element			
Method	– Instruction manual – Construction process – Collaborative knowledge production – Triangulation – Voice recording	– Negation searching – Intellectual wandering – Insight gathering – Writing as a method of inquiry	– Anti-method – Morality elevator – Scene-setting – Story generators

The dominant metaphors of methods, such as instruction manual, construction process, collaborative knowledge production, triangulation and voice recording, emphasize method as a set of specific rules and procedures that researchers need to follow in order to develop truthful scientific knowledge about reality.

The alternative metaphors of methods, of negation searching, intellectual wandering and writing inquiry, counter this prevalent view by highlighting that methods in various ways generate specific data and versions of reality that are researcher-produced and in a sense artificial and far from 'pure' or innocent. They tend to emphasize the role of the researcher and his/her moves, as well as a more open-ended and explorative orientation of research.

The additional metaphor of anti-method emphasizes even more strongly the idea that the development of more original knowledge often requires a much more explorative orientation in the conduct of research. The anti-method, morality elevator, scene-setting and story generators metaphors illuminate still other sides of method that perhaps may also encourage wild ideas and a lack of discipline and rigour – and therefore need to be balanced with considerations of coherence and careful reasoning.

Reflexivity means considering and playing out various ideas about being systematic and accountable versus emphasizing other values and operations, such as broader sweeps leading to unexpected ideas and insights. Often some ingredient of both is needed, but most research projects follow a main route, typically something indicating a clear guideline and procedural steps, but modified to various degrees. It is perhaps common that deviations are more salient in actual research practice than in the method section of a research report. Apart from choosing a major version of method, projects can have ingredients or stages where a non-dominant metaphor plays a role. In a primarily insight-gathering study, where the selected 'star material' from interviews is emphasized, there may also be elements of voice recording or triangulation supplementing this with other voices. More strictly, instruction manual ideas may also guide some (parts of) expert interviews in order for the researcher to have some control over the process and to be able to check and compare data. Reflexivity around the interactionist aspects is vital here, including thinking carefully about the risks of selecting and highlighting insights that support the researcher's conviction. It is easy to let one's preferences guide what one views as highly valuable statements, being central in the research.

DATA

'Data' is one of the most frequently used terms in research texts, particularly in regard to 'data collection' and 'data analysis'. Data are typically seen as specific units of information in terms of people's experiences, perceptions, beliefs, behaviours, social practices, episodes, etc. about some phenomena, such as family, death, healthcare service encounters, leadership or trust. The researcher wants to know more about these phenomena, and therefore needs to 'collect' data about them. In the words of Merriam and Tisdell (2015: 105), 'data are nothing more than ordinary bits and pieces of information found in the environment'. They can be concrete and measurable, as in pupils' classroom attendance and talk frequencies in social interactions (e.g. in meetings between social welfare officers and clients), or invisible and difficult to measure, as in feelings, beliefs, values and social practices. Whether or not a bit of information becomes data in a research study depends solely on the interest and perspective of the investigator. The researcher does something in order to get data, either more proactively, such as accessing informants, or more passively by reading the newspaper, or listening to conversations at the research site where something of interest may pop up. If these activities lead to note-taking (on paper or in the researcher's head) of information and then that information is used in an inquiry, one can talk about data collection.

In order to access data about phenomena, the researcher is typically claimed to use different 'methods of data collection' (Hesse-Biber & Leavy, 2011: 92). In the words of Willig (2011: 16), 'qualitative data collection methods are designed to minimize data reduction. In qualitative research, the objective of data collection is to create a comprehensive record of participants' words and actions.' Similarly, Hatch (2002: 7) states that '[t]his chapter is about how to collect qualitative data, and ... I devote separate sections to the primary data gathering strategies of qualitative research (observation, interviewing, and unobtrusive data collection).' Judging from the terms used, such as 'collecting' and 'gathering', it seems that data are usually seen as something more or less given (pieces or bits of information) that lay around in the environment and/or in the heads of people targeted for inquiry, which the researcher can collect if s/he uses the right instruments (in a similar way as we pick fruit and vegetables in the garden). The view of data as given is well entrenched as it is also aligned with the Latin root 'dare', which means 'to give' (Brinkmann, 2014: 721).

An alternative expression for data is 'empirical material'. While data may sound fixed, distinct and manageable, more like bricks, empirical material may indicate 'data' as less robust and objective, something less formed, like clay. Regarding 'data' as empirical material signals something more uncertain and open for the 'material-handling' of the researcher, as being in need of some degree of formation. We mainly stick to the dominant expression of data in this section (and in most parts of the book), but sometimes vary terminology in order not to reproduce the understandings associated with data, as something rather firm and reliable to proceed from.

Dominant metaphors

A dominant or at least commonly used set of metaphors for data emphasize the robustness and objective reality-like qualities of data, such as in terms of interview statements, field observations (e.g. tape- or video-recordings or written notes) of 'naturally occurring' events or behaviours or texts. Most researchers probably acknowledge some degree of uncertainty and arbitrariness regarding data, such as what interviewees say, but bracket doubts and tend to take a pragmatic view. The fact that data are always – or at least in most cases – theory-impregnated is perhaps recognized, but many research orientations see this as a less important issue and emphasize data as being not really, or only marginally, contaminated by theory, the researcher's interpretative leanings and subjectivities. Data are seen as offering a strong foundation for research. They are often seen as 'showing' something – a direct expression of reality: the facts.

Data are commonly seen as the basic building blocks for knowledge development, offering the raw material for, and the major input to, the knowledge production process. Richardson (2000: 523) also uses the overarching material metaphor to highlight the meaning behind data, but suggests that data are more 'like wet clay, it is there for us to shape'. A similar, but not the same, metaphor is data as *picture fragments* of reality. Here data are seen as a myriad of reality fragments that researchers put together to generate a rich and accurate description, leading to a map or portrayal of a specific phenomenon. Data are therefore not seen as distinct building blocks for theory building, but rather as forming part of the description of research phenomena. In this view, good data may lead to a qualified description, which may in itself form the key ingredient of a study, such as descriptions of the life of a transgendered person, or the situation of sexual harassment in a workplace, or the detailed account of a significant political process. In other words, the (thick) description itself offers an ambitious representation of the phenomenon in question, and is therefore seen as contributing to the overall accumulated picture of the studied phenomenon. The assembly of data then provides the basis for the finding, typically a pattern of something, for example, the views of Norwegians on new asylum centres for refugees (Bygnes, 2020) or the experiences of legal constraints for sex workers in legal brothels in Nevada (Blithe & Wolfe, 2017).

A similar but, at the same time, reverse logic emphasizes data as something that confirms or disconfirms theoretical ideas and hypothesis. Although qualitative research is typically not focused on hypothesis testing, there is very often some idea that data can support or reject or, more commonly, show where theories work or 'match' reality. Here data can be regarded as a *referee* (or judge), who decides whether a knowledge claim is true or false, under specific circumstances and in certain domains, that is, if the claim is supported by data. The referee job of data may be more or less clear or (un)problematic, as the level of ambiguity makes the referee use of data complicated. Still the idea is that data have the quality of saying yes or no (pass or fail) to knowledge claims. Data then enter relatively late in the research process, compared to what is suggested by the metaphor of data as building blocks. The block work is assumed to lead to theory, the latter coming late, while the referee metaphor and the judging of hypothesis or ideas means that theory comes first and then is checked with data.

Similarly to the building blocks and the referee metaphors, data can be seen as *road signs*, showing the way to knowledge/theory in line with grounded theory and other data-istic inductivists (Alvesson & Kärreman, 2011). The road sign metaphor indicates data's path-showing or discovery-facilitating qualities. The idea is that you follow the data in a process leading to a novel theory or another intellectual contribution (idea, insight) that moves beyond the pure empirical finding. There are building block-qualities as part of this, but data are rather seen as leading the way to theory than as being crucial for the accumulation of evidence loosely leading to a strong empirical statement about how the world operates or how people think about certain issues. Compared to the referee image, the road sign metaphor downplays issues of confirmation/falsification (or other notions around support for or rejection of theoretical ideas).

A problem with the above views is that they separate data from theory and from cultural norms, the performative effects of research (e.g. interviewer or observer effects) and other phenomena influencing data. The views assume that we are, in principle, supposed to identify and collect data about the unconscious independently of psychoanalysis, to collect data about leaders without consulting leadership theory or simply to observe conflict, group dynamics or inequality without a clear theoretical idea of what to observe, such as the meaning of a group (as opposed to an assembly of individuals). Brown (1976) suggests that these views regard data as true reflections of reality, that is, as *reality recorders*. 'The data itself are thought of as sending out their own self-identifying signals; as researchers, all we must do is tune our receiving instruments to the right channel and screen out our subjective noise' (Brown, 1976: 187). However, not only theory affects how data are produced, but also social norms and cultural understandings inform participants' accounts. How people in interviews talk about their poverty, gender equality, etc. may be affected by the cultural, social and political context at a particular time. Accounts in interviews or questionnaires about sexual harassment may, for example, vary before, during and after the peak of #MeToo, as the latter affects informants' ways of talking about the subject matter, being highly context- and cues-sensitive. There are therefore reasons to recognize the uncertainties around what data really say. This can open up consideration of other approaches to, and metaphors for, data, acknowledging their limited reliability.

Alternative metaphors

If research is about point-making, data may be seen more as *rhetorical tropes* that can be lined up to make the point forcefully. Data offer illustrative and supportive material for a specific perspective or key point that the researcher wants to make. Data (or perhaps better empirical material) are then mainly employed by the researcher in order to make her or his case with some empirical grounding that increases the readability and credibility of the text. A gender researcher may, for example, be able to say something about females' experiences based on a number of interviews that offer such experiences (rather than problematize the notion of their being specific female experiences in contrast to human, occupational, classed, ethnic, highly idiosyncratic or whatever 'non-female specific' experiences). The case is then supported by data – the latter mainly being used for the purpose they are being set up for. This does not imply that there is no learning or revision of ideas following from empirical encounters, only that a major purpose of data being reported is to support and illustrate the point/thesis/idea proposed by the researcher.

When research is regarded as knowledge demolition and reality creation, the idea of data as basic building blocks of reality becomes problematic and even misleading. Instead, data are seen as *artefacts* rather than direct mirrors or reflections of something. As artefacts they live more or less their own lives, in an uncertain relationship to what they are supposed to represent. That is, as something constructed and produced through human activities, giving rise to what Baudrillard (1994) called 'hyper-reality'; a situation in which what is 'real' and what is 'map' are an entangled whole impossible to distinguish from each other. In hyper-reality, various clear, accessible representations of reality become more 'real', more present and impression-creating than 'reality' itself, that can't really be assessed and are too ambiguous and messy to compete with hyper-reality. The latter, in the forms of interview statements, text chunks or observation protocols, then become the core elements of data, having an uncertain relationship to reality being out there somewhere. Data indicating motives, attitudes or values may, for example, be seen as expressions of cultural conventions or politically correct statements that can be studied as such, that is, as cultural artefacts carrying some significance but not necessarily saying much about 'real' drivers or sentiments, which are perhaps almost impossible to access. But we can, as Mills (1940) suggested, study the vocabularies of motives of a range of discourses or narratives, without jumping to conclusions about something outside these discourses or artefacts.

Another metaphor is to see data as *clues*, that is, as more or less subtle indications of what type of hidden, interesting phenomenon or ways of understanding or explaining something can be detected and identified as valuable pieces of information to be unravelled. The clue metaphor may be connected to the idea of the researcher as a detective or explorer, following subtle and often unreliable indicators of what and how to study something. Some data are false or non-informative, while others are more reliable or valuable. This is something that is crucial for objective hermeneutics, engaged in source critique trying to sort out different kinds of more or less unreliable data (Alvesson & Sköldberg, 2018).

Data may be seen as naturally occurring, untouched by human (researcher) interventions, but in most cases, there is a clear awareness of the actual or potential audience, leading to data being about *impression management*. In diary studies, people write their diaries with an awareness that someone will read and use them. People being observed may perform as on stage, aware of the researcher-observer. Interviewees are of course aware that their statements may make some social and political difference, but, more generally, they are also aware of how they will appear, and are likely to engage in impression management. Interviews may be seen as specific sites for data construction in a complex interaction between the interviewer and the interviewee involved in impression management, political action or identity work (Alvesson, 2011).

Additional metaphors

Other metaphors suggest that data can be seen as a *lightning rod* that attracts insights around which new categories can form (Grodal et al., 2020: 15). This is somewhat similar but much stronger than the road-sign metaphor, as the function of the lightning rod is to prevent lightning-like unsupported interpretations damaging the knowledge building by filtering out these unsupported interpretations before they become part of the actual knowledge building. This metaphor has some resemblance to the beachcomber metaphor suggested earlier, where the insight-generating element is being prioritized, compared to broader work with all or most data. Regarding data as *puzzle pieces* echoes the jigsaw puzzle metaphor, but also that we partly have to create the pieces of the jigsaw puzzle as they are not ready-made. In fact, it suggests that we can create different jigsaw puzzles from the same set of data depending on how we categorize the data, that is, create pieces of the emerging jigsaw puzzle.

The reporting of data, not least observations, may also be seen as an *artistic portrait*, perhaps of an impressionist or confessional nature (Van Maanen, 1988). Of course, artistically portraying data does not mean that the researcher is free to invent or make up any kind of knowledge claim or story. The use of artistic qualities in observations may simply mean taking a less 'square', superficial and conventional approach and finding more imaginative, lively, insightful and deeper ways of portraying something (e.g. Geertz, 1973).

Summary

Table 7.2 Summary of metaphorizing data

Metaphors **RP element**	*Dominant*	*Alternative*	*Additional*
Data (collection)	– Picture fragments – Referee – Road signs – Reality recorders	– Rhetorical tropes – Artefacts – Clues – Impression management	– Lightning rod – Puzzle pieces – Artistic portrait

The two most common metaphors underlying data are data as building blocks and picture fragments, which conceptualize data as thing-like pieces of reality 'out there' which can be collected with specific methods. They are reality recorders and are therefore also often seen as a referee and final arbiter regarding the truthfulness of our theories – are they supported in the data or not? Data are seen as the robust foundation of research, to be taken very seriously and respectfully.

The four alternative metaphors offer a counterview of data by emphasizing their more constructed features, as artifacts, or their more rhetorical function in research texts. Here the researcher more actively does something that leads to data being produced, which calls for the handling of the artificial, contingent and uncertain nature of observations, interview statements, questionnaire responses or whatever indicators of reality the researcher is working with. The metaphor clues also point to the ambiguous and often unreliable nature of data, calling for the careful assessment of the quality of data in terms of reliability and value, and perhaps sorting out untrustworthy material. The additional metaphors offer further unconventional views of data in research.

Reflexivity over how data should be considered and perhaps reconsidered may be facilitated through the various domains we have indentified: me-ism, we-ism, etc. Most apparently relevant is here interactionism, that is, how the interplay between the researcher and those being studied affects the research. It is common to rely on metaphors that indicate the interviewee as a reliable and truthful supplier of accurate research data, a servant of science. These are part of the building blocks or reality-recording metaphors. More sceptically, various problems with the 'data supply' may be considered, reflecting the imperfections of the data suppliers, for example, interviewees are not necessarily capable or willing to simply express their experiences and meanings. The people being studied may have their own political, social or ego-agendas or may simply be poor informants, producing confused or contradictory statements about what interests the researcher (Alvesson, 2011). Sometimes the researcher–participant relationship may be one of a barely hidden coalition. The social welfare researcher and welfare clients may have a joint interest in producing knowledge supporting requests for welfare reforms. Leadership researchers and managers may easily agree on the importance of leadership and all the good things that come from the right type of leader and leadership, thus increasing the status of managers and leadership experts. People interviewed by gender researchers may be inclined to emphasize discrimination or other forms of 'gender trouble'. Given these complications, the reflexive researcher may seriously reflect on data as uncertain clues and work hard to move beyond the study of the impression management that most data may express. Sometimes recognizing the difficulties of using data, such as in terms of building blocks or picture fragments, may lead to caution, and therefore addressing data less ambitiously. They could, for example, be seen as rhetorical tropes or artistic portraits, used more for illustrations and idea generations than as a basis for strong knowledge claims about findings.

More generally, interactionism reflexivity may encourage the researcher to consider what is the nature of the relationship between the researcher and the participants being studied, such as struggles to control the agenda (where there are different views of comfort zones/areas of special interests) and issues of exploitation (where all parties try to exploit the other). Interactionism may also include how the research participant is to be conceptualized: informant, participant, co-researcher, expert, reluctant witness, politician may all be relevant metaphors to consider here. (For space reasons, we do not address these metaphors in this book.)

ANALYSIS

When 'data' have been 'collected' or 'produced' about a phenomenon (religious beliefs, trust in authorities, childrearing, decision making about terminally sick cancer patients, etc.), the next step in the research process is to handle these data in some reasonable way. Often this is formulated in terms of data *analysis*, with the aim of identifying patterns and connections about the phenomenon under investigation. 'In conventional terms "analyzing" signals the terminal phase of qualitative inquiry or data collection, to implement analytic procedures to produce interpretations, which are integrated to theory' (Denzin & Lincoln, 1994: 479). Analysis is commonly described or seen as carefully examining the data by 'taking them apart', that is, separating them into their smallest parts and thereafter coding or categorizing them 'in ways that allow researchers to see patterns, identify themes, discover relationships, develop explanations, make interpretations, mount critiques, or generate theories. It often involves synthesis, evaluation, interpretation, categorization, hypothesizing, comparison, and pattern finding' (Hatch, 2002: 148).

This analysis, the taking apart of data and then connecting them on a higher level to find patterns and connections, often follows some specific procedure, such as the grounded theory approach (Glaser & Strauss, 1967) or the 'Gioia method' in management (Gioia et al., 2012), for coding or categorizing the data with the aim of developing a theory. In the words of Charmaz (2014: 113), 'coding is the pivotal link between collecting data and developing an emergent theory to explain these data'. For example, the grounded theory approach or the Gioia method follows a specific coding procedure consisting of first-, second- and third-order coding, leading to a theory of the phenomenon in question.

The analysis is often described in a neat, logical and smooth way. Blithe and Wolfe (2017: 733), for example, in their study of the constraints affecting sex workers in legal brothels in Nevada, write that their 'analysis proceeded inductively, grounded in data, and happened through iterative waves. ... We formed initial codes and then refined, reduced, expanded and collapsed categories as some themes proved more salient than others ... [After] refining the data, some themes emerged' (p. 733).

An alternative conceptualization of data analysis is the *interpretation* of data. While analysis often focuses on taking apart and analysing specific parts of the data, and relating these externally to each other, interpretation tries to interpret some non-obvious meaning in light of the whole and some context (Alvesson & Sköldberg, 2018). In contrast to analysis, which tends to focus on the explicit, literal meaning of the data, taking the data at face value, interpretation involves some guess-work about underlying meanings. Here, the researcher-subject is more actively engaged and responsible for the development and specification of themes, which are an outcome of the researcher's interest, interpretative inclinations and choices rather than simply emerging from the data and from a rational process. There is less of an analysis in a strict sense and more emphasis on intuition, interpretation and context sensitivity in this type of project.

Dominant metaphors

When data are approached as building blocks of reality, the analysis is typically seen as taking a reliable control over the often complex and messy qualitative material, made up of interview statements, field notes and written document material. Key here is the ideal and practice of the *coding* of data. It involves classifying and sorting the collected data into distinct categories and gradually abstracting those categories into a new piece that will add to the never-ending theoretical jigsaw puzzle. Here one may somewhat ironically see the code as a way of turning the well-known into something cryptic and secretive, as it tends to transform something that may appear to be natural into something de-contextualized, abstract and standardized – often with the loss of sensitivity for social context and meaning (Brinkmann, 2014; Potter & Wetherell, 1987). The defence for this type of coding would be that this loss is acceptable, as it is necessary to attain rigour and reliability – and just loose and open readings may make the researcher inclined to insert his or her favourite opinion or truth on the data.

Other aspects of the data analysis could be indicated by the metaphor *data-processing*, indicating a factory-like treatment of empirical material. The researcher then engages in a sort of refinement project, where the raw material through the analysis becomes processed, filtered, refined and combined, leading to knowledge products. Here, the analysis is seen as a fairly straightforward production process, where the raw material is gradually transformed into something refined and sophisticated. Data-processing may of course be carried out partly in the form of codification, but there are other options, such as thematic analysis, where specific issues or themes are the key part of the process. Data-processing may also lead to more empirically-oriented accounts, where the rich map of a terrain is aimed for. This is then different from coding, which typically aims to support a theory-building process.

In cases where research is seen as picture generation, analysis can be seen as *deciphering*, that is, to discover the meaning of the picture, what it tells us. Many liken the process of pattern findings in the analysis as completing a jigsaw puzzle. However, as Bogdan and Biklen's (1992) note, 'you are not putting together a puzzle, whose picture you already know. You are constructing a picture that takes shape as you collect and examine the parts' (cited in Hatch, 2002: 10). Hence, in analysis as deciphering, data are commonly seen as pieces in an emergent picture of some phenomenon, an evolving jigsaw puzzle.

A commonly used metaphor for capturing the interpretative nature of data-processing is *thick description*. It means addressing 'a multiplicity of complex conceptual structures, many of them superimposed upon or knotted into one another, which are at once strange, irregular, and inexplicit, and which [the researcher] must contrive somehow and then to render' (Geertz, 1973: 10). Just recording what interviewees say they mean is not sufficient. The challenge is to set in motion 'the power of the scientific imagination to bring us into touch with the lives of strangers' (p. 16). Thick description, with an emphasis on empirical detail and a thorough knowledge of the site that has been studied – the researcher having been there or having accessed the inner life – is then central. Thick description calls for rich empirical material but moves beyond just summarizing this material. It emphasizes the ambitious interpretative nature of the enterprise – here, it is not so much the marshalling of a great body of data as the strength of the (ambitious) interpretation that matters, typically going far behind just presenting empirical detail. Instead, thick description calls for moving beyond facts or registration of 'espoused' meanings. It thereby goes against surface-scratching and response-registering work, including the idea of codification (i.e. imposing a standardized meaning). Thick description calls for a hermeneutic approach, searching for hidden or barely visible meanings. Key elements, such as source-critique, moving between pre-understanding and understanding, relying on intuition and making informed guesses are part of the picture (Alvesson & Sköldberg, 2018).

Alternative metaphors

For some researchers, data are seen as *surprise-providers*. Data analysis provides or at least it is hoped it will provide 'the opportunity for surprises the researcher did not anticipate'

(Gray & Silbey, 2014: 111). This is of course a matter of serendipity – sometimes data offer very few candidates for surprises, apart from the surprise that they are mundane, trivial and uninformative. But sometimes data have potential, and with enough effort in the empirical work, especially in qualitative work, there should be material that could provide surprises – at least for the imaginative researcher who is capable of avoiding dumping everything into standard categories. The metaphor would then encourage researchers to try to produce data that are surprising, such as through asking unconventional questions ('is your workplace/family/life sometimes a madhouse?'); to try to see the surprising in a first glance at conventional material (de-familiarization); and to neglect or more briefly address totally predictable material and then concentrate efforts on what the researcher finds surprising. This may be connected to the design idea of research as mystery-creation and solving, as discussed earlier, but data as surprise-providers may also be used in other ways and on a smaller scale.

Researchers who tend to interpret rather than analyse data often take the standpoint that although data, in some ambiguous sense, are 'out there' (to be 'collected'), they do not speak for themselves or cannot be easily and reliably codified but must be interpreted. (Codification means that there is no or minimalistic – or disguised – interpretation.) This is because data are always experienced or understood from a subject's point of view. This kind of interpretative work can be seen as *intelligent guess-work* (Geertz, 1973). Also referring to Geertz and the field of anthropology, Freeman (2014: 828) describes the work as 'one of mediating between an unending maze of contextual, historical, semiotic, and affective accounts' based on some hermeneutic that mediates these multiple perspectives.

A possible counter-metaphor to the dominant ones could be to see analysis as *free imagination* (to borrow an expression from phenomenology) or promiscuous analysis (Childers, 2014). These metaphors/images encourage researchers to release themselves from strictly following a specific recipe and instead to be more responsive and sensitive to the complexity of reality. Brown (1976: 180) emphasizes scientific creativity and sees this as

> the ability to play two language games at once, to speak formal deduction while hearing one's own words translated into induction, to see the empirical evidence while simultaneously visualizing their purely formal relations, to understand the 'is' of experiment and the 'must' of deduction as metaphors for each other, each retaining is autonomy while at the same time insinuating itself into the other.

A very different metaphor for analysis would be one pointing at filtering away much of the data that a large number of interviews or days of observation normally generates. We pointed at beachcombing as a research design. Some key aspects of analysis here could be metaphorized as *crap removal*. One of the researcher's first concerns could be the filtering out of a large amount of material that is routine and predictable. Much data are of limited interest in generating new and original insights, but also of low or negative value in producing reliable descriptions. Much data may simply be outcomes of interviewees' inclination to produce socially suitable accounts, to be politically correct or to use available social scripts for how you talk about something, react with the interviewer, etc. (Alvesson, 2011). Sometimes interviewees find it hard to produce revealing accounts and to express their thoughts in words, and not all people have good communicative skills. We know that people filling in questionnaires are very sensitive to clues about the sender of the questionnaire, the purpose of the study, the exact formulations on items, the scales used, etc. (Schwarz, 1999). Often questions 'force' people to respond on issues in a misleading and irrelevant way (Einola & Alvesson, 2021). Interviews are sometimes of equally questionable value as mirrors of reality. Irrespective of its reliability, most empirical material is more or less a repetition of what is already known.

> Being able to claim that a large number of interviews were conducted and that they yielded a huge number of words when transcribed may be an important part of a game that qualitative researchers play, and it may even earn them some respect and credibility. To me this seems irrelevant, ritualistic and pointless. (Gabriel, 2015: 334)

The crap removal metaphor would then point at the significance of working more intensively with limited material that is assessed to have some potential in offering something novel in terms of ideas or insights. Here, the metaphor for data analysis would resonate with the purpose of the research as insight generator and a researcher role and identity that circulates around this.

Additional metaphors

While a fairly common metaphor for data analysis is interpretation, an alternative could be to regard data analysis as *diffraction* (Barad, 2007). In contrast to interpretation, which emphasizes patterns and coherence, diffraction encourages researchers to focus on central differences within data about one and the same phenomenon. An additional metaphor can be to see data analysis as *swimming*. The idea here is that the researcher swims around in her/his data more or less randomly and in that way reaches different insights. As Grodal et al. (2020: 10) proclaim, data analysis is like different swimming strokes, which 'enable researchers to swim differently through their data and reach diverse destinations'. Another metaphor is to regard analysis as *doubt-cultivation*, particularly in studies that are discovery-oriented. Locke, Golden-Biddle and Feldman (2008: 908) argue that 'doubt – experienced as not knowing – motivates a search for understanding. Living doubt is necessary to energize inquiry.' Of course, doubt only reaches so far, but from doubt can emerge some unexpected idea, as the business-as-usual analysis is interrupted and the researcher thinks a bit differently. A perhaps more unconventional metaphor for data analysis is one of *crystallization*. Richardson (2000) opposes the notion of triangulation and suggests that at least in her genre, postmodernist mixed-genre texts, we don't triangulate, we crystallize. Against the rigid, fixed, two-dimensional triangle, the crystal 'combines symmetry and substance with an infinite variety of shapes, substances, transmutations, multi-dimensionalities, and angles of approach. Crystals grow, change, alter, but are not amorphous' (Richardson, 2000: 522).

Summary

Table 7.3   Summary of metaphorizing analysis of data

Metaphors	Dominant	Alternative	Additional
RP element			
Analysis (of data)	– Coding	– Surprise-providers	– Diffraction
	– Data-processing	– Intelligent guess-work	– Swimming
	– Deciphering	– Free imagination	– Doubt-cultivation
	– Thick description	– Crap removal	– Crystallization

The prevalent metaphors of coding, processing and deciphering all portray data as fragments of reality and regard analysis as a more or less rigorous (or, as critics may say, mechanical) procedure of categorizing and ordering the data in specific ways that highlight particular patterns and relations and, based on that, develop new knowledge. The temporal separation and later joining together separated parts are thus key elements.

In contrast, the unconventional but fairly often used metaphor of thick description portrays analysis as an interpretative exercise where the separation of data is seen as problematic: what do these data indicate about a specific phenomenon? Here going beyond processing explicit material and trying to do 'deeper' or more bold, speculative interpretations are important.

The alternative metaphors counter the prevalent view of analysis as a rigorous process by portraying data analysis more as surprise generation, intellectual guess-work, free imagination or crap removal. Analytical elements always form part of research, but these can be downplayed in favour of something more intuitive. (Critics may say fluffy or unscientific, involving dangerous subjectivity and arbitrariness.)

While the additional metaphor of swimming indicates that the pathway to theory may be less mechanical or linear than is assumed by the dominant views of analysis, the other metaphors (diffraction, doubt, crystallization) point to analysis as a far more precarious and enigmatic enterprise. These latter, more unconventional metaphors emphasize the creative more than the rational and rigorous aspects of research.

Most analyses aim to find and report patterns. This type of analysis may be confronted by alternative modes of analysis. The construction of patterns ('findings') may be exposed to alternative patterns or even deconstructions ('anti-findings'), which open up some alternative ideas, out of which perhaps something creative and insightful can be carved out: something that is possibly quite different from what may be the case if seen only as a matter of 'building theory' or doing rigorous data management. Alternatively, the researcher who is more inclined to work with bold interpretations – informed by intelligent guess-work or swimming metaphors, for example – may confront these with more rigour-aiming metaphorical understandings and then be more aware of alternative approaches, encouraging new angles on the material.

The reflexive researcher may approach empirical material (data) in many different ways. This can be done in a holistic and consistent way: all material is processed, deciphered and targeted for codification or thick description. Alternatively, different materials may be approached more selectively. Sometimes analysis and interpretation may be joined together where coding is seen as appropriate. In other instances, there may be material that lends itself to other ways of approaching it, such as swimming or intelligent guess-work. Combinations may also include a round of coding, then analysis including free imagination, swimming and working with doubt, followed by a new round of coding, which may then require re-coding. It can result in more novel ideas and interesting fragmentations or it may lead to more than one set of interesting research results. Different metaphors may work in tandem, in line with our smorgasbord (and to some extent our supermarket) metaphor, supporting or challenging each other.

CHAPTER SUMMARY

In this chapter we have addressed the method, data and analysis elements of the research process. These may loosely be referred to as the processing, 'middle' or midstream elements of the research process. These metaphors (middle, midstream) are of course somewhat misleading in terms of the temporality of the distinct parts of research. Many elements are in operation simultaneously and boundaries between stages, parts or aspects are always arbitrary. The grounding and framing elements are also more or less actively processed throughout the entire project. Still, we see a point in dividing up research in the way we do it in this book, and just want to alert the reader to not take this too seriously. To remind the reader and ourselves: reflexivity in research means refraining from unreflective imitation and reproducing conventions without good reasons. Of course, sometimes it makes sense to follow templates, either for pragmatic reasons or where the social costs of non-compliance are high. But before placing oneself in a particular cage of 'musts' and risk-minimization, other options and the possibility that a bold, innovative move may be successful should be carefully considered.

The processing elements refer to the interactions with the empirical phenomena being studied, how empirical material is generated, seen and analysed. One principal approach is the data management route, which relies on construction process thinking, following an instruction manual for collecting the data and then processing the data analytically, emphasizing the taking apart of and the reconnecting of data elements. A different approach sees the empirical work as much looser in nature. Method may involve an intellectual wandering, searching for negations of what is expected, addressing data as clues or outcomes of participants' impression management; and then motivating a less systematic and predictable data analysis and instead engaging in more careful interpretative work, trying to get some interesting ideas, interpretations or findings out of ambiguous materials. Of course, different routes and metaphors can be combined in interesting ways. It is fully possible to approach the field armed with an instruction manual, do diligent data gathering and then be inspired (also) by alternative metaphors – seeing data as potential surprise-providers or as a source of free imagination – in interpretation. Combining and crossing conventional routes and mixing different types of metaphors may generate creativity and original results from studies.

NOTES

1. As we have mentioned before, the expression 'construction' may hide rather different metaphorical meanings. One is the construction, in the sense of producing building blocks as part of an individual and collective research project, leading to knowledge accumulation. Here, we can talk about building-construction, a clumsy but perhaps informative expression.

2. A quite different example could be to counter something commonly regarded as self-evident with an alternative, negation logic. One could, for example, consider the dominant idea that universities facilitate learning and then offer a countering claim that universities' main role is to lower the unemployment rate or provide (for many false) promises of acquiring a qualified job, that is, selling aspiration, hope and credentials rather than being in the learning business.

8
METAPHORIZING THE DELIVERING ELEMENTS OF THE RP

The delivering elements entail writing and contribution, which are mainly involved in expressing and communicating the finished research and its contribution. Even though these elements are key issues a long time before the researcher starts to craft the text and formulate the contribution, they typically become more salient and significant when most of the intensive empirical stages and analytic work have been carried out. We do not, as said before, want to emphasize a linear approach to the research process (RP). Elements that seemingly enter early may emerge more fully closer to the delivering stages. Researchers may, for example, carry out a significant part of the literature review when they have arrived at their empirical findings and try to make sense of their findings and connect these to existing literature, perhaps finding a gap 'backwards', compared to what a more rational approach would suggest.

Departures from conventional setups and steps in the research process may be particularly likely if the research is based on an open, ethnographic approach, not guided by a specific research question but more oriented towards finding out 'what's going on here', within a wide and open domain where unexpected paths may be taken. Researchers may then try to pull various pieces together in a text where cited references support or allow for an interesting debate around a specific empirical account, not necessarily following directly from an early literature review or other traditional framing elements. Researchers may also have what appear to be more delivering stages clearly in mind very early in the process. For example, it is possible to develop an idea or thesis even before starting the research, so that the research work mainly demonstrates, illustrates or fine-tunes the contribution. But the norm of empirical findings being the key driver in a qualitative study may inspire the researcher to emphasize that 'data show' more than what the researcher wants to show.

Alternatively, an ambition to produce a particular type of text may guide the design and data of the empirical study, so that the imagined final text – perhaps written for a specific journal – then drives the design of the study rather than these elements being first and the writing simply being an effect of these earlier moves.

We therefore acknowledge that research is not necessarily linear. However, we would still suggest that in most cases the writing and contribution elements are likely to be more salient in the later or final stages of the RP. We address them here as delivering elements in the flow of research.

WRITING

The production of texts may be seen as a more or less central part of the research process. Methodology textbooks often tend to downplay the significance of writing research as well as in terms of the effort, pain and pleasure of the researcher-author. It is sometimes marginalized as a matter of writing up the results in accordance with the standards for academic writing. Journal articles tend to look fairly similar, whereas there is more variation in books and sometimes in dissertations. But there are very different views on the writing up results issue, and many upgrade writing as a key issue for social research, particularly for qualitative research, and even more so for interpretative researchers. There is a difference between (entirely) interview-based studies and ethnographies, as summarizing interview accounts and writing an ethnography are quite different. To produce a text based on 'having been there' and communicating direct experiences of social situations is more complex and demanding than accessing these in the mediated and pre-packaged form of accounts encountered by the interview researcher. As a consequence, ethnographers are often more interested in writing issues (Van Maanen, 1988, 1995).

More generally, many emphasize the need to write continuously or at least frequently during the research process. One may start to write down ideas, make comments about literatures reviewed, and document encounters with interviewees, not only through recordings but also through writing about one's impressions and aspects of the interview situations that are not captured by the recording. Of course, in ethnographic work, intensive note-taking is necessary and forms a very large part of the research process. All this text material may be produced to function as building blocks or as clues for the researcher's detective work or interpretative endeavours. Revised versions of notes may also appear in publications, more so in books than in articles.

The 'writing up' of the study/findings is commonly seen as the final element in the research process. All the reviewed methodology textbooks in one way or another point to the centrality of writing up the research findings as effectively as possible to ensure 'that our research endeavors contribute to the larger knowledge base on our topic' (Hesse-Biber & Leavy, 2011: 333). The conventional view of writing is that researchers should, through the writing up, provide an accurate representation of the investigated phenomenon. It is about presenting the results in a way that truly represents what is being studied. Moreover, dominant conventions for writings in journals stipulate a fairly strict procedure for reporting research, such as introduction, literature review, methods, findings and discussions-conclusions (e.g. Barney, 2020; Cornelissen et al., 2012; Patriotta, 2017). We follow this structure in the present book but encourage the reader to consider alternatives.

According to the most dominant form of writing (Sword, 2017), which is sometimes called the realist style (Van Maanen, 1988), the study should be written in such a way that the researcher is not present (i.e. as a subject doing this and that), almost as if the scientific method itself is writing the text. There are also, but less commonly, various non-realist styles, which give the researcher and sometimes also the research participants a stronger presence in the writing. These texts are often intended to overcome the problem of studies that are, according to the many critics, 'restricted in range, full of jargon, and stuffed with remote facts, as if to satisfy some fetish of documentation or legitimation; they exhibit little interpretive nerve' (Van Maanen, 1988: 23). Given the extensiveness of such critique, there are many suggestions for alternatives that offer more engaging modes of writing research texts (Richardson, 2000; Sword, 2017).

Writing is, as we mentioned in the *section of method* and will elaborate further below, not only a matter of writing for an audience; it is also 'auto-communication'. Much writing is about the researcher thinking, exploring, sharpening, reflecting upon the research and the contribution. It is when we write that we think and find some perspective of thinking. Much of the intellectual and creative work is done at the keyboard.

Dominant metaphors

In writing, language is commonly seen as a *representation tool*, a transparent medium for the objective transport of information about reality. Writing is then the transmission medium between the analysis and findings from the researcher to the audience. Or in the words of Hatch (2002: 211), writing is about 'turning the hard-earned products of design, data collection, and analysis into findings that communicate what has been learned'. Writing is, as Flick (2018: 569) notes, not only an instrument for documenting data, but also an instrument 'for mediating and communicating findings and knowledge'. These metaphors often guide ideas on data collection, such as the assumption that questionnaires or interviews are transport vehicles for transferring the participants' knowledge to the researcher (Potter & Wetherell, 1987). Regarding language and writing as a representation tool is directly aligned with seeing research as picture generation. Seeing research as knowledge building is also closely linked to writing as a representation tool, in that the researcher builds knowledge in language. The house of knowledge is built with the help of a set of concepts related to each other in a specific way. The writing should then effectively transmit a well-selected part of reality out there in a textual representation to an audience and then mirror the phenomenon under study.

Writing is often viewed as a *template-driven exercise* for the effective communication and transmission of results. Academic writing means, according to dominant views, a particular genre. The established format stands for superior rationality, viewed as a recipe for effective and rigorous reporting. Texts, then, are broadly similar, indicating a rational, clear-cut process where the researcher shows that s/he has ticked off all the boxes. Or rather that the almost subject-free research process does so. Often, no subject seems to be writing the text. Instead, scientific rationality, manifested in 'the study' or 'the article' seems to write the text. Richardson (2000: 517) sees this as based on a model that 'requires the authors to silence their own voices and to view themselves as contaminants'. Templates may sound negative, but offer clear guidelines, both for author and reader, so that expectations tend to be similar and the risk for misunderstandings and complexities are reduced. Journal reviewers sometimes find templates-compliant text easier to evaluate and push for standardized texts.

Another metaphor for writing is *conversation*. The understanding is that research is not really about producing monologues, but contributing with texts that are dialogic and relate to previous texts and ongoing talks between people wanting progress in the knowledge areas.

> The metaphor of writing as a conversation suggests a step by step approach to conceiving a paper and developing powerful contributions. This type of approach foreshadows a text building strategy that unfolds according to the following 'moves': 1) identifying a 'good' conversation, 2) analyzing the conversation, 3) adding to the conversation. Conversations provide the baseline for a contribution: that is, they fix a reference point for establishing what is known in a particular area of investigation. If a contribution extends or challenges what is known, then joining a conversation will help authors identify and address gaps that are in urgent need of attention. (Patriotta, 2017: 753–754)

A conversation may include challenges and critique, but is perhaps best seen as cautious, polite and aiming for mutual understanding, not merely serious or hard-hitting debate and questioning. The conversation metaphor can, of course, be used rather loosely, only pointing at that there is always some exchange of ideas and mutual influencing among authors and texts in a specific field. But the metaphor can also indicate something more ambitiously dialogic, where the text is inviting and anticipates the active reader, who is encouraged not only to accept the message but to think for him- or herself and respond to the text. The response is then different from writing authoritatively, trying to establish 'how it is' with a case that is as watertight as possible, and which is difficult for the reader to approach in an open-minded way.

Often texts may be seen as *monologues within a conversation*, that is, there is a conversational element and context but the monologue elements still dominate. The author addresses an audience with an issue it is supposedly interested in, refers to well-known reference points (literature citations, the issues being debated, the use of specific language familiar to the audience) in the beginning and the end. But the major part of the study is 'tighter' and makes an authoritative case without many openings or invitations for the audience to directly join the conversation before the author-monologue has ended. Some kind of conversation-framed monologue is sometimes difficult to avoid when you write a book, and perhaps even more so an article, as the author drives the piece and no other voices in a conversation are directly heard.[1] There is, of course, the genre of dialogues or exchanges of views, but this is outside the research process as we address it.

Alternative metaphors

When research is seen as point-making, writing can be portrayed as a *rhetorical exercise* – the text as a piece of rhetoric (Richardson, 2000) – rather than as a correct representation of reality. The purpose is to convince. Here, aesthetics is sometimes emphasized. Of course, issues around the relationship between the correctness or credibility of the 'facts' and rhetoric can never be disregarded. Nothing speaks for itself in research: a persuasive text is needed. Both data reflecting reality and/or persuasive writing can be emphasized as key elements in thinking about research texts. Seeing writing as a rhetorical exercise does not therefore imply it is fake or that it disregards empirical material. Rather, the point is to present findings that have strong persuasive appeal and make the reader accept and possibly see the aesthetics of them. Rhetoric can certainly take the upper hand sometimes and lead to a text that appears to be persuasive but has difficulty in standing up to critical scrutiny.

Alternatively, writing can be seen as *exploration* – you think when you write (Richardson, 2000). We addressed this in writing as method. Now we say the same but from another angle: exploration as writing. Writing sharpens thinking and/or leads to associations and encouragement to explore new pathways. The pace of writing and the concentration of shaping a message make the reader think in a way that differs from other phases in the research process. The text is then auto-communication, an expression of an act where the author engages in an idea generation, specification and clarification project. Editing is needed to consider another audience than the author, but this is a secondary project, compared to the primary one of writing as a (self) exploration process. The text as exploration may, as with all metaphors, be seen as indicating general aspects – all texts bear some imprints of explorative work. But text can also be strongly guided or best understood through this metaphor. Here, it is possible that the preliminary texts – drafts – bear the strongest imprint of exploration, but also a finished, published text may be characterized by an exploratory style, being open, indecisive, searching, preliminary and rich on demonstrated reflexivity.

Alternatively, writing may be seen as *path-making* in the sense that 'to write … is to carve out a new path through the terrain of the imagination' (Solnit, 2001: 72). Here the social construction of reality in texts is the key element. This view encourages experimental writing and alternative forms of expression. According to Barad (2007), Dreyfus and Taylor (2015) and others, we need to move away from the representational metaphor of language and writing that holds us captive and guides our habits of thoughts and the way we conduct research. Barad (2007: 135) suggests that we move on to performativity, regarding discursive practices such as writing as performative. According to her (and many others), we are trapped in a geometrical optics view of the world, that we are somehow standing outside the world and observing it, and, based on that, we objectively represent it in the written text. Instead, the notion of performativity suggests that researchers not only or primarily represent reality, but rather enact social reality through their writing. In this case, language use is not seen as separate from, but constitutive of, social reality.

It is common to refer to writing and writings through metaphors of *story-telling*, which merges with the metaphor of research as a whole – overall purpose, method and contribution – as story-telling. Writing and research become one and the same thing. Van Maanen (1988) uses the notion of tales of the field to point at variations of ethnographic writing. He uses the term to highlight the 'representational qualities of all fieldwork writing. It is a term meant to draw attention to the inherent story-like characters of fieldwork accounts' (Van Maanen, 1988: 8). He identifies three major tales: realist tales, where the text is narrated in a dispassionate, third-person way, confessional tales, which emphasize the fieldworker's personal authorship and point of view, and impressionist tales, where the author is inspired by 'the impressionists' self-conscious and, for their time, innovative use of their materials – color, form, light, stroke, hatching, overlay, frame – that provides the associative link to fieldwork writing' (Van Maanen, 1988: 101).

Although non-conventional writing metaphors do not mean anything goes, such as neglecting some or even all empirical grounding, it may lead to richer and more vivid representations of empirical contexts (e.g. Grey & Sinclair, 2006; Kunda, 1992; Rosen, 1985). There is an emphasis on the author's voice and on how researchers do something actively and more or less creatively with the empirical material – the latter typically not being seen as a very strong determinant behind the text but is addressed more as being inspirational. This is partly because, irrespective of view, there are always many different ways in which you can produce specific representations and a full text. Unless research is about repeating the words used by those being studied, there are always large degrees of freedom for how to put together a text for a book, essay or even – although to a lesser extent – a journal article.

Additional metaphors

Another possible metaphor is to regard writing as *enlivening*, that is, as making something more entertaining and livelier. Rather than the distant, neutral, disengaged author and text, something that invokes a response in the reader is necessary. Writing styles such as irony and self-irony are possible here (for examples see Alvesson & Spicer, 2016; Grey & Sinclair, 2006). Writing may be viewed as a *rendering of reality*. In contrast to representing reality, in rendering reality the researchers deliberately create new terms, concepts and distinctions that illuminate reality in a specific way. As Hass (2008: 177) notes, such rendering of reality 'requires that one creatively reconfigure words, phrases and perhaps even syllables that are at one's disposal so that they are infused with new articulating sense and power'. An additional metaphor to story-telling is *emplotment*. It emphasizes that it is through the writing that the researcher constructs the plot of the story that s/he wants to tell about a phenomenon. The idea is that the plot is what orders the findings into some coherent story or interpretation of the phenomenon investigated.

Summary

Table 8.1   Summary of metaphorizing writing

Metaphors	*Dominant*	*Alternative*	*Additional*
RP element			
Writing	– Representation tool – Template-driven exercise – Conversation – Monologue within conversation	– Rhetorical exercise – Exploration – Path-making – Story-telling	– Enlivening – Rendering of reality – Emplotment

Writing is commonly seen as a representation and template-driven exercise that truthfully reports the findings from studies. The most common view of (academic) writing, the realistic tale, has an objectivistic tone in which the researcher as a subject is eliminated or at least downplayed. Texts tend to be formulaic. Counter to this prevailing view, the set of alternative metaphors emphasize writing as being more about crafting compelling and convincing stories. Here the researcher-author is central and is much more of an author than a transmitter of information, and more of a performer, although of course all academic writing is a mix of different elements. The additional metaphors go one step further by highlighting writing as performative, which creates rather than represents reality through a focus on the reader's experience.

The qualitative researcher is very much an author, although awareness of, and interest in, this may vary. Text crafting may follow established conventions and the author may want to copy text types that are successful in terms of acceptance for publications in leading journals. S/he may also want to gain a large (and appreciative) readership, which probably calls for some deviation from following standards, quite a lot of text work and some risk-taking. On the other hand, well-crafted texts can find a balance between different ideals, moving away from boring, impersonal and alienating styles as well as from producing texts that appear esoteric or egocentric or just so different that the reader finds them difficult to comprehend. Non-conventional writing is difficult, as there are fewer sources of inspiration and considerable writing skills are needed. Some self-critique and careful attention to the reader's responses to drafts can therefore be important, calling for both discursivism, me-ism and we-ism reflexivities.

CONTRIBUTION

The conventional view is that 'contribution' means adding something to existing knowledge about an area in some important ways. 'Part of the logic of doing research of any kind is to add to the body of knowledge, and part of the rationale for many projects is that they fill a gap in the literature' (Hatch, 2002: 41). This formulation highlights the common metaphor of contribution as adding to a body of existing, valuable research. It is about adding value. In Elsbach and van Knippenberg's (2020: 1277) words, 'we advance knowledge through programs of research in which studies help build on previous work and set the stage for future research'. Contribution is predominantly seen as adding another piece to existing knowledge about a phenomenon. To contribute is therefore largely about filling an empty space. You contribute by filling a gap in the existing body of literature in an area that you have spotted through the review of that literature (Alvesson & Sandberg, 2013a).

Sometimes the contribution means something on the border or even outside what is indicated by a gap-filling metaphor. Research contributions can be about 'extending extant literature with a new concept' (Charmaz, 2014: 253) or confirming/revising/falsifying/problematizing a particular theory or reporting an empirical finding. Of course, these contributions may also be formulated as gap-filling: a new concept may be about a lack of a much-needed concept or theory checking (hypothesis testing) may reflect a relative absence of such studies in a knowledge field.

Adding positively to established knowledge by filling in holes in it, or adding details, on the overall knowledge map is only one aspect or version of the ways we may think about research contributions. Contributions may also involve raising new, unexpected questions and ideas, challenging existing knowledge and arriving at normatively valuable contributions that suggest ways for tackling practical problems, such as in policy or professional practice. This may also be seen as finding and filling a gap – at least researchers need to scan existing knowledge in order to not re-invent the wheel and show the novelty of a contribution – but this type of more radical, innovative research is not really captured by the gap-filling metaphor.

A really significant contribution may lead to or be a push for paradigmatic change. Kuhn's (1970) idea of paradigms and paradigmatic revolutions may be debatable in social science – being generally multi-paradigmatic or pre-paradigmatic – but this does not prevent the appearance of contributions that question earlier knowledge and suggest something quite different. They may open up new avenues or encourage the understanding of something in quite novel ways. This is certainly very rare, but rather than the marginal, footnote-adding studies that dominate, one may also imagine more significant contributions in between more-of-the-same contributions and paradigm-revolutionary contributions.

Dominant metaphors

As we have pointed out at several places in the book, much research is based on the understanding of research as an accumulative enterprise. Research is predominantly about positively adding to earlier studies and suggests progress and ongoing growth of human knowledge. This is not necessarily accomplished in a linear and frictionless way, as most researchers recognize the uncertainty and imperfections of knowledge production. All are aware of mistakes, dead ends and unproductive paths taken that do not deliver much. But, still, individual studies typically mean the *expansion* of valuable knowledge. Here size and growth are part of the imaginary. This expansion or accumulation idea is the overall metaphor guiding many ideas of contributions. The metaphor can be expressed in somewhat different ways: expand, extend, increase, improve knowledge through research. Studies add to existing knowledge. The more (good) studies there are, the more we know. Quantity is thus important, as a greater volume of research means that we know more (although more does not always mean better). Human knowledge is like a library, with any new, good study added to the library as we make progress in the accumulation of knowledge, and with each new addition we add resources for reflection and better informed decision making and actions.

This means that when research is seen as knowledge building, contribution tends to be seen as *bricklaying*. The particular study adds another brick to the ongoing knowledge building in an area. Knowledge 'accumulates vertically, building higher and higher on tested foundations' (Pratt et al., 2020: 4). The bricklaying or building metaphor is overlapping the expansion metaphor but is a bit more specific, as expansion can be accomplished also in other ways than through building work. The bricklaying metaphor signals a move upwards, a vertical project, although some horizontal work is also needed in order to form a base.

Accumulation may also be considered in other ways, expressed by alternative metaphors. One is the picture generation or mapping metaphor that we have referred to before. The contribution can then be seen as *map-making*. Here the emphasis is not on building but on adding to knowledge through identifying and conducting studies that supplement them through findings in domains not yet sufficiently studied or understood, or sometimes in entirely new domains. White spots on the map need to be filled in with accurate information. We may, for example, conclude that we do not know enough about a particular group's view on vaccination or the experience of clients with personal assistant providers, and therefore need to conduct a study to fill this white spot on the knowledge map.

Another take on accumulation means the adding of perspective. Here the accumulation is less about supplying more robust studies aiding knowledge building or map-making, and more about adding to a diversity of perspectives on some phenomena. Here the researcher supplies additional knowledge – empirical studies, concepts – in a more pluralistic way.

> A horizontal notion of knowledge accumulation may be more effective as it furnishes a stock of broad principles generated across many past situations, each of them unique. In a changing, complex world, where every circumstance is different, safety lies in doubting previous experience and having available wide repertoires of tentative theories and concepts with which to address always-novel conditions. (Pratt et al., 2020: 6)

Sometimes this perspective-adding is through introducing a more or less unknown thinker and add his or her perspective on something. The thinker may be a dead French philosopher. Some new combination of sociomateriality and/or discourse is also possible, as is adding a process or practice perspective on something that was not previously blessed by these. But also, a more down to earth perspective or a new metaphor is possible.

We can here refer to the *supermarket* metaphor to illuminate the general adding of a new perspective ideal and then broadening the repertoires of tentative theories and concepts. (Here, supermarket is used in a somewhat different way from when we talked about meta-metaphors, such as smorgasbord or supermarket, for illuminating a variety of metaphors for research.) By comparison, extension, bricklaying and map-making contributions refer to stricter processes, including the rigorous adjustment to other knowledge pieces. Studies need to be positioned and plugged into earlier research. Different studies need to connect and fit, build on each other, and can be compared with these, work in tandem, etc. Adding to a construction project or a supermarket means rather different types of contributions, pointing at rigorous, consistent, synthesized and robust knowledge versus a more diverse set of various perspectives, theories and studies. While the expansion and bricklaying metaphors emphasize a robust knowledge base, a supermarket is more open about diverse qualities and reliabilities of knowledge products in a less controlled and more pluralistic setting. As said in the beginning of this book, we partly rely on this supermarket metaphor in proposing the various sets of metaphors. But here we propose the metaphor for the specific contribution of adding perspectives, concepts or ideas to a variety of other contributions, forming a conceptual toolbox for people who supposedly benefit from research.

A very common motivation for research is a response to a call. Someone has expressed a wish for, or highlighted a need for, something to be studied and the researcher demonstrates responsiveness through responding. The contribution is then a demand-driven delivery. Contribution as *response call*. Someone makes the call and the research contribution is the answer. Blithe and Wolfe (2017: 726), for example, write that their study 'responds to calls for more research on the work-life management practices of marginalized populations and people in non-normative work situations'. Their contribution, then, is about possible legislation/policy revisions, and attention to the ways legislation constrains people. Similarly, Currie, Tempest and Starkey (2006: 755) contribute to the area of new career fields by 'respond[ing] to calls for more research that discusses the impact of new career boundaries upon employees and employers'. In a sense, the response to a call leads to another call, and so on, leading to an endless call for more research, turning contribution into a perpetuum mobile, going on without energy added from the outside. The only fuel it needs is the call for more research. One may imagine the research community as hearing a voice from somewhere – 'more research on X is needed' – and then someone feels obliged to respond, and then they send out another call – 'still more research on X+ would be a good thing'. Research collectives are then a form of call centre. This may, as with all metaphors, but perhaps especially when contribution is seen as a response to a call, invite some we-ism reflexivity.

Alternative metaphors

When contributions are seen as *idea generation* they may be start- or beginning-heavy; the author has a point or theoretical idea that drives the text. Here, the thesis (the more or less original point or line of reasoning emphasized and carrying the text), the new framework or idea is offered. The idea may have emerged before a study or be emergent in the process, but it tends to put imprints on the entire text. The reader may encounter it as already clear from the start. Of course, the subsequent parts of the process may mean refinement, modifications, rethinking and up- or downscaling of the thesis, but still, later stages play a less dominant role. Idea generation means an idea developing paper, where there is constant work with developing or supporting the idea driving the study rather than it being an outcome of it.

In cases when contribution is in the form of a *story*, hopefully a rich one, the contribution may be seen as mid-heavy, focused on following the account, where the author presents empirical material or reason so that the reader is stimulated to get an in-depth understanding, such as in thick description (Geertz, 1973), or follow (be inspired or upset by) the text's reasoning. This is different from box-and-arrows and general findings types of texts, as the story qualities in these are fairly weak or thin. (Of course, the story-telling metaphor can be used in relationship to all texts, but an understanding of research contributions as good story-telling encourages other modes of writing than the effective presentation of well-packaged results in tables and formulaic writing.) The story-contribution commonly needs clear empirical and theoretical support to demonstrate logics and rigour, but it can still be seen as a story (or narrative), in the sense that there is a plot, development and someone driving the account forward. You may follow a patient in a health system, or the trajectory of a political decision.

When the point of research, as within strongly 'constructionist' (discursive) understandings, is seen as reality creation, contributions may be understood more as 'reality invention'. Here, any truth claims are seen with suspicion and the contribution is often one of *disruption*, of obstructing the conventional construction of reality in a specific way, with its truth creating and normalization effects, for example categorizing people into two sexes or claiming there is such a thing as distinct psychiatric conditions revealed by a diagnosis or that superior/subordinate relations of people at work are improved through 'transformational leadership'. As Foucault (1980) emphasized, a problem with knowledge is that it creates reality. That is, it does not just simply tell a truth, but creates the truth via categories, as well as through the naturalization and normalizations of the social world and people, by adapting to knowledge-driven conceptions of childhood, adolescence, ethnic groups, personality tests, formulas for leadership, consumer identities, etc. Here the disruption or even the demolition of (dominant, reality-creating constructions) knowledge may be the contribution. Socially fixed and controlling categories and concepts are then unfixed and their arbitrary and socially contingent nature explored.

Still another metaphor for a contribution is about *mystery solving*. As we have addressed earlier, the ideal research process could be seen as including two key elements: (i) to create a mystery; and (ii) to solve it (Asplund, 1970). A mystery is then empirical findings that deviate from what is expected and lead the researcher into a (temporary) stage of bewilderment and loss: a mystery appears when we cannot understand something, calling for a new set of ideas, which deviate from established assumptions and wisdoms, in order to resolve the mystery. The solved (or well-illuminated, and thus 'de-mystified') mystery means that a puzzle, quiz or mystery – a finding or question that is surprising and counterintuitive – is being explained or illuminated through a good interpretation or a new theory. The contribution is relying on the researcher having developed (or in a study faced) a mystery, but in the end it is the solving of the mystery that is the pay-off for the reader (Alvesson & Kärreman, 2011).

Additional metaphors

Additional metaphors could be to see contribution as a *path switching* or *conversation starter*. Here, the meaning of contribution is to change the direction or broaden the discussions and agenda in a specific research field. A key element in a novel contribution is the researcher being led away from old to new theoretical insights (Timmermans & Tavory, 2012: 170). Another metaphor, rarely seen but perhaps important to consider, is to see contributions in terms of *show-stoppers*. A show-stopper indicates a contribution that says that we should end this type of study, that is, stop using a method (in a particular area), continue with a research programme or do research based on a certain assumption and using a particular line of inquiry. Alvesson, Hallett and Spicer (2019), for example, argue for a moratorium of the use of the term 'institution' and the temporary ending of using institutional theory as a claimed theoretical perspective as it has expanded to include almost everything and leads to confusion, almost beyond repair. With the expansion of so many areas of social science, concepts become stretched and more and more ambiguous (Alvesson & Blom, 2021). As mentioned above, there is often a call for more research, but sometimes it may be more motivating to call for less research, at least in certain areas or within certain schools.

Summary

Table 8.2   Summary of metaphorizing contributions

Metaphors	Dominant	Alternative	Additional
RP element			
Contribution	– Expansion – Bricklaying – Map-making – Supermarket – *Response call*	– Idea generation – Rich story – Disruption – Mystery solving	– Path switching – Conversation starter – Show-stopper

The dominant metaphors of contribution – bricklaying, map-making, supermarket and perpetuum mobile – all in various ways regard contribution as a knowledge expansion, that is, an enlargement of existing knowledge about some phenomena. Contributions are about increasing size through growth. The alternative metaphors, on the other hand, suggest that contribution may be more about generating new ideas, solving mysteries and disrupting established knowledge. More radically, one can also regard a contribution as a path switching or a conversation starter, as proposed by the additional metaphors. Even more radical would be to see contribution as a conversation stopper, suggesting a selective – or a broad brush – discontinuation of studies that do not lead to much added-value for others except for those who benefit career-wise from it.

An important topic for reflexivity is whether the research really offers something of value. Here the elevator pitch idea – is there a clear contribution that can be communicated within a short time – may offer a good test. Is this study worth all the money? Who will benefit from reading this? Will those I have studied understand things much better if they spend time reading my report? These are good questions to ask. If there are no good answers, perhaps the researcher needs to expend more effort and try to do a better job – read more, discuss more, do more follow-up empirical work and look at possible interesting threads that are not sufficiently explored or do some re-interviews, or look for alternative metaphors on the project.

CHAPTER SUMMARY

In this chapter we have addressed two elements that typically become more salient for both the researcher and the audience (if there is one) late in the research process: writing and contribution. The contribution is often more or less given at the start and framing of a project, but sometimes there is a surprise and the researcher can change direction or at least modify the character of the result in a different and unexpected way. Both writing and contribution can, of course, be metaphorized and researchers are typically guided by metaphors in their approaches to text and contribution crafting. Writing can be viewed as everything from an effective transmission of information, a condensed mirroring of the research process, a conversation, to a more artistic and freely crafted text. The contribution may be seen as spanning from accumulation of knowledge, similar to bricklaying and map-making, to idea generation, story-telling and even show-stopping. As in previous chapters, our ambition is to show how the elements of the research process may be targets for metaphorization. We offer a range of suggestions in order to support mind-stretching and imagination, and – based on that – less of pre-structured and imitation-governed paths and more of reflexively grounded, free choices.

The five domains for reflexivity we have suggested and connected to in earlier chapters may also be applied to writing and contribution, in order to facilitate careful thinking through of the research process. Me-ism and we-ism may consider and rethink individual inclinations and collective standards for writing. It could encourage reflections about what non-familiar genres or author tactics can be considered, marginalized by one's author history or the mainstreaming effects of the research tribe. Interactionism would suggest a greater interest in the interplay between researcher-author and audience-reader – spanning far beyond considering an accommodation to reviewer requests. (Interactionism reflexivity would, at the final stages addressed here, move from researcher-people studied to researcher-audience, but in some cases the groups may overlap, particularly in policy-oriented or practitioner-relevant research.) Criticism reflexivity could carefully fuel consideration of how research contributions may have consequences on societal ideologies, interests, institutions and identities. Sometimes contributions have a conservative influ-ence or legitimize certain ways of understanding social phenomena. Behind what appears to be 'progressive' or supportive of good causes – resistance at workplaces, new teaching philosophies, more human rights – may be less innocent. Finally, discursivism means a careful consideration of how text is used. Apart from considering writing more generally, a careful look at the claimed contribution in terms of language use and the way of making a persuasive knowledge claim can be scrutinized.

Reflexive interpretation may encourage the researcher to reconsider text and contribu-tion, de-familiarization to support a more radical outlook and thinking of the possible strangeness of the entire project. For example, how can a complex reality 'out there' be packaged in 10,000 words, the average length of a journal article, in which most space addresses other elements than direct reporting of data?

As highlighted throughout this book, reflexivity of all kinds may be accomplished through moving between different metaphors, some comparing and others challenging each other. The writer may, for example, play out the metaphors of writing as a represen-tation tool, a conversation or an exploration and consider which one or which combina-tion may enrich the text most. Or s/he may seriously consider what type of contribution it is: is it bricklaying, adding to existing knowledge, a part of a call-centre enterprise, a story or the solution to a mystery? Considering and confronting a range of options may inspire creativity and a more interesting text. Reflexive exercises closer to the delivery stage may mean some reconsiderations of what has been done and how it can be made more interesting through challenges to the researcher's business-as-usual thinking and invite re-conceptualizations.

NOTE

1. However, sometimes the author's monologue may reflect a heavy input from reviewers and occasionally there are complaints (seldom praise) about articles bearing the imprints of committee-work, which are full of compromises and cleansed of the author's voice.

III
A KALEIDOSCOPE OF RP METAPHORS

9
PROPOSING A KALEIDOSCOPE OF RP METAPHORS

We have suggested the kaleidoscope as a 'super-metaphor' for working reflexively with metaphors during the research process (RP). As elaborated in the four previous chapters, all the elements of RP can be re-imagined at times, for example, in various stages of the RP. The aim of this chapter is to formalize the kaleidoscope of RP metaphors together with a set of general guidelines for putting the kaleidoscope to work. The kaleidoscope of RP metaphors is summarized in Table 9.1, and further developed below.

In most conventional understandings, the research process follows a linear path, at least this is what it looks like in methodology textbooks, as rigour and consistency are valued. Interest and literature review lead to a research question, the elaboration of a firm theoretical position informs and specifies the latter, gives a framework for analysis, the precise research question points to a specific design, followed by planned and predictable data collection, thereafter data analysis that produces findings, which subsequently informs writing and research contributions. Linearity and adherence to conventions may appear convincing on paper, but is sometimes largely a fabrication, aiming to portray the researcher as rational, rigorous and truthful. It also tends to reduce recognition and amplification of creative elements in research. Linearity is seldom the route to good ideas and stimulating research texts (Knapp, 2016; Maxwell, 2012).

However, as said before, the main purpose with this book is not to add to conventional methodology textbooks and their advice for how to maximize rationality and rigour and to accomplish a more or less predictable delivery of findings. Instead, the aim is to challenge conventional thinking and ways of conducting research by offering a repertoire of alternative ideas and understandings of the RP. We thus want to suggest ways to counteract this linear tunnel vision of the RP, as well as the production and shaping of researchers with a particular, somewhat 'square' way of being. We are worried that contemporary academic regimes produce research technicians more than scholars (Alvesson, Gabriel & Paulsen, 2017). Through providing a kaleidoscope of metaphors – where alternative ways of doing and writing research are being suggested – we hope to aid reflexivity and help researchers to develop not only their research but also themselves as researchers, teachers and as academics in general.

Table 9.1 A kaleidoscope of RP-metaphors

Metaphors RP elements	*Dominant*	*Alternative*	*Additional*
	Grounding elements		
Overall point of research	– Knowledge building – Picture generation	– Knowledge demolition – Story-telling – Point-making – Reality creation	– Cultural capital- investment – Institutionalized myth – Game playing
Researcher's role	– Instrument – Bricoleur – Technician – Truth-finder	– Provocateur – Destroyer – Insight generator – Story-teller	– Puzzle-solver – Artist – Reformer – Partisan – Advisor
Research collective	– Community – Conversation – Field – Trade association – Marketplace	– Tribe – Chain-gang – Lynch mob – Social box	– Societies for internal admiration – Political coalition – Genre – Social movements – Think-tank

Research phenomenon	– Piece of nature
	– Social object
	– Thing-like social
	  construction
	– Process
	– Domain-specific,
	  e.g. gender as
	  performance
		– Researcher invention
		– Co-produced artefacts
		– Off-centre domain, e.g.
		  gender as trap
			– Discourses
			– Appearances
			– Political acts
			– Off-centre domain,
			  e.g. gender as
			  comedy

	Framing elements		
Literature review	– Knowledge packaging – Jigsaw puzzle – Gap-spotting – Construction project	– Fault-finder – Blinker – Sparring partner – Dialogue partner – Assumption digger	– Insight producer – Idea-picking – Reservoir of narrative material – Vacuum cleaning
Theory	– Mirror – Lens – Variable connector – Reading device – Worldview	– Performative force – Eye-opener – Potentializer – Cage	– Reflexivity-stimulator – (Anti-)religion

Metaphors	Dominant	Alternative	Additional
Design	– Blueprint – Composition – Legitimizing account – Pattern following	– Plot plotting – Journey – Beachcombing – Mystery creation	– Dance routine – Garbage can – Path of discovery – Grammar
Process elements			

Method	– Instruction manual
	– Construction process
	– Collaborative
	  knowledge production
	– Triangulation
	– Voice recording
		– Negation searching
		– Intellectual wandering
		– Insight gathering
		– Writing as a method of
		  inquiry
			– Anti-method
			– Morality elevator
			– Scene-setting
			– Story generators

Data (collection)	– Building blocks – Picture fragments – Referee – Road signs – Reality recorders	– Rhetorical tropes – Artefacts – Clues – Impression management	– Lightning rod – Puzzle pieces – Artistic portrait
Analysis (of data)	– Coding – Data-processing – Deciphering – Thick description	– Surprise-providers – Intelligent guess-work – Free imagination – Crap removal	– Diffraction – Swimming – Doubt-cultivation – Crystallization
Delivering elements			

Writing	– Representation tool
	– Template-driven
	  exercise
	– Conversation
	– Monologue within
	  conversation
		– Rhetorical exercise
		– Exploration
		– Path-making
		– Story-telling
			– Enlivening
			– Rendering of reality
			– Emplotment

Contribution	– Expansion – Bricklaying – Map-making – Supermarket – *Response call*	– Idea generation – Rich story – Disruption – Mystery solving	– Path switching – Conversation starter – Show-stopper

The idea of the kaleidoscope is to try different metaphorical combinations and not simply to proceed with the tunnel-vision version, which we commonly do. Reflexivity means some variation, trying new angles and combining elements in new ways. A kaleidoscope of RP metaphors does not mean that everything goes or that the researcher can move around without friction and confusion. There are impossible or at least highly difficult combinations. Some caution is therefore necessary before combining the proposed RP-metaphors. Even if we see playfulness as important for creativity, it is a matter of intellectual, careful, serious play. It provides an opportunity to increase *disciplined imagination* (Weick, 1989) in the sense that it allows researchers to generate greater heterogeneity in research. As Weick notes, 'a greater number of diverse conjectures produce better theory than a [theorizing] process characterized by a smaller number of homogenous conjectures' (Weick, 1989: 522).

In the spirit of Weick's disciplined imagination, the kaleidoscope of RP-metaphors enables what can be called *disciplined disruption* of the RP in that it provides a tool for researchers to disrupt the way we think about the RP and its different elements in a disciplined way. It means considering different metaphors of overall purpose, researcher identity, data, writing, etc. Apart from suggesting positive alternatives, it is very much a matter of blocking the continued reproduction of dead metaphors, that is, the researcher's taken-for-granted notions of the RP elements – including the habitual use of seemingly progressive (but possibly worn-out and dead) metaphors like discourse, construction and narrative. Looking more specifically, the kaleidoscope offers four broad sets of metaphorized RP elements that aid the researcher to generate more interesting and imaginative research, namely grounding, framing, processing and delivering elements of RP.

The metaphorized *grounding* RP elements provide resources for creating an intellectual space for doing research differently and potentially more creatively than through following received wisdom in the starting phase. Energy is used to imagine the range of options for the overall point of research (knowledge building, point making, knowledge demolition) and researcher role (technician, provocateur, insight generator), etc. This may then lead to either a revision (or reinforcement) of a grounding position or the clarification of some possibilities being accessible (and creatively exploited) in interacting with emergent ideas and choices unfolding during the RP. This could encourage researchers to seriously think through the overall purpose of their research and, relatedly, their research identity and researcher role. Such thinking through is likely to lead to some opening up and ongoing reflection rather than radical changes – metaphor jumping is unlikely. For example, a truth-finder or instrument researcher role may be softened up or be reconfigured a bit differently if a destroyer or missionary identity is being considered.

To repeat our overall message, against an institutionalized logic that drives researchers into strong conformism in terms of basic orientations, it is possible to re-imagine one's work and re-position it into something more novel and unpredictable, including offering surprises for one's sub-tribe. The poststructuralist provocateur could try to take seriously the possibility of mapping the world by not seeing process, fragmentation, fluidity and discourse as ruling the world as much as considering stabilities, patterns and the frozen nature of some phenomena. The gap-spotting knowledge builder could take a devil's advocate position and aim for knowledge demolition. Rather than searching for gaps, a quest for cracks in the building may lead to new forms of inspiration. Similarly, the established tribe-member (e.g. a gender or practice theory scholar) may shift to see her/ his community more as an open marketplace with strong competition rather than as a closed tribe. What are the most productive ways of regarding the research phenomenon, as a piece of social nature or as discursively made up? Something creative and unexpected may arise when one is trying to think in 'alien' or counter-mainstream ways, and to do work inspired by the (temporary) different subject positions of doing research, perhaps using de-familiarization to avoid falling into the trap of staying within the domain of the well-known and comfortable.

Using (one or several of) the metaphorized *framing and processing* elements as resources means starting research more or less as usual but then during the inquiry engaging in more ambitious framing and processing reflexivity than what is common. Is the literature review an effective compass for leading my study straight or an occasion for critical questioning and problematization? Does the literature review provide a firm platform for building on further, or is it better approached as a conversation partner or perhaps even as a cognitive straitjacket? Does the used theory function as an eye-opener, a potentializer or a blinker, or perhaps as all three more or less at the same time, allowing more precise but also limited thinking? What are the best ways of imagining the nature of the data/empirical material? ('Best' is of course as assessed by the researcher and his/her critics, given the project, ambitions and abilities.) Is the material to be viewed as building blocks for authoritative knowing (mirror of reality) or as uncertain hints for informed guesses (creative portrayals)? Is the empirical material suitable for rigorous codification work? Or does it consist of a mix of more or less well-informed/questionable empirical accounts of the research object, calling for intensive detective work and source-critique to sort out who and what is worth one's attention, that is, seeing data as clues. In particular, what can be regarded as valuable clues for finding out what is the truth or 'truth' (accurate descriptions, insightful statements) behind all confusing and possibly sometimes misleading empirical materials?

The framing and processing elements offer a range of options for breaking away from habitual modes of thinking and doing research. For example, through planning the research and/or when working with data, one could seriously consider a variety of approaches based on a spectrum of metaphors. Am I controlling data to make a rigorous knowledge-building case? Can data be mobilized as elements in a story, where the accuracy of details matters less than the credibility and insightfulness of the narrative, or are data potentially most relevant and valuable through kicking back at established frameworks and discourses, being a vehicle for knowledge demolition and the inspiration of rethinking? In a similar way, other framing and processing elements and their metaphors can be compared and confronted, which may lead to new ideas, descriptions, results and contributions.

Using the metaphorized *delivering* RP elements means that the ambitious work is done mainly during the later stages of research in real time, as they are related to the previous RP elements (grounding, framing, processing) and often follow these. It is of course possible that the researcher also can actively think about options for the text production before starting the actual research. Nevertheless, fairly late in the process there are choices regarding how to write, although much of the writing is formed much earlier, when making notes or writing about texts that have been read or taking down observations. The researcher may early on in the RP choose between publication outlets, such as a book, an essay, a chapter or a journal article. Doctoral students may choose between a monograph and a collection of articles. Sometimes, choices about writing have implications for what empirical material to work with. But the researcher may also later in the research process rethink the text and compare and confront different modes of writing. Sometimes it may lead to some additional theory and literature work as well as some supplementary empirical work. Text and supporting material need, of course, to be aligned. Again, being careful and reflexive about the type of writing style is central for interesting studies. Rather than imitating others and following the formula, researchers can seriously consider alternative writing styles, select and embrace a chosen style or a combination thereof (e.g. through reading inspiring texts and practising, getting feedback and support, etc.) and then try to write a good text. Hopefully, our book can help in providing some legitimation through lining up alternatives and pointing out the non-given nature of the writing project. Similar ideas are relevant for views of contributions – as well as all the other elements in the RP.

The kaleidoscope of metaphors, then, enables researchers to combine different metaphors from different elements or steps in the RP. Rather than following a well-trodden path – whether neo-positivistic, interpretative, critical theorist or poststructuralist – the researcher tries, at times, to seriously consider alternatives for thinking about everything from the purpose of research to writing. The combination of metaphors that inspires the researchers does not necessarily mean the reproduction of a favoured line of reasoning, but will give added, unexpected insights and fuel for imagination. For example, understanding the researcher's role as being a technician in combination with seeing the research phenomenon as researcher invention trigger another imaginary than seeing the phenomenon as an object of social nature. Approaching data as building blocks, but then considering path-switching compared to a picture-supplying metaphor for contribution will lead to somewhat different re-imaginings of the building-block material. And so on.

However, how the metaphorized elements of the RP can work together is often a complex issue calling for careful consideration. Some combinations of metaphors may lead to creative frictions, others may simply be too contradictory to work together or inconsistent for a specific research project and the specific researcher. For example, seeing the research collective as a chain-gang or a lynch mob instead of how it is commonly viewed, as a community, may trigger a departure from conformism and encourage a freeing of the spirit, at the same time as overdoing it may lead to problems such as alienation and exclusion, but also the researcher being prepared to handle these.

Taken together, the value of using a kaleidoscopic view of the RP is to provide ideas and support for rethinking, picking and/or developing metaphors that can generate some new insights or increased (or more disciplined/self-critical) playfulness, creativity and opportunity-spotting when doing research and writing research texts. Such metaphor mobilization enables researchers to both become aware of, and distance themselves from, conventional and 'dead' metaphors (or one's own habitual thinking, where things are taken for granted and the metaphorical nature of issues are not considered) and to discover new ways of generating ideas and communicating their research. Perhaps the researcher thinks, 'Aha, I can approach the research task, my self-understanding, the literature I am struggling with, design issues, my view on the nature of data or writing quite differently than I thought earlier and/or what the "mainstream" prescribes and, thereby, produce less predictable and dull ideas and texts than are common.' (We hope that the reader is not drowning in metaphors. If so, a selective – cherry-picking – approach may offer a lifeline.)

SOME GENERAL GUIDELINES FOR PUTTING THE KALEIDOSCOPE OF RP METAPHORS TO WORK

Below we outline some general guidelines for how the proposed kaleidoscope of RP metaphors can be used for generating ideas, empirical material and texts that are seen as novel, interesting and less predictable and formulaic than is common. The guidelines are not to be read as a set of formulas or recipes, but as potentially helpful ideas and resources in order to generate more varied and imaginative studies and engaging texts.

1. *Identify* the current, taken-for-granted metaphors in use. This means stepping back and thinking through the varieties of meanings of what the researcher and his/her research tribe are doing in terms of basic understandings of the RP. Researchers then make a serious effort to approach their research project/subfield with critical distance, making an effort in de-familiarization. The key question then becomes 'what is really going on here that is not self-evidently sensible?' And even what appears to be sensible or rational may only stand for one version of several sensibilities or rationalities. What appears self-evident may not be the case. This identification work can be done during or in between projects. One may – possibly together with others, within or outside the academic subtribe – look at a previous project and re-read one's text or scrutinize the work of those of similar inclinations in the subfield with the aim to uncovering some peculiarities and oddities of the ways one does (or is claiming to do) research. The metaphors in use are thus clarified.

2. Awakening the *dead* metaphors. Part of the identification exercise is to make what is not directly acknowledged as underlying images or ideas more accessible for reflection. Apart from bringing these out, it is especially important to identify those metaphors that are *dead* – not in any absolute sense but for the researcher and her/his community – and awaken them, for him- or herself and others. Perhaps some metaphors should rest in peace, but others may be targets for revival. (We may talk about zombie metaphors, the half-dead ones.) The researcher should try to get some intellectual control over what is normally controlling him or her in the research process. This is not only about targeting the usual suspects, like 'gap', 'design', 'data', or 'theory building'. It is also about pursuing seemingly progressive and live metaphors, particularly those that have been taken for granted so much that they have received a zombie-like status, such as 'narrative', 'resistance', or 'discourse as a reality

constructor'. These ideas, novel once upon a time, easily become taken for granted and used in a routinized and unreflective way. Discourse constitutes reality and research as story-telling may be, for some people or academic tribes, dead or at least zombie metaphors, incapable of evoking much energy.

3.   Identifying *zombie* metaphors. It is very easy to use a standard, familiar vocabulary and thus put thinking on auto-pilot. Identifying zombie metaphors – metaphors that are taken for granted but easy to 'wake up' and (self) critically addresss – is often as productive as identifying stone dead metaphors as objects for life-saving enterprises. This is not entirely easy, but the metaphorical kaleidoscope and examples in this book may be helpful. Addressing a novel metaphor and see others with this in the back of the mind opens up. In particular, based on an awareness of what is used or taken for granted, it is possible to mobilize a number of alternative metaphors that are not typically used in the researcher's work or in the subfield, but are nevertheless possibly relevant. Here, a spectrum of options can be put forward, some of which encourage a break with the researcher's routinized way of being and doing. Such alternatives can stretch thinking and challenge the researcher and clearly add something in the sense of framing and conducting research in a novel way.

4.   Identifying *useful* metaphors for the specific research project. Far from all the metaphors suggested in this book are relevant and valuable for specific people in their specific projects. It is therefore important to identify what metaphors could be beneficial for a specific research project. The list should not be too long – and typically much shorter than our lists – and a criterion is the intuitive feeling that all can possibly be put into productive use. As we have said, a good metaphor combination needs to be situated in the individual and the social research context. Specifically, the list of identified metaphors could work as a resource base for the selection of one or several anchoring points in the research process, as well as offering resources for confrontation and mind-stretching. When used as anchoring points, these metaphors ensure there are at least some key issues in the RP where alternative metaphors (to the ones conventionally used by the research field/researcher in question) are available for reflection. Pursuing alternative metaphors means that the researcher is challenging his/her comfort zone as well as his/her research habits in some respects. Guiding criteria here are a mix of familiarity with unfamiliarity and a good initial grasp of a new metaphor – or seeing a well-used metaphor as strange and problematic.

5.   Developing an *operative strategy* (or tactic) for metaphorizing the RP in a specific project. This strategy focuses on privileging a certain set of key elements that works well for the researcher, being different from his/her business as usual, but not so different or alien that s/he can't really understand or handle them competently. This operative strategy means the careful selection and combination of alternative, contrasting metaphors to work with. It may focus on selective parts of grounding, framing, processing and/or delivering RP elements or a combination. It may involve two or more metaphors of, for example, purpose, literature review, phenomena, data analysis and contribution metaphors, that the researcher will work with more intensively, in combination with some reflexivity domains. (Other elements of the research process may not be targeted for metaphor work, as it may become too complicated and the effects of metaphor considerations/reflexivity on some parts may have positive effects on others.) Specifically, this strategy enables the researcher to

combine the opening up associated with new metaphors with a tactic for reducing variation and attaining some closure in order to provide direction and produce some discipline in order to create a convincing study.

6. Using *metaphorical reflexivity* as a meta-strategy. In addition to the specific work of identifying metaphors, including awakening or abandoning the dead, and playing with alternative metaphors, the researcher may try to have an overall view for how to critically think about the whole research project. Crucial here is often to organize support from other people – all this is difficult to do in splendid isolation and the lonely heroic researcher (or small team of similar-minded co-researchers) may easily fail. Finding one or more devil's advocates may be a good idea. So is the reading of counter-literature, so that other points of view are offered as valid theoretical and methodological alternatives to the path the RP takes. De-familiarization as a specific tactic for reflexivity can be useful here in the effort to break away from the intellectual orientations and social boxes most of us are caught in and comfortable with.

CHAPTER SUMMARY AND CONCLUDING COMMENTS

In this chapter we have further developed how one can use the kaleidoscope of RP metaphors for imagining a more varied set of options for thinking about and doing research. The kaleidoscope offers a super-metaphor for a metaphor-stretching and reflexivity-stimulating way of addressing the RP.

One may do kaleidoscopic work spontaneously and playfully, perhaps occasionally engage in brainstorming, or having a clear overall strategy or design – although hardly a blueprint version – for doing this. A range of options can be considered here. We have advocated some overall ideas for a loose strategy. It is easy to get lost when there is so much to consider when doing research, so some structure for employing kaleidoscopic thinking may be necessary. It may be wise not to include too much but to see the supermarket of possibilities as offering a selection for choices, no obligatory routes through the shopping aisles. The researcher needs to economize and not overdo the metaphorical reflexivity. Sometimes less is more. It calls for a more systematic effort than just spontaneously thinking creatively and differently.

In most cases, it may be relevant to primarily consider and confront dominating metaphors with alternative ones, or for the person who is much into alternative metaphors to contrast these with dominating metaphors or other alternative or additional ones. We have consistently pointed out the problems with dominant, conventional metaphors being taken for granted and establishing rigid norms for how to conduct research. This does not mean that for all researchers, in all fields, it is a good thing to celebrate what we have presented as 'alternative' metaphors. These do not simply stand for something more progressive or interesting than the more commonly used metaphors or images. The 'alternative', non-conventional metaphors can be equally constraining and lead to predictable, boring studies, or failed attempts to appear 'interesting'. What we have presented as alternatives are, for some people, normal and normalized metaphors, which are sometimes dead for them, because they are taken for granted. Our issue is not with metaphors being good or bad *per se*, but with the tendency that researchers freeze their understanding of themselves and their research processes and let favourite or taken-for-granted metaphors control their work. Here, it is important to see dominant metaphors not only as dominant on a broader scale or in absolute terms – dominating research as a whole – but also dominant within specific research fields or groupings. What is 'alternative' on the grand scene may be dominant or conventional within a specific orientation, for example constructionism, feminism or LGBTQ studies. We have in this book addressed the larger scene, so here we only comment about how to consider dominant and alternative metaphors to specific research traditions.

Our key point is that researchers should consider, for themselves and their research tribe, not only dominant metaphors, but also (and more importantly) alternative metaphors, and use these considerations throughout the process of conducting research. In some cases, research traditions are often caught in their own, favoured alternative metaphors, which may be better seen as field conventions rather than as a straitjacket of the individual researcher. In many areas of critical theory, feminism, poststructuralism, intersectionality and narrative studies, researchers may be careful about celebrating and reproducing their favoured metaphors and consider ways of being productively linked to conventional metaphors as well as other alternative ones. Linking may be supplementary or dialectical – with metaphors working in parallel, adding to smorgasbord pluralism or leading to a (hopefully) productive tension, where the negation and friction fuel creativity.

10

ILLUSTRATING THE KALEIDOSCOPE OF RP METAPHORS

In this chapter we discuss how the metaphorical kaleidoscope proposed in the previous chapter can be used for generating alternative ways of conducting research by applying it to two examples. It is not entirely easy to demonstrate how to use the kaleidoscope more concretely based on published texts. We cannot apply all the ideas suggested in previous chapters, as it would lead too far, and we are not familiar with the researchers' specific situation or the subfield at the time of the study. Most studies can also be conducted in an almost infinite number of ways. However, in their published texts researchers try to make a persuasive case for a specific way of doing research. Authors typically aim for closure, rather than openness. They are therefore seldom generous in terms of showing alternative ways of thinking as this would easily reveal the shortcomings of a study and invite unwanted critique. Although researchers often insert sections on limits and shortcomings, these sections rarely open up radically different ways of conducting studies. Instead, they focus on the need for additional research, typically along more or less the same lines as the study presented, but using another sample, better techniques or following up certain questions. Even though research can be understood as dialogues, many texts demonstrate little of this quality and are primarily monologues. Sometimes they are even written as impenetrable fortresses, which are very difficult to open up and thus encourage closure and mimicking.

However, we think that taking a renewed look at a couple of well-known and celebrated studies, published in highly ranked journals, may be instructive and perhaps inspirational for how the kaleidoscope of RP metaphors can be used. We have chosen the following two studies for careful scrutiny: Barley's (1986) study of how technology is structuring work roles and relations, and Pratt, Rockmann and Kaufmann's (2006) study of how medical students do identity change when becoming residents in a teaching hospital.

We have access to the authors' texts only and make assessments based on these, assuming that the metaphors used come through in the publications. It is of course possible that the metaphors guiding the researchers during the actual conduct of research – often spanning over several years – may have been different. But our interest here is to point at how studies could have been imagined differently, and for this purpose it is sufficient to consider the metaphors that are traceable in the final reports.

EXAMPLE 1: HOW TECHNOLOGY IS STRUCTURING WORK

In this example, we apply our kaleidoscope of RP metaphors to Barley's (1986) highly influential and praised paper 'Technology as an occasion for structuring: Evidence from observations of CT scanners and the social order of radiology departments', which was voted by a number of prominent academics (the editorial board of a major journal) as the most interesting paper in the entire management and organization studies field in terms of being counterintuitive, an example of good writing, and offering new theory and strong practical implications (Bartunek et al., 2006). This may say more about the field than the paper's qualities in terms of having interesting things to say. Although we find it impressive in various ways, though not necessarily that interesting, we think it is a good example to scrutinize through our metaphorical kaleidoscope, particularly as many people view it as exemplary research.

Would it be possible to turn Barley's study into something even more 'original' and 'interesting' (the concern of our book)? That is, could further research learn not only from the reported study, but also of alternatives ways of approaching his research topic? Our metaphorization of Barley's study is not meant to suggest an entirely new 'design' of his study, but rather to show how alternative metaphors in selected phases of the research process could lead to other (perhaps more) interesting ways of conducting such a study. It is of course a thin (or perhaps a thick) line between doing more or less the same study (or rather a similar study) guided by alternative metaphors of the RP and being so inspired by these that it means doing a rather different type of study.

Barley (1986) begins his paper by noting that evidence for technology's influence on organizational structure is confusing and contradictory. As a way of overcoming and making sense of the contradictory evidence, he proposes structuration and negotiated order theories. From a combination of these theoretical perspectives, 'technologies are better viewed as occasions that trigger social dynamics which, in turn, modify or maintain an organization's contours' (p. 81). Using the framework of structuration theory as a basis,

Barley then conducted a study of two radiology departments in hospitals and observed how new technology affected the interaction patterns between radiologists and technicians. Exactly what ideas/metaphors informed the various parts of the study is hard to tell. The text is also 'tight', convincing and protected, leaving few openings and encouragements for the reader to think differently about the research undertaken by Barley. Nor does the study contain any signs of doubt, reflexivity or self-critique, as we suggest in this book. A sense of rationality and rigour dominates.

Metaphors guiding the study

When it comes to *the metaphors in use*, Barley presents the study as rationally carried out according to the plan, where all the ingredients fall neatly into place. It appears almost to be a transportation along a fixed route, where all the stations (literature review indicating unexplained phenomena, theoretical framework, data collection, analysis) are passed without frictions or surprises, or reason to, at times, rethink or re-route a well-planned trajectory. At least there are no signs of such disruptions or reasons for radical rethinking. All data have a uniform, clear-cut meaning that can be reduced to standardized categories for interaction (e.g. role reversal, direction giving). The research is presented as a carefully planned and managed labour process, largely following the logic of a well-run factory. An efficient research machine is in operation: it is well-thought through, processed and with a high-quality, predictable delivery of results to the audience. The researcher comes out as a very clever operator of the scientific machinery, contributing to knowledge building.

When it comes to the literature review, Barley argues that 'as most investigators admit, after two and a half decades of research our evidence for technology's influence on organizational structure is, at best, confusing and contradictory' (p. 78). The literature review is thus easily summarized as inconclusive, leaving room for an effort to address the contradiction and the knowledge development failures it is supposed to reveal. (One could argue that inconclusiveness is inevitable, but that would draw upon another metaphor.) The literature review is about gap-spotting. Earlier studies are deficient in an important sense and therefore require something new/different, the reader is told. However, the text downplays any substantive challenge of the existing literature. Instead, Barley portrays his study as relating positively to the community, reassuring the reader that 'to view technology as an occasion for structuring is not to deny the worth of previous work on technology's relation to structure, but rather to modify and specify that work' (p. 106). He then politely contributes to the knowledge community through simply suggesting some modest changes and specifications.

The theoretical framework proposed by Barley (structuration theory) seems to function as a mirror offering an authoritative source for truth-telling. It allows us to see how the relation between technology and organizational structure really works, if studied carefully. The structure is mapped and explained by theory emphasizing structuration. However, the major anchoring point for the study is not the theoretical framework but the data. In fact, two-thirds of the article concerns data and modes of dealing with them. The collection and analysis of data are absolutely crucial to the study, which appears to be strongly data-driven. The robustness of a massive amount of data, very cleverly and diligently handled, gives the study authority. The paper appears to be a true masterpiece of data management.

The operative strategy Barley follows, at least in the article, is an established methodology with a strong technical focus on data collection. The researcher comes out as a technician and truth-finder, the phenomenon is a piece of nature, and data are robust building blocks, while the writing is template-driven. Participants' interpretations were 'sought and recorded', 'field notes revealed', while observations provided 'raw data for the analysis' (p. 85). Research as a mirror of reality was then the modus operandi of the study. Here the formal roles/labels/occupations of radiologists and technicians are taken for granted and invite the portrayal of workplaces populated by units, where the only further differentiation is the degree of experience with the technology. Gender, age, ethnicity, personal characteristics are never mentioned. Subjects are stripped of human characteristics and come out as one with their occupation, that is, addressed as cloned. There is nothing wrong with that; we only indicate other possible approaches to the phenomena studied.

In fact, the research that is reported appears almost to have been conducted without a researcher (facing dilemmas or ambiguity, using judgement, having to deal with the complexities of accessing reality). There is a statement 'I began observation' (p. 84) and there is a reference to 'my field notes' (p. 86), but otherwise, and in all-important respects, it is the research (Science) that is the subject. The text is full of passive formulations like 'were observed', 'field notes revealed' and 'scripts traced'. Furthermore, claims like 'authority was centralized' are made without any hint that this may be an interpretation; or that the construction of something as 'centralized' may not only be an outcome of objective reality but, rather, an effect of the researcher being more than a skilled operator of the Science Machine.

Dead metaphors. The question of 'dead' metaphors is difficult, as it is sometimes a matter of dead for whom. An entire field may take a concept for granted so that it loses its metaphorical quality, as there is no imagination-stimulating interaction between source (modifier) and target (principal subject). That is, the modifier metaphor and the principal subject become one and the same thing, like the 'brain' is a 'computer'. It is often hard to know if a person is using an expression in a conscious metaphorical ('live') way or not. However, certain expressions indicate some underlying understandings in the text where the metaphors may have been taken for granted – or perhaps encourage the reader to confuse the metaphor for the literal and precise meaning. For example, Barley has a section named 'mapping the evolution of structure' (p. 81). Here, the 'evolution' of 'structure' is simply there to be 'mapped', like the course of the Nile. All data are addressed as robust building blocks for the study. Data were 'gathered'. They were easily turned into something standardized. 'Each episode was then reduced to an initial plot' (p. 85). Expressions like 'distribution', 'centralization' and 'roles' are used in the paper as if these were unproblematic representations of underlying phenomena, lacking any metaphorical quality. They seem to be employed in order to make the link between the interactions among people from two occupations and a credible case for organizational structure. Another possible dead metaphor enacted by Barley is 'coding', such as 'measures of centralization were constructed by coding instances of routine decision making' (p. 86) and 'dummy variable that coded each scan's date' (p. 105), further emphasizing research as map-making.

Alternative metaphors worth considering

Let us suggest some *alternative* metaphors that could have guided the research, that is, that could have led to a different but similar study. Instead of Barley's 'knowledge building enterprise', one could imagine 'point-making' as the key purpose of the study. This could be done through the idea of 'knowledge demolition', where the researcher radically challenges and provokes the mainstream views of technology and structure. This demolition should then be followed by the launching of a structuring perspective. A more radical view of the methodology needed for understanding technology in relationship to organizational structure could then be put forward. Writing that follows 'templates for result transmission' could be confronted with a more challenging and upsetting 'path-making' understanding. Here, the established literature in the field could be addressed as problematic and a superior alternative could be put forward and advocated as part of a paradigm war or confrontation. Such confrontation would not only make Barley's contribution stronger and more brutal, but would also open up space for clearer alternatives. The author would then be a 'provocateur' rather than, as embraced and communicated, a 'cautious reformist'.

Alternative themes could suggest work that moves away from the rather strict application of theory and data management. If we, inspired by Barley's title, change the view of theory application to an occasion for alternative thinking, we could move from viewing the theory as a mirror for mapping reality and a guide to the truth (providing perfect theory/data fit), to seeing it as a 'lens' giving a selective and sharp picture or inspiring a rich portrayal of the possibly, for most readers, exotic world of radiologists and technicians. Making (some of) the episodes studied into a set of richly constructed events, portrayed in ways that allow the reader to get a feeling for what goes on, including their meanings (considering more fully the views of those studied), could have been an alternative. Here, data are not so much neat objects to be collected and coded than occasions for thick (or at least not anorexic) descriptions of encounters between the people at the site, which are not entirely easy to reduce to standardized categories.

As alternatives to the metaphors of mapping and gathering data, it would be possible to consider a spectrum of construction possibilities. Instead of Barley's choice of the theoretical categories of distribution, centralization and roles, one could imagine a somewhat less 'neutral' approach and the empirical phenomena respectively could be portrayed as social inequality, domination and re-positioning. The latter could be opened up even more, and not, as in the paper, be closed and fixed (at least in specific episodes), by using process thinking and its talk about temporal subject positions. Rather than 'role negotiations', the material could be addressed as the doings of 'social class work' in the med-tech context. (One could then highlight a strong class element in the relationships and interactions of the people studied, where the radiologists and technicians come out as upper- and lower-class groups, respectively.) In doing this, we simply point out other options than the more 'conservative' or 'neutral' ways of claiming what data mean, through identifying other constructions – in opposition to the mirroring or data management-guided possibilities.

An alternative strategy could also include thinking about elements in the process through metaphors such as empirical material as 'inspirations for insights', 'appealing to intuition', or 'raw material for confessional or impressionistic writing', allowing for richer portrayals (Van Maanen, 1988). One could, for example, keep most of the metaphors of the entire RP used by Barley more or less as they are but view data as reality constructions and see writing as telling a personal story of a 'structurationist/negotiated order enthusiast' entering the world of radiology at the time of the introduction of a new technology. The researcher could then declare: 'Let the drama begin'. Here, the writing would be more like emplotment.

Summing up

The (re-)metaphorization of Barley's study, the tensions between some key metaphors underlying the central elements of his research and the set of alternative metaphors for those elements, open up different ways of thinking and doing research about the technology–structure relationship. In the published study, Barley is largely portraying himself as a cautious reformist who is effectively running the scientific machine: he scans the literature and identifies a confusion gap in the sense of contradictory evidence about how technology influences organizational structure; he proposes structuring theory as a sharper mirror of reality and as a way to overcome and transcend the perceived contradictory evidence; he collects data through close observations and interviews; he analyses the data by coding and reducing them to standardized categories; he portrays the findings as they mirror reality; and, thus, he delivers a significant piece to the theoretical jigsaw puzzle of the technology–structure relationship.

In contrast, our *alternative* metaphorization of Barley's study suggests that the researcher could engage in point-making, trying more strongly to engage in a specific line of reasoning, rather than trying to tell the truth. This would give more agency to the researcher than to the data being the source behind the results. Instead of identifying gaps in the existing literature to be filled, the researcher could, for example, work as an insight generator, identifying and challenging some of the assumptions underlying the existing literature as flawed. Based on that the researcher could provide a set of alternative assumptions that offer a more novel space for inquiry. Moreover, instead of regarding structuration theory as a mirror of reality in the sense of perfect theory/data fit, one could see the theoretical framework as a lens that offers an interesting but selective perspective of the technology–structure relationship. Instead of approaching data as stable building blocks of reality, the researcher could treat data as ongoing constructions made by the researcher and the research participants. Finally, instead of regarding writing as a template for delivering yet another piece to the existing jigsaw puzzle of how technology influences organizational structure, the insight-generating researcher could use writing as a rhetorical exercise and exploration of idea generation and rich stories about the technology–structure relationship, perhaps shaking up parts of the research collective, which could be addressed as a community (to be gently shaken up) or as a social box (to be challenged less politely).

The ideas suggested here – following from other metaphors than those guiding Barley – do indicate a somewhat different study from Barley's. But we are not suggesting something radically different. The point is to encourage expanding the set of considerations and efforts to re-imagine a study, not to suggest something completely different. Given our alternative metaphors, one can still study and say something about how technology is structuring work and relations. However, the use of the alternative metaphors would lead to a study, text and contribution that would be moderately or significantly different, depending on how far one wants to push the alternative metaphors. Hence, even an exemplary study can be rethought in interesting ways and inspire not only more of the same but also something that stands out as different. Working with alternative metaphors shows how this can be done.

EXAMPLE 2: BECOMING A PHYSICIAN

In our second example we apply our metaphorical kaleidoscope to Pratt, Rockmann and Kaufmann's (2006) well-cited study of how people construct their professional identity when they become medical residents, that is, when they go from being students to becoming qualified doctors, during a structured programme at a teaching hospital. The residency serves as an important boundary-crossing from student to practitioner. Pratt et al. motivate their study by claiming that 'despite a growing interest in matters of identity in organizational studies, researchers know relatively little about how identities are formed among professionals, being a group of outmost importance' (p. 235).

The aim of this article is to 'build and enrich theory around how professionals construct their own professional identities' (p. 236). The researchers examined this process in the context of medicine. They see their sample as an extreme case, arguing that such cases facilitate theory building because the dynamics being examined tend to be more visible than they might be in other contexts. Applying this criterion, they chose to study medical residents in the specialties of primary care, radiology and surgery. The primary method of data collection was semi-structured interviews with the 29 medical residents in the three specialties, who were interviewed four times each over 3–6 years, based on a common set of questions that allowed the researchers 'to see changes in members' responses to questions over time' (p. 239).

The major finding concerned how the residents dealt with 'identity violations', that is, discrepancies between what people did and who they thought they were, between doing and a sense of being. The outcome of the study was that instead of adopting a whole new identity while being a medical resident, individuals can enrich an existing identity, patch together two (or more) identities (e.g. a specialist and a general doctor), or use another identity as a temporary splint, for example, falling back on a student identity (p. 256).

Pratt et al. claim that their findings show 'how professionals build identity over time ... [findings which] provide new insights into extant conclusions (e.g., why perceived competence accompanies identity construction), refine current ways of thinking (e.g., the importance of the magnitude of integrity violations rather than task newness as a trigger for identity change), and show how findings from these separate literatures are linked in the identity construction process' (p. 259).

In the above text quotes, we note many metaphorical expressions to indicate the subject matter. The authors write that they show how professionals *build* (i.e. develop or construct) identity, which *provide* new *insights* (thus supply new resources for understanding the phenomenon), illuminate (our metaphorical expression) competence as an escort (*accompanies*) to the production of *identity* (the meaning of this metaphor is not entirely clear in the paper), offer *refinement* of thinking, for example, about breaks of coherence (*integrity violations*) being a *trigger* for change, as well as demonstrating (through putting on an *exhibition*) discoveries (*findings*) through linking separate literatures in the 'identity construction process'. (We put their chosen words with a strong metaphorical meaning in italics.) We will address the metaphor(s) behind these expressions below.

Metaphors in use to indicate the subject matter

Pratt et al. see their research phenomenon – identity – as more or less given 'out there', a piece of social nature that can be easily studied with the right equipment. The word 'identity' is also connected with other words in the article, such as learning cycles, construction, integrity violation, formation, evolves, changes, conversion, work, dynamics, customization, claims, descriptions, enriching, belief, set, build, patching, composite, developed and strengthened. Pratt et al. also talk about identity 'components' ('one's clothes and other possessions are often an integral part of identity. Dress is an especially potent component of identity among physicians', p. 248).

Many of these words indicate metaphors pointing in rather different directions. An identity 'learning cycle' suggests that identity is something you learn in a rotating and predictable way. 'Construction' and 'build' point at some active production effort with a clear direction, perhaps not so 'cycled'. 'Work' points at something more ongoing and open. 'Integrity violations' indicate something being originally united, now being mismatched or broken apart. A 'formation' seems to suggest something robust, with a clear shape, and changing in a less decisive way than perhaps 'build' and 'construction' would indicate. 'Patching', 'component' and 'composite' appear to be some type of assembly phenomenon, less of formation and integrity, made up of parts, and also a bit different from evolving. 'Enriching' points at the adding of value while 'strengthened' indicates power and solidity.

Through these remarks, we do not want to suggest critique by claiming the paper to be incoherent and confused. Whether the variety of expressions and mixing of (root) metaphors for the subject matter of Pratt et al.'s text indicates a paper that itself scores high on integrity violation, evolvement, patching, composition or on enrichment and construction can be debated. Many, if not all, papers exhibit some pluralism or mixing of metaphors – sometimes consciously, and sometimes the play of metaphors acts beyond the control and intentionality of authors and makes them appear stuck in mixed discourses. Often, the patching of a study and paper calls for the blending of a multitude of metaphors, perhaps making a paper not so much rigorous as interesting and insightful.

Generally, the metaphorical reflexivity we advocate here tends to see the limits, as well as the unfruitfulness, of conventional claims to rigour. Nevertheless, Pratt et al.'s metaphors indicate something more than just trivial opaqueness regarding what the authors actually mean by 'identity'. The authors do not provide a systematic discussion or define the key concept, but remain elusive in the text. Many of the data claimed to indicate identity do not always clearly do so. Having 'responsibility for patients', being a consultant, being residents at the institution or a student (p. 241) are rather crude identity indicators. One could possibly ask for much richer material on the meaning of having responsibility, being a resident or student etc., that is, moving beyond organizational or sociological factsheet categories. But Pratt et al. are similar to most authors – social science is often much less rigorous than it appears. This is hard to avoid due to the fleeting nature of phenomena and often unreliable or 'clumsy' data. Language use is seldom precise, and we need to be tolerant and open about some looser or inconsistent thinking, empirical work and writing.

Metaphors guiding the study

Moving on from metaphors indicating the research phenomenon of identity, Pratt et al. see the *purpose of their research* in terms of adding to the knowledge map through gap-filling. They find shortcomings in the explanatory power of existing theories and the lack of studies on the subject matter. The authors 'identified three literatures as especially helpful in understanding the identity construction process, broadly defined: careers and role transitions, socialization, and identity work. Though we ultimately found that each perspective held important pieces of the puzzle of identity construction, none adequately accounted for our findings' (p. 236). There is, thus, a gap, the authors conclude: 'there is a paucity of literature on the topic' that is 'under explained' (p. 235).

Addressing the gap and engaging in *puzzle solving* form parts of what, for Pratt et al., is basically a *building* exercise. The aim of the paper is to build theory in the area of professional identity construction and to extend existing theory by making it 'denser by filling in what has been left out – that is by extending and refining its existing categories and relationships' (p. 238).

Building theory is mentioned repeatedly in the paper. Sometimes Pratt et al. supplement 'build' with 'enrich' or 'elaborate' theory. At one point, they say that the study 'builds and extends research'. This is combined with the idea of gap-filling. Theory needs to be extended and made 'more dense by filling in what has been left out' (p. 238). Their ambition is to build knowledge that both contributes to build something bigger, more densely and tight, where what has been missed ('left out') by earlier, perhaps more negligent builders, will be taken care of. All this building aims to contribute to 'theory', seen as something that fits and explains data. The building metaphor even spills over into their discussion about identity construction, that the residents 'build identity' (p. 259), indicating its strong grip over Pratt et al.'s thinking and way of theorizing.

When it comes to *design*, Pratt et al.'s study is clearly structured from the beginning, and the entire research process follows a strict blueprint, without any interesting surprises or new ideas being triggered:

> We represent the segmentation of this profession by examining medical residents in three specialties: primary care, surgery, and radiology. The choice of these three physician groups maximized differences along two dimensions thought to be particularly relevant to the work of physicians: generalist versus specialist, and high to low degree of patient contact. (p. 238)

In terms of *data* collection, semi-structured standardized interviews were used, apparently conducted in a linear and production-line oriented manner outlined in their blueprint for research:

> Interviews were performed at the hospital and lasted approximately one hour on average. The first and third authors recorded the interviews as well as took notes, and interviews were transcribed verbatim. (p. 239)

All interviews seem to be taken at face value and all interview statements are presented as if they mirror or give reliable indicators of the identities and identity change of the people being studied. (There is no explicit recognition of the possibility of data being about how people adapt to/perform in the interview setting, and thus data can be seen as *artefacts* more or less loosely connected to issues around self and experiences in people's lives and developments 'outside' interview talk situations.) Data are seen as a means of transporting information from the 'subjectivities' of the people studied to the world of academic knowledge. Data mirror reality and become objects for rational data management.

Regarding *analysis*, Pratt et al. write that they 'analysed the qualitative data by traveling back and forth between the data and an emerging structure of theoretical arguments' (p. 239). They went through the steps of open coding, axial coding and then looked at how generated 'categories fitted together into a coherent picture' (p. 240). The process is described as diligent, rigorous and straightforward work, involving a refinement and abstracting process.

> We brainstormed alternative conceptual frameworks or models that described how these themes related to one another and to available organizational theories. Once we had identified a possible framework, we reexamined the data's fit/misfit with our emergent theoretical understanding. (p. 240)

The brainstorming metaphor indicates something quite different from other parts of the research process, which seem to be tight, rigorous and smooth, with a clear, objective and logical process, where Pratt et al. 'identified', 'examined' and could establish fit/misfit. One may assume (or at least hope) that this leads to a framework that offers a valuable knowledge contribution in terms of better theory.

In terms of *contribution*, Pratt et al. claim that their 'research points to the importance of looking at work-identity *integrity* as motivating identity construction', and they argue for the need to examine how work and identity reinforce each other rather than concentrating on work–identity fit' (p. 259). The paper leads Pratt et al. to propose 'a more general theoretical model of identity customization among professionals. Our study concludes with a discussion of the implications of our model both for theory related to identity construction and, more practically, for the training and management of health care and other professionals' (p. 240).

Dead and live metaphors

As with most research, Pratt et al.'s study includes some metaphors that seem to be taken for granted – or at least they are not made the topic of explicit recognition – and belong to the standard repertoire, including building, gap and codification. One could perhaps say that this disguises some of the ambiguity and arbitrariness that are unavoidable when studying non-distinct, vague phenomena such as identity, which may give rise to a misleading, although institutionalized, impression of the phenomenon in question, understood as a piece of nature, ready for picture-taking. That 'identity' has emerged as a topic for social research may be a source of reflexivity – there are other ways of approaching human subjectivity than through the idea of 'identity' (Alvesson, 2010; Meyer & Allen, 1987) – but this metaphor has a strong grip over contemporary Western society and large research collectives.

As noted above, the *building* metaphor is the major metaphor for the research process of Pratt et al. The project is one of building theory through finding various building blocks that are carefully tested for fit/misfit and then processed in such ways that a knowledge contribution comes out of all the work. For example, they talk about 'an emerging structure of theoretical arguments' (pp. 240–241). The authors conclude that available theories did not 'adequately account[...] for our findings' (p. 236), which could be interpreted as they lack quality to be fully used in the knowledge project. The statement 'data's fit/misfit with our emergent theoretical understanding' (p. 240) also indicates a view where the various parts that 'fit' together (which is a key element in the building project) stand in a friction-free relationship to each other in order to make the enterprise work. The researchers appear to be technicians skilfully dealing with the components of the RP.

The self-evident nature of codification and the assumption that the empirical material of identity change lends itself to being codified, thus leading to aggregations, also reflect a metaphor that is not addressed as a live one in the paper. Expressions like 'different categories fitted together into a coherent picture' (p. 240) indicate that research is about arriving at a coherent picture. The picture metaphor may be productive but it seems to be taken for granted here. The possibility that identity change is about movements, circulations, twists, reversals etc., leading to an incoherent, fragmented multidimensionality of identity (and something less identity-bound, i.e. fluctuating subjectivity) is not considered here.

The paper, of course, also works with more novel, live metaphors, less in order to capture the research process than in order to illuminate the phenomenon, where identity change is seen in terms of customization and violations, that is, novel and consciously used (one may assume) metaphors:

> we found that differences in these work-identity integrity assessments resulted in different *identity customization* processes. We use the term 'identity customization' to denote that identity is tailored to fit the work at hand, and not vice versa. (p. 242, original italics)

Pratt et al. also use expressions like *violations, customization types* – enriching, patching and splinting – and talk about 'the *identity sets*, or "raw materials" used to customize these identities' (p. 246). All these words are metaphorical and encourage the reader to think in novel ways, partly through the use of imagination-stimulating metaphorical qualities, combining the target or focal object of subjectivity with sources or modifiers like violence (violate), marketing (customize), tailoring (patching), etc. It is perhaps important to point out that conventional metaphors like building and picture do not prevent innovative ideas.

Alternative metaphors

It is not entirely easy to identify alternative metaphors in a tight case like Pratt et al.'s paper, which – as most papers – has been written to be convincing and defended against critique and possible loopholes. As with most papers, the dialogic or conversational qualities are not particularly pronounced, and the reader faces closure rather than encouragements to think differently and outside the logic of the text. One learns about the routes taken by the research team, while options to engage in other trajectories, guided by alternative metaphors, can only be discussed from 'outside' the text. This is not inevitable, and texts encouraging more open readings are possible, as suggested by our alternative metaphors. Let us therefore suggest some alternative paths, based on other metaphors for the research process than those characterizing the paper.

As noted, Pratt et al. are clearly guided by the knowledge building metaphor, which suggests that the point of research is to develop knowledge in an accumulative manner, which is exactly what they emphasize in the paper. An alternative could be to follow the path of *knowledge demolition*, where the point is to challenge, rather than extend, existing knowledge. One option here is to not take the phenomenon of 'identity' as a given, but to question the self-evident 'truth' that identity is something that everyone develops and has in one form or another. Perhaps identity does not always matter as much as is commonly assumed? We could, for instance, follow Alvesson and Robertson (2016: 7) and ask if 'workers perceive certain situations and events as less of an identity issue and, if this is the case, how is this accomplished?' Pratt et al. appear to take the phenomenon of identity and identity change for granted. The medical residents may not always be engaged in identity production when transitioning from being a student to a practitioner. Something else may matter more, such as curing people's ill health or earning good money or temporarily saving the self in esteem-threatening situations. Taking this alternative path, either in combination with Pratt et al.'s existing one or on its own, could be one way to open up more frame-breaking theory: questioning assumptions about identity, and not just reproducing and adding to these assumptions, and thus cementing the notion of 'identity' being something self-evident and important.

Opening up rather than building knowledge by problematizing identity – viewed as an unproblematic and straightforward 'it' in the paper – could be another path forward.

In the paper, the phenomenon 'identity' is addressed as simply being there, more or less ready-made, to be investigated by the researchers who then arrive at certain findings. An alternative to this could be to see 'identity' as something 'made up' – perhaps for good (or less good) reasons – by the research community, thus forming a 'we' of identity researchers, agreeing upon and then imposing a specific way of forming reality, where 'identity' is a significant phenomenon. Identity is then addressed as an artefact, an invention by the research collectivity.[1]

As indicated above, Pratt et al.'s literature review is strongly guided by a jigsaw puzzle metaphor, with some limited elements of the dialogue partner metaphor. Pratt et al. see some minor shortcomings in the literature in the context of their specialized interest. The theories referred to are well packaged in the shape of three coherent streams, each of which is summarized briefly and without any recognition of diversity or problems within each of these. Yet an opening up exercise may reveal very different understandings of these literatures and their shortcomings, and indicate alternative ways of building or adding to or critically questioning theory. An unpacking or demolition metaphor could thus lead to another engagement with existing literature on the topic.

An alternative to gap-spotting as a literature review approach could include assumption-digging or more radical dialogues, with some challenges and critique. For example, the idea of identity could be problematized – in terms of importance and meaning – and also the assumption of a steady trajectory during the years as resident – in terms of identity change – could be critically discussed.

Moving on to method issues, the strict design and logical and linear work with collecting and analysing data through codification following three clear steps – only marginally supplemented with a reference to a sudden instance of brainstorming – could be challenged by an alternative approach such as intellectual wandering. This could mean long interviews with a few residents, searching for clues and inspiration and then following the lead, for example, about people to interview or situations to observe. Observations could for example include a group of residents interacting with senior people at the institution or following them to the bar or having lunch with them, looking out for identity construction clues. The researcher could also try to spot other clues in a similar sphere of interest, including non-identity issues like role playing. (What is and is not identity is seldom clear.) Even though the wandering metaphor suggests a more open approach, some sense of direction and interest is part of any research, even those versions that suggest an intellectual adventure or wanting to find a mystery, that is, something unexpected.

Taking 'the native's point of view' together with 'thick description' could be alternative metaphors that could have guided the design and method. Here, the research project would emphasize getting much closer to the experiences, feelings and thinking of the people being studied. Some of those studied could have been encouraged to more fully develop their views of the transition from students to independent or fully-fledged practitioners. Against the data collecting interview – tapping informants on their 'inner life' during one-hour, semi-standardized interactions – one could imagine more complete human encounters, aiming for confessions, insight generations (from informants) or otherwise more extensive and varied accounts, relying on alternative metaphors for data collection.

Compared to Pratt et al.'s template-driven, representation-oriented style – a style dominating journal publications – alternative writing styles could be considered. More explorative impressionistic styles could have been adopted, or the focus could have been on carefully describing rich episodes or drawing detailed portraits of interesting and/or representative subjects. Some identity studies look in some depth at individuals, who become more visible and alive than is the case if all interview statements are disconnected from the people who uttered them, as in Pratt et al.'s paper. (Sennett, 1999, is a good example.) More path-making or emplotment-oriented styles could be considered. These may appear less scientific, but they possibly convey a more reader-friendly text and in some ways provide a better understanding of the phenomenon.

Summing up

Pratt et al.'s study effectively delivers a contribution to building theory through a gap-spotting approach and skilful data management. Alternative metaphors could mean different ways of illuminating identity change themes, and possibly lead to different, although not necessarily contradictory, results. The study could be guided by another objective, such as knowledge demolition or telling a rich story, making theory building not the only purpose. It could also be informed by another researcher role – a less objective and technical one – where the research group becomes more involved, engaged and interpretative. In terms of considerations of 'we', the research collective, the study could be based on a notion of the research collective as less community-oriented and as more competitive, fighting for ideas and recognition in a marketplace of ideas, perspectives and research results. At the other end of the spectrum, story-telling, a rich account, inspiration for rethinking – a conversation (re-)starter – could have been imagined, and the writing could have borne greater imprints of the authors as explorers or plot-producers. Perhaps they could have followed the medical students on their sometimes bumpy and anxiety-ridden way to more secure professional identities, or become involved in the processes, where there perhaps is no such thing as a clear identity outcome, only more ongoing insecurities and fragmentations in life (Knights & Clarke, 2014).

All these suggestions do not, of course, necessarily lead to a better study. Pratt et al.'s study is of high quality and is frequently cited. The purpose – including developing generalized knowledge – differs from what would be the case if our alternative metaphors had inspired the research. Our purpose here is only to highlight additional options to those typically favoured and to open up research using conventional and not so conventional metaphors in research in combined ways, making research possibly more imaginative and interesting.

CHAPTER SUMMARY

In this chapter we have illustrated how a kaleidoscopic view can be applied. We have chosen two high-quality and widely cited studies representing fairly normal (even normalized) qualitative research and how it is being reported in leading journals. As most studies are eager to score highly on rigour and discipline, scientific rationality is in the driver's seat in these studies, which give the texts a strong sense of closure. There are few reported or hinted at possible loopholes and clues for thinking differently about the texts are absent or minimized. There are no explicit signs of reflexivity – the researchers do not demonstrate any doubts about what they are doing, discuss alternatives and non-obvious choices and how they approach the various parts of the research process. The researcher me, we, the character of interactions with those studied, the societal context and its imprinting on the phenomenon (e.g. identity and power issues in relations between physicians and technicians in healthcare and the situation of medical students transitioning to residents) are not considered in the texts. There are no explicit reflexive considerations of the discourse aspects of the texts – how they are constructed and construct the research process (presented as rational, rigorous, authority, cleansed of ambiguities) and the phenomenon to be studied (the object for clear-cut findings and generalization).

These comments are not to be read as critique of the studies discussed (as said, they are in many ways admirable), but as invitations to consider alternative ways of relating to various parts of the research process. Alternatives may lead to studies of less quality in many respects, but we suggest serious consideration of at least a few alternative ways of thinking about the doing and writing research. An awareness and consideration of various research options may lead to a healthy variation in studies, as well as helping researchers to find their own style – and not merely to mimick others. As a result, it may rejuvenate social research and make it more imaginative and interesting.

NOTE

1. We could add here that one of us has done extensive work on identity, so we don't have any particular issues with identity research as such – *more than we see that* the identity concept tends to be over-used and becomes an uncritically employed research topic, a 'hembig', i.e. a hegemonic, ambiguous big concept, as Alvesson and Blom (2021) call it.

11
GENERATING MORE INTERESTING RESEARCH THROUGH METAPHORICAL REFLEXIVITY

In this final chapter we further discuss how the proposed kaleidoscope of RP metaphors can contribute to the development of more imaginative and interesting research and writing within the social sciences, particularly qualitative research but also research based on mixed methods and social research in general. We also add some reflexive, self-critical notes, encouraging some caution before becoming too enthusiastic about metaphors and trying to be imaginative.

As we described in Chapter 1, there are numerous complaints about the shortage of interesting and influential ideas in many fields within social science. Articles are often viewed as abstract, incremental, unimaginative and tedious to read (Alvesson, Gabriel & Paulsen, 2017). Many studies fail to deliver an original idea or insight and often come across as rather flat, with efforts to beef up a trivial contribution with social science jargon.

There is also the triple crisis of representation, legitimation and praxis in social science (Denzin & Lincoln, 2005: 19). While the central purpose (and ideal) of research has been to represent, mirror or tell a truth about a part of social reality, there is now an increasing scepticism of this ambition. Qualitative researchers cannot any longer lay unopposed claim to truly capture and represent the lived experience of social actors. It is now well established that the researcher's own subjectivity and group belongingness (tribe membership) as well as the idiosyncrasies of a research project affect the research outcomes. The knowledge developed is therefore always contingent upon the researcher, such as his/her social characteristics and loyalties and the specifics of a study, including who has been interviewed or observed at a particular time by the researcher.[1] Legitimation is undermined by the questioning of the (im)possibilities of validity, generalizability and reliability of research results. The replication crisis in positivism is also well documented, and the trust in qualitative research in the aforementioned respects is probably much lower. Praxis is questioned through doubts about social science being capable to effect change in the world. Most people outside academia are not particularly interested and see social research primarily as an intra-academic enterprise – academics writing for other academics, with limited concern for others and sometimes driven by ideological agendas. The research–practice gulf appears to be expanding.

The reasons for the current gloomy state of affairs and developments are many. Mass production of higher education being accompanied by mass research is one explanation. Part of this is global competition, where higher education institutions need to demonstrate their qualities, and here research publication is a key element. New Public Management, with an emphasis on measurement and competition on the national level, is also part of the same syndrome. Another issue is that so much has been said already, so it may be difficult to add something significant. It is often better to read or re-read classics than to consult the research 'front', as contemporary work often seems to have backed down from trying to say something interesting and important and instead has fallen back into formulaic and 'safe' work. On a more individual level, university teachers have experienced a fall in status, which has resulted in increasingly uncertain and vulnerable identities, and here it becomes important to show one's value and quality to oneself and others. This is often done through research publications, preferably in leading journals. Research then becomes more of an ego-saver than a knowledge-enriching enterprise. A high level of instrumentalism and compliance seem to characterize 'successful' academics nowadays. A shortage of talented researchers – academia appears to be decreasingly attractive as a workplace and occupation – adds to the explanations for the depressing state of affairs.

These factors – and the increased pressure to demonstrate publishability, which is key to employability – mean that bold, time-consuming and imaginative research suffers. The ego and the CV can't wait for the confirmation, so a quick and certain output is given priority. Few nowadays conduct ambitious ethnographic studies where the researcher really learns about the site, reads extensively, and deviates from research collectives, which are increasingly becoming specialized and turned into micro-tribes or chain-gangs. Delivering what social science should be all about – formulating an original, distinct idea, having rich empirical material (that is not easily squeezed into a data management grinder), bearing the imprints of the researcher's creativity, and producing an appealing text – becomes a rarity, almost out of the question. Few academics come close to leading journalists in terms of key qualities in knowledge development and presentation. Compare, for example, Klein's (2000) *No Logo* with academic work on marketing and consumption.

It may be an overstatement to say that social science research is a failure or that very little of significant value is being accomplished. There are different views and probably variation between fields. But there are reasons for concern and it seems counterproductive to suggest more of the same conventions and templates for conducting research today. Continuing to follow dominant templates for conducting research may facilitate the career prospects for researchers and improve the relative standing of metrics-fixated institutions, but surely, we, as social scientists, as a collective, cannot be satisfied with these selfish and shortsighted ambitions.

Although we cannot do much about, or in this book seriously discuss, most of the drivers behind these unfortunate developments, we optimistically and strongly believe that as individual researchers and as research collectives it is fully possible to increase the likelihood of doing social research leading to significant contributions. The ambition of this book is restricted to highlight one problem area and suggest the rethinking of it: how we conceptualize and approach the research process and its key elements. Here, the increasingly dominant and constraining formula for success can be targeted for critical scrutiny and rethinking. What appears to be the solution to the problems of good research is, perhaps, often the source of the problems. Following the dominant conventions and templates for doing social research may work for many people and many projects, but not for all. Our target is not conventional ideas and recipes *per se*, but their domination and the lack of serious consideration and use of alternative understandings of conducting research. More reflexivity about this and, as a result, greater heterogeneity needs to be encouraged.

Researchers, from their PhD and onwards, rather predictably, often start with finding a 'gap' in the literature as a potential for their contribution, followed by a methodology section in which 'some pious platitudes about ontology and epistemology' (Gabriel, 2015: 332) are outlined that justifies the use of a set of semi-structured interviews to address the gap. These are then diligently collected and processed through a carefully detailed coding procedure aided by a program. 'This has now become highly mechanized as the qualitative equivalent of number-crunching in quantitative research, leading to a findings section involving a variety of verbatim quotes from the interview transcripts, often summarized in a number of tables' (Gabriel, 2015: 332). It ends with knowledge claims that fill the gap, the identification of some further gaps and acknowledging certain shortcomings in the research, especially regarding the method of study.

The aim of this book has been to counteract these sedimented and ingrained conventions and templates, which hold a firm grip over qualitative researchers, and, instead, offer support for researchers' imagination and thus autonomy and choice. Presenting and legitimating options may encourage mind-stretch and less predetermined and more carefully arrived at routes of research through an awareness of alternatives. Such awareness may be of value to those who are not entirely comfortable with dominating views. But also, those who are well adapted to the dominant views may be intellectually inspired by some provocation and inputs to think differently and reflexively about the dominant views. Such inspiration may hopefully also affect their thinking about themselves, their research collectives, the societal context in which they are embedded, as well as how text is being constructed and social orders are being (re)formed and sometimes cemented in research. We have suggested me-ism, we-ism, interaction-ism, criticism and discursivism as domains or themes for reflexive exercises. As we have said a few times in this book, these are options to choose from (or to replace with other themes and angles that the researcher feels work better for him/her), not a mandatory set of boxes to tick off. Even ambitious reflexive work cannot consider all aspects and should not be spread too thinly.

The conventionality of our ordering and presentation of the metaphorization of the RP elements is a source of concern and needs to be commented upon. Many of our proposed metaphors suggest alternative ways of thinking about the ordering of the RP elements and the very different ways of reporting it, perhaps more loosely. Research following a detective story approach to mystery creation could, for example, start with a perplexing, curiosity-evoking empirical observation and move on from there, and avoid the conventional ingredients or the partitioning of a text, perhaps referring to literature if and when it supports – and not disrupts – the account. Method issues could enter when the author is discussing path choices or the reliability and value of documents, observations and interviews, while a separate method section could be skipped or marginalized. The reader is encouraged to think about alternative ways of structuring the research process and the resulting text, and not necessarily to think in terms of the standard elements, but rather to consider alternative metaphors for all or most of these. Nevertheless, in this book, following a conventional form can be defended as it may be easier for many readers to understand our more unconventional and perhaps provocative message as wolves in sheep's clothing.

THE KALEIDOSCOPE

Our metaphorizations generated a variety of dominant and alternative as well as additional metaphors. We have summarized these in Table 9.1. In contrast to existing approaches, which predominantly focus on single RP elements and, thus, only provide limited and fairly narrow ideas for generating more imaginative research, the kaleidoscope of RP metaphors proposed here provides a more comprehensive view *and* broader platform for generating more imaginative and engaging research. Taken together, the proposed kaleidoscope of RP metaphors and associated guiding principles provides the researcher with reflective resources for (i) becoming aware of, and breaking out from, the sedimented conventions and templates for existing ways of doing research and writing research texts, and (ii) creating new and perhaps more novel ways of conducting research that potentially can lead to more interesting, impactful and engaging research.

We do not, of course, suggest that researchers should consider all the proposed metaphors in conducting their research. Instead, the kaleidoscope of metaphors offers a metaphorical toolkit that enables researchers to pursue different avenues of conducting and writing more interesting and imaginative research. Specifically, the proposed kaleidoscope offers two key contributions in relationship to the earlier work of trying to broaden the picture through targeting various limited parts or elements of RP.

First, in comparison to existing recommendations for generating more imaginative and impactful research, which mainly point at single RP elements, for example, design, inter-pretation or writing, the proposed kaleidoscope of RP metaphors provides a considerably *broader and stronger input to combinations and the interactive effects* of RP metaphors in the pursuit of generating more interesting and engaging research results and texts. Although focusing on a single key element in the RP can be important for being able to open up alternative options of doing research, the much wider and holistic set of metaphorization possibilities offered by the kaleidoscope of RP metaphors gives additional input to creativ-ity. We do not do so directly – we are not proposing alternatives to brainstorming poetry or sex, drugs and rock'n'roll – but indirectly, in the sense of how researchers approach their subject matter, communities, themselves and the overall purpose of research. In other words, the kaleidoscope of RP metaphors offers a 'prism' through which the ele-ments of the RP can be viewed and comprehended more imaginatively than the prevail-ing conventions and templates for conducting and writing research.

Here, we propose that researchers avoid the conventional choices between the usual suspects of paradigms and perspectives – neo-positivism, interpretivism, critical theory, poststructuralism, etc. – and do not follow the resulting silos in terms of group loyalties, views of theory, data, writings and so on, but rather try to consider non-predictable combinations of metaphors. Creativity means that you work with unexpected combina-tions and tensions. As we have said, not all metaphor combinations work well. Many mixes may fail to encourage interesting confrontations and mind-stretching, either because metaphors are too similar or they are too different. But there are often other possibilities than just working with a list of metaphors that are regularly seen as hanging together without friction. Some friction is part of creativity and part of novel thinking. Some movement outside the comfort zone is important.

Second, the proposed kaleidoscope of RP metaphors and associated guiding principles offers a *meta-approach* rather than a specific methodology for generating more imagina-tive and engaging research. Most existing recommendations for dealing with the current 'crises' suggest a specific path from 'a' to 'b' – for example, moving from gap-spotting to problematization (Alvesson & Sandberg, 2013a), focusing on problem-oriented rather than theory-developing research (Corley & Gioia, 2011) or advocating hermeneutics, critical realism, following in the footsteps of Foucault or another stream. Instead of going from 'a' to 'b', the proposed kaleidoscope of RP metaphors acknowledges that there is a spectrum from 'a' to 'n' images of RP elements to consider and perhaps further develop.

Hence, rather than focusing on a single RP element or embracing a particular established perspective or template, we encourage the researcher to work at a meta-level with a variety of metaphors, as well as going back and forth between these, and then to choose the one(s) that appears to offer the best framework for saying something interesting. Alternatively, the researcher can develop new metaphors that can provide better support for something new in the specific case of research. Of course, the researcher needs to carefully relate the (novel, unconventional) understandings to established knowledge/theory and consider reasonable ways of using the empirical material and writing in such a way that it is understood and seen as credible by the intended audience. Here, we need to consider the conventionalism and conservatism that many people in academia face. But in most cases, a sufficiently large audience should be able to grasp well-argued new ideas emerging from empirical studies that are a bit more imaginative, creative and offer more originality than what we are witnessing today.

The proposed kaleidoscope of RP metaphors is not intended to be an instruction manual. Instead, the very idea is that the researcher must think through issues and make more broadly considered choices, which is the opposite of offering strict guidelines. There is no formula for being more imaginative in research. Just repeating the slogan 'Be imaginative' is self-defeating. But this ambition can be indirectly supported by introducing various images – in our case, formulated as metaphors – that generate some mind-stretching and at least inspiration for wider, less predictable thinking. Our ambition with this book is to encourage moves that bring more 'life' into academic work through metaphorizing the RP. It means both identifying and waking up common and 'dead' metaphors and targeting them for reflection, and identifying and mobilizing some alternative metaphors that open up possibilities to do research in more varied and imaginative ways. Our pluralistic and promiscuous kaleidoscope of RP metaphors – a dialectical smorgasbord of metaphorical possibilities – aims to highlight the wealth of options, rather than to follow the conventional, narrow route of 'adding-to-the-literature', through a focused and limited message carving out a small piece of novelty.

We suggest that the kaleidoscope approach and the variation of metaphors are considered in all respects of academic life. They can be considered in the planning and conducting of research, in seminars, in lunch and pub talk, and in the assessment of research proposals, book ideas and journal submissions. It may be of less relevance for the highly inexperienced and uncertain rooky postgraduate students, who often benefit from clear guidelines rather than a wealth of possibilities. But having overcome the earlier-career stage (and the often-attached experience of not knowing anything and feeling totally worthless), then some adding of metaphors to the most basic, mainstream ones may be a good idea. For senior researchers, it may be a matter of increasing their repertoire or trying to challenge their, over time, often more and more fixed, convenient modes of thinking, rooted in metaphors that are seen as given (and thus dead). Metaphorization may here work as a vitamin injection, a cure of premature intellectual ageing. As we have said, a (re)turn to the kaleidoscope may also be liberating (as well as annoying) for the established researcher, who is easily caught in box thinking. However, although we think our proposed kaleidoscope framework can enable researchers to generate more imaginative and interesting research, we do not see it as a miracle cure. It has its side effects and may create a lot of problems in the wrong hands (or on the wrong keyboard).

A SELF-CRITICAL NOTE

We have in this book offered many critical comments, in particular about established conventions and templates for conducting and writing research, which, according to our view, are too dominant. To repeat, we have no problems with dominant templates for conducting research and the metaphors they build upon, as long as the researchers using them are guided by careful choices and are not just expressing received wisdom, imitation and compliance. Too often the latter, un-reflexive auto-pilot inclinations take over and we want to challenge that.

There are, however, good reasons – following a reflexive spirit – to be self-critical. One great risk of a calling to arms for imagination and working with alternative, and supposedly creative, ways of doing research is that not much good comes out of this, as such high ambitions may not be fulfilled. Working with a spectrum of metaphors may also lead to confusion and indecisiveness. Moreover, working with metaphors that are not well anchored in tradition is difficult – particularly without broad collegial support and a lack of good examples to be inspired by and follow. It therefore requires a lot of extra effort from the researcher. It also requires a rather high level of talent. Following the spirit of this book may also lead to an increased risk of failure. People who are less resourceful in terms of background knowledge, time, secure employment, analytical and writing skills, social support, etc. may be warned not to move too far from established routes. Adapting to what is institutionalized and following templates is easier and often leads to acceptable, although seldom remarkable, studies and results. Hopefully, the scholars reading and being inspired by this book will not encounter the dangers of looking into the kaleidoscope of metaphors too late in their research. We often discover that while the spirit was high, the body was weak. Being inspired to do something one can't accomplish can lead to tragedies.

A second problem we want to raise concerns about is the difficulty in coming up with and formulating a good range of metaphors for covering and conceptualizing all options. Sometimes there is no easily available metaphorical expression to catch an underlying image or discourse, and efforts to develop one may not lead to a metaphor that is short, punchy and evokes the intended associations. Sometimes language has its shortcomings and may, at times, make our efforts to metaphorize a bit clumsy. We are certain that the reader may have felt this while reading our book, which of course also reflects the limited ability of us as authors not being poets. Complicated ideas and understandings may not always be easily translatable into an elegant metaphor. Hence, although we can benefit tremendously from using metaphors, we need to realize that they can only do certain things and have their shortcomings.

A third problem is that metaphors sometimes capture something but in a vague way that may mean the many nuances are lost and that the metaphorical expression loses precision and, thus, has a weak capacity to communicate meaning. A building metaphor may be rather crude, as 'building' may stand for many different things, from craft to mass production, to more intuitive, trial-and-error projects to the careful and detailed following of the blueprint. A building may also vary from being a shed, a bunker, a bungalow or a palace. A narrative may also mean very many different things. Sometimes much work is needed to get behind the false simplicity that a metaphorical expression may communicate and it is easy to stop thinking too soon.

Finally, we should confess that we have struggled quite a bit to find an informative and creativity-inspiring set of metaphors – both dominant, alternative and additional ones. Often candidates for metaphors are not obvious; sometimes it is not at all clear which dominant, alternative and somewhat more esoteric ones can be added to the list. We don't claim to be exhaustive or to get everything right. Our purpose is simply to offer a sufficient spectrum of options, mainly to inspire the reader to think differently about the research process and to be able to work with alternative metaphors when it appears productive to do so, whether in a single part of the RP or across the entire RP. Here, the researcher needs to think through issues for him- or herself and not rely too much on authority – not even ours, the authors of this book – or convention.

Hopefully, this somewhat cold shower of potential problems should not prevent the reader from feeling warm about the prospect of using the proposed kaleidoscope of metaphors more systematically and ambitiously in studies. Moving on with appropriate speed is to be recommended, bearing in mind the bumps on the way. We see the suggested use of metaphors as a mixed blessing – as with virtually everything – but potentially a great resource for doing more imaginative and interesting research. The researcher needs to self-critically consider when and when not to use metaphors more ambitiously. This needs to be done on a project-by-project basis, as neither one size nor one metaphor fits all situations.

CONCLUSION

Metaphors offer excellent, although far from unproblematic, reference points for bringing out and dealing with more creativity and imagination in research. Metaphors help us to see things in a new light and communicate this in an often inspirational way. With a playful metaphorization of the entire RP, or selected parts of it, we can become a bit less dull, predictable and cautious in studies and texts. Increasing the joys of doing research and, perhaps even more urgent, of reading the fruits (or deliveries) of it appears to be impor-tant. This could increase the attraction of social science. Reading a typical research paper – formulaic and unimaginative – does seldom do much good PR for the academic industry.

More imaginative ideas and stimulating research texts are needed, then, calling for a more playful and alternative mode of relating to work. This is not to deny the need for rigour, discipline and credibility, nor the shortcomings and complications of emphasizing metaphors. We are, however, less concerned about these qualities in the present book. We emphasize options and do think there is a general overrating of the ideals of rationality and rigour. 'Rigour' often means sticking to conventions and reproducing taken-for-granted assumptions (relying on dead metaphors) and treating data at face value, to be processed in data management procedures. Often data – as we have pointed out – can be understood in other ways than mirrors of reality forming building blocks or pixels for knowledge building or picture taking. Sometimes conformism means the covering up of problematic practices, seen as self-evident or superior, just because they are taken for granted and 'everybody else' does things in a particular way. Objectivity is often a convention, upheld by a part of the research society. Conformism means the suppression of awareness of debatable metaphors. Often dead or zombie metaphors – design, building knowledge, mapping, codification, growth of knowledge – are mistaken for rationality and rigour, and addressed as the only or superior way to do research.

Imagination and novelty are hardly visible virtues in contemporary published research. Too often, many complain that they are rarely surprised or encouraged to think more than marginally differently when reading contemporary academic books, dissertations or journal articles (e.g. Gabriel, 2015; Richardson, 2000). Perhaps we are at a stage where (too) much research has been conducted and it is difficult to say much of interest any longer. But this depressing idea may also inspire new efforts to reconsider what we are doing. What is badly needed is more imagination and creativity in the development of ideas, understandings of the research process and forms of writing. The kaleidoscope of RP metaphors offers one comprehensive way of generating new and novel patterns of doing more imaginative and, hopefully, also more influential research. If the reader feels highly uncertain about what to do after reading this book, it may say more about the reader's over-socialization into dominant journal article formulas – and perhaps his/her participa-tion in too many journal publication workshops or 'meet the editor' events – than the relevance of the ideas suggested here.

NOTE

1. Quantitative studies face similar issues. Questionnaires, for example, are heavily affected by how questions are formulated, what scales are used and who is the sender of a questionnaire/responsible for a study. The outcomes of questionnaires can vary substantially and findings may say little about phenomena out there, behind unreliable numbers (Schwarz, 1999).

REFERENCES

Abbott, A. (2004). *Methods of discovery: Heuristics for the social sciences*. New York: Norton.

Abend, G. (2008). The meaning of 'theory'. *Sociological Theory*, *26*(2), 173–199.

Abend, G., Petre, C., & Sauder, M. (2013). Styles of casual thought: An empirical investigation. *American Journal of Sociology*, *119*(3), 602–654.

Abutabenjeh, S., & Jaradat, R. (2018). Clarification of research design, research methods, and research methodology: A guide for public administration researchers and practitioners. *Teaching Public Administration*, *36*(3), 237–258.

Agar, M. H. (1986). *Speaking of ethnography*. Beverly Hills, CA: Sage.

Alvesson, M. (2002). *Postmodernism and social research*. Buckingham: Open University Press.

Alvesson, M. (2010). Self-doubters, strugglers, story-tellers, surfers and others: Images of self-identity in organization studies. *Human Relations*, *63*(2), 193–217.

Alvesson, M. (2011). *Interpreting interviews*. London: Sage.

Alvesson, M. (2013a). *The triumph of emptiness: Consumption, higher education and work organization*. Oxford: Oxford University Press.

Alvesson, M. (2013b) Do we have something to say? From re-search to roi-search and back again. *Organization*, *20*(1), 79–90.

Alvesson, M., & Blom, M. (2021). The hegemonic ambiguity of big concepts in organization studies. *Human Relations*, [in press].

Alvesson, M., Blom, M., & Sveningsson, S. (2017). *Reflexive leadership: Organizing in an imperfect world*. London: Sage.

Alvesson, M., & Deetz, S. (2021). *Doing critical research*. London: Sage.

Alvesson, M., & Einola, K. (2019). Warning for excessive positivity: Authentic leadership and other traps in leadership studies. *Leadership Quarterly*, *30*(4), 383–395.

Alvesson, M., & Gabriel, Y. (2013). Beyond formulaic research: In praise of greater diversity in organizational research and publications. *Academy of Management Learning & Education*, *12*(2), 245–263.

Alvesson, M., Gabriel, Y., & Paulsen, R. (2017). *Return to meaning: A social science with something to say*. Oxford: Oxford University Press.

Alvesson, M., & Gjerde, S. (2020) On the scope and limits of identity. In Brown, A. (Ed.) *The Oxford handbook of identities in organizations*. Oxford: Oxford University Press.

Alvesson, M., Hallett, T., & Spicer, A. (2019). Uninhibited institutionalisms. *Journal of Management Inquiry*, *28*(2), 119–127.

Alvesson, M., Hardy, C., & Hardy, B. (2008). Reflecting on reflexivity: Reappraising practice. *Journal of Management Studies*, *45*(3), 480–501.

Alvesson, M., & Kärreman, D. (2011). *Qualitative research and theory development: Mystery as method*. London: Sage.

Alvesson, M., & Robertson, M. (2016). Money matters: Teflonic identity manoeuvring in the investment banking sector. *Organization Studies*, *37*(1), 7–34.

Alvesson, M., & Sandberg, J. (2013a). *Constructing research questions: Doing interesting research*. London: Sage.

Alvesson, M., & Sandberg, J. (2013b). Has management studies lost its way? Ideas for more imaginative and innovative research. *Journal of Management Studies*, *50*(1), 128–152.

Alvesson, M., & Sandberg, J. (2014). Habitat and habitus: Boxed-in versus box-breaking research. *Organization Studies*, *35*(7), 967–987.

Alvesson, M., & Sandberg, J. (2018). Metaphorizing the research process: Reflexivity, imagination and novelty. In C. Cassell, A. Cunliffe & G. Grandy (Eds.), *The Sage handbook of qualitative business and management research methods: Methods and challenges* (pp. 486–505). London: Sage.

Alvesson, M., & Sandberg, J. (2020). The problematizing review: A counterpoint to Elsbach and van Knippenberg's argument for integrative reviews. *Journal of Management Studies*, *57*(6), 1290–1304.

Alvesson, M., & Sandberg, J. (2021). Pre-understanding: An interpretation-enhancer and horizon-expander in research. *Organization Studies*, published online.

Alvesson, M., Sandberg, J., & Einola, K. (2021). Reflexive design in qualitative research. In U. Flick (Ed.), *The Sage handbook of qualitative research design*. London: Sage.

Alvesson, M., & Sköldberg, K. (2018). *Reflexive methodology* (3rd ed.). London: Sage.

Alvesson, M., & Spicer, A. (Eds) (2011). *Metaphors we lead by: Understanding leadership in the real world*. London: Routledge.

Alvesson, M., & Spicer, A. (2016). *The stupidity paradox*. London: Profile.

Alvesson, M., & Sveningsson, S. (2003). Managers doing leadership: The extra-ordinarization of the mundane. *Human Relations*, *56*(12), 1435–1459.

Aspers, P., & Corte, U. (2019). What is qualitative in qualitative research. *Qualitative Sociology*, *42*(2), 139–160.

Asplund, J. (1970). *Om undran inför samhället*. Lund: Argos.

Barad, K. (2007). *Meeting the universe halfway*. Durham, NC: Duke University Press.

Barley, S. R. (1986). Technology as an occasion for structuring: Evidence from observations of CT scanners and the social order of radiology departments. *Administrative Science Quarterly*, *31*(1), 78–108.

Barney, J. B. (2020). Contributing to theory: Opportunities and challenges. *AMS Review*, *10*, 49–55.

Bartunek, J. M., Rynes, S. L., & Ireland, D. R. (2006). What makes management research interesting, and why does it matter? *Academy of Management Journal*, *49*(1), 9–15.

Baudrillard, J. (1994[1981]). *Simulacra and simulation*. Ann Arbor, MI: University of Michigan Press.

Becker, H. S. (1982). *Art worlds*. Berkeley, CA: University of California Press.

Becker, H. S. (1998). *Tricks of the trade: How to think about your research while doing it.* Chicago, IL: University of Chicago Press.

Bell, E., Kothiyal, N., & Willmott, H. (2017). Methodology-as-technique and the meaning of rigour in globalized management research. *British Journal of Management*, *28*(3), 534–550.

Benson, K. J. (1977). Organizations: A dialectical view. *Administrative Science Quarterly*, *22*(1), 1–21.

Berg, B. L. (1998). *Qualitative research methods for the social sciences*. Boston, MA: Allyn and Bacon.

Bernstein, R. (1983). *Beyond objectivism and relativism*. Philadelphia, PA: University of Pennsylvania Press.

Bishop, R. (2005). Freeing ourselves from neocolonial domination: A kaupapa approach to creating knowledge. In N. K. Denzin & Y. S. Lincoln (Eds.), *The Sage handbook of qualitative research* (3rd ed., pp. 109–137). Thousand Oaks, CA: Sage.

Black, M. (1962). Metaphor. In Max Black, *Model and metaphor* (pp. 25–47). Ithaca, NY: Cornell University Press.

Blithe, S. J., & Wolfe, A. W. (2017). Work–life management in legal prostitution: Stigma and lockdown in Nevada's brothels. *Human Relations*, *70*(6), 725–750.

Bluhm, D. J., Harman, W., Lee, T. W., & Mitchell, T. R. (2011). Qualitative research in management: A decade of progress. *Journal of Management Studies*, *48*(8), 866–891.

Blumer, H. (1954). 'What is wrong with social theory?' *American Sociological Review*, *18*(2), 3–10.

Bogdan, R. C., & Biklen, S. K. (1992). *Qualitative research for education: An introduction to theory and methods*. Boston, MA: Allyn and Bacon.

Bono, J. E., & McNamara, G. (2011). Publishing in AMJ—Part 2: Research design. *Academy of Management Journal*, *54*(4), 657–660.

Bourdieu, P. (1984). *Distinctions*. Cambridge, MA: Harvard University Press.

Bourdieu, P., Chamboredon, J.-C., & Passeron, J.-C. (1991). *The craft of sociology*. Berlin: Walter de Gruyter.

Bourdieu, P., & Wacquant, L. J. D. (1992). *An invitation to reflexive sociology*. Chicago, IL: University of Chicago Press.

Brinkmann, S. (2014). Doing without data. *Qualitative Inquiry*, *20*(6), 720–725.

Brinkmann, S., Jacobson, M. H., & Kristiansen, S. (2014). Historical overview of qualitative research in the social sciences. In P. Leavy (Ed.), *The Oxford handbook of qualitative research* (pp. 17–42). Oxford: Oxford University Press.

Bristow, A., Robinson, S., & Ratle, O. (2017). Being an early-career CMS academic in the context of insecurity and 'excellence': The dialectics of resistance and compliance. *Organization Studies*, *38*(9), 1185–1207.

Brown, R. H. (1976). Social theory as metaphor. *Theory and Society*, *3*(2), 169–197.

Burke, K. (1969). *A grammar of motives*. Berkeley, CA: University of California Press.

Burrell, G., & Morgan, G. (1979). *Sociological paradigms and organisational analysis*. London: Heinemann.

Butler, J. (1990). *Gender trouble*. New York: Routledge.

Butler, N., & Spoelstra, S. (2012). Your excellency. *Organization*, *19*(6), 891–903.

Bygnes, S. (2020). A collective sign of relief: Local reactions to the establishment of new asylum centers in Norway. *Acta Sociologica*, *63*(3), 249–266.

Calás, M., & Smircich, L. (1992). Rewriting gender into organizational theorizing: Directions from feminist perspectives. In M. Reed & M. Hughes (Eds.), *Re-thinking organization: New directions in organizational theory and analysis*. London: Sage.

Capaldi, N. (1998). *The enlightenment project in the analytic conversation*. Berlin: Springer.

Chalmers, A. F. (1999). *What is this thing called science?* Brisbane, Australia: University of Queensland Press.

Charmaz, K. (2008). Grounded theory as an emergent method. In S. N. Hesse-Biber & P. Leavy (Eds.), *Handbook of emergent methods* (pp. 155–172). New York: Guilford Press.

Charmaz, K. (2014). *Constructing grounded theory*. London: Sage.

Childers, S. M. (2014). Promiscuous analysis in qualitative research. *Journal of Qualitative Inquiry*, *20*(6) 819–826.

Clark, T., & Wright, M. (2009). So farewell then … reflections on editing the *Journal of Management Studies*. *Journal of Management Studies*, *46*(1), 1–9.

Cohen, M., March, J., & Olsen, J. (1972). A garbage can model of organizational choice. *Administratively Science Quarterly*, *17*(1), 1–25.

Corley, K. G., & Gioia, D. A. (2011). Building theory about theory building: What constitutes a theoretical contribution? *Academy of Management Review*, *36*(1), 12–32.

Cornelissen, J. P. (2005). Beyond compare: Metaphor in organization theory. *Academy of Management Review*, *30*(4), 751–764.

Cornelissen, J. P. (2006). Metaphor in organization theory: Progress and the past. *Academy of Management Review*, *31*(2), 485–488.

Cornelissen, J. P. (2017). Preserving theoretical divergence in management research: Why the explanatory potential of qualitative research should be harnessed rather than suppressed. *Journal of Management Studies*, *53*(3), 368–383.

Cornelissen, J. P., & Durand, R. (2014). Moving forward: Developing theoretical contributions in management studies. *Journal of Management Studies*, *51*(6), 995–1022.

Cornelissen, J. P., Gajewska-De Mattos, Piekkari, R., & Welch, C. (2012). Writing up as a legitimacy seeking process. In G. Symon & C. Cassell (Eds.), *The practice of qualitative organizational research: Core methods and current challenges* (pp. 185–203). London: Sage.

Cornelissen, J. P., & Kafouros, M. (2008). Metaphors and theory building in organization theory: What determines the impact of a metaphor on theory? *British Journal of Management, 19*(4), 365–379.

Cornelissen, J. P., Oswick, C., Christensen, L. T., & Phillips, N. (2008). Metaphor in organizational research: Context, modalities and implications for research – introduction. *Organization Studies, 29*(1), 7–22.

Creswell, J. W. (2009). *Research design: Qualitative, quantitative, and mixed methods approaches*. Thousand Oaks, CA: Sage.

Crossan, M., & Apaydin, M. (2009). A multi-dimensional framework of organizational innovation: A systematic review of the literature. *Journal of Management Studies, 47*(6), 1154–1191.

Currie, G., Finn, R., & Martin, G. (2010). Role transition and the interaction of relational and social identity: New nursing roles in the English NHS. *Organization Studies, 31*(7), 941–996.

Currie, G., Tempest, S., & Starkey, K. (2006). New careers for old? Organizational and individual responses to changing boundaries. *International Journal of Human Resource Management, 17*(4), 755–774.

Czarniawska, B. (2013). What social theory is, and what it is not. In H. Corvellec (Ed.), *What is theory?* (pp. 99–118). Stockholm: Liber Copenhagen Business School Press.

Darbelley, F., & Stock, M. (2011). Tourism as complex interdisciplinary research object. *Annals of Tourism Research, 39*(1), 441–458.

Daveson, B., Callaghan, C., & Grocke, D. (2008). Indigenous music therapy theory building through grounded theory research: The developing indigenous theory framework. *The Arts in Psychotherapy, 35*(4), 280–286.

Davis, M. S. (1971). That's interesting! Towards a phenomenology of sociology and a sociology of phenomenology. *Philosophy of Social Sciences, 1*(2), 309–344.

Deetz, S. (1996). Describing differences in approaches to organization science: Rethinking Burrell and Morgan and their legacy. *Organization Science, 7*(2), 191–207.

Denzin, N. K., & Lincoln, Y. S. (1994). Introduction: Entering the field of qualitative research. In N. K. Denzin & Y. S. Lincoln (Eds.), *The Sage handbook of qualitative research* (pp. 1–17). Thousand Oaks, CA: Sage.

Denzin, N. K., & Lincoln, Y. S. (2000). Introduction: The discipline and practice of qualitative research. In N. K. Denzin & Y. S. Lincoln (Eds.), *The Sage handbook of qualitative research* (2nd ed., pp. 1–29). Thousand Oaks, CA: Sage.

Denzin, N. K., & Lincoln, Y. S. (2005). Introduction: The discipline and practice of qualitative research. In N. K. Denzin & Y. S. Lincoln (Eds.), *The Sage handbook of qualitative research* (3rd ed., pp. 1–32). Thousand Oaks, CA: Sage.

Denzin, N. K., & Lincoln, Y. S. (2011). Introduction. In N. K. Denzin & Y. S. Lincoln (Eds.), *The Sage handbook of qualitative research* (4th ed., pp. 1–19). Los Angeles, CA: Sage.

Denzin, N. K., & Lincoln, Y. S. (2018). Introduction. In N. K. Denzin & Y. S. Lincoln (Eds.), *The Sage handbook of qualitative research* (5th ed., pp. 1–26). Los Angeles, CA: Sage.

Dilthey, W. ([1894] 1977). Ideas concerning a descriptive and analytical psychology. In W. Dilthey, *Descriptive psychology and historical understanding* (pp. 21–120). Dordrecht: Springer.

DiMaggio, P., & Powell, W. W. (1983). The iron cage revisited: Collective rationality and institutional isomorphism in organizational fields. *American Sociological Review, 48*(2), 147–160.

Dreyfus, H., & Taylor, C. (2015). *Retrieving realism.* Cambridge, MA: Harvard University Press.

Einola, K., & Alvesson, M. (2021). Behind the numbers: Questioning questionnaires. *Journal of Management Inquiry, 30*(1), 102–114.

Eisenhardt, K. M. (1989). Building theories from case study research. *Academy of Management Review, 14*(4), 532–550.

Elsbach, K., & van Knippenberg, D. (2020). Creating high-impact literature reviews: An argument for integrative reviews. *Journal of Management Studies, 57*(6), 1290–1304.

Fabian, F. H. (2000). Keeping the tension: Pressures to keep the controversy in the management discipline. *Academy of Management Review, 25*(2), 350–371.

Ferraro, F., Pfeffer, J., & Sutton, R. (1993). Economics language and assumptions: How theories can become self-fulfilling. *Academy of Management Review, 30*(1), 8–23.

Feyerabend, P. (1975). *Against method: Outline of an anarchistic theory of knowledge.* London: NLB.

Finlay, L. (2002). Negotiating the swamp: The opportunity and challenge of reflexivity in research practice. *Qualitative Research, 2*(2), 209–230.

Fischer, T. (2018). Leadership: Processes and ambiguities. PhD thesis. Lausanne: University of Lausanne Press.

Fleming, P. (2020). Dark Academia: Despair in the neoliberal business school. *Journal of Management Studies, 57*(6), 1305–1311.

Flick, U. (2018). *An introduction to qualitative research.* London: Sage.

Foley, D., & Valenzuela, A. (2005). Critical ethnography: The politics of collaboration. In N. K. Denzin & Y. S. Lincoln (Eds.), *The Sage handbook of qualitative research* (3rd ed., pp. 217–34). Thousand Oaks, CA: Sage.

Fontana, A., & Frey, J. (2005). Interviewing: From neutral stance to political involvement. In N. K. Denzin & Y. S. Lincoln (Eds.), *The Sage handbook of qualitative research* (3rd ed., pp. 695–727). Thousand Oaks, CA: Sage.

Foucault, M (1976). *Discipline and punish.* Harmondsworth: Penguin.

Foucault, M. (1980). *Power/knowledge.* New York: Pantheon.

Freeman, M. (2014). The hermeneutical aesthetics of thick description. *Qualitative Inquiry, 20*(6), 827–833.

Gabriel, Y. (2002). Essai: On paragrammatic uses of organizational theory – a provocation. *Organization Studies, 23*(1), 133–151.

Gabriel, Y. (2010). Organization studies: A space for ideas, identities and agonies. *Organization Studies, 31*(1), 757–775.

Gabriel, Y. (2015). Reflexivity and beyond – a plea for imagination in qualitative research methodology. *Qualitative Research in Organizations and Management, 10*(4), 332–336.

Gabriel, Y. (2018). Interpretation, reflexivity and imagination in qualitative research. In M. Ciesielska & D. Kozminski (Eds.), *Qualitative methodologies in business and management: New approaches to current research dilemmas* (pp. 137–157). London: Palgrave.

Gabriel, Y., & Lang, T. (2015). *The unmanageable consumer.* London: Sage.

Gardner, H. (1987). *The mind's new science: A history of the cognitive revolution.* New York: Basic Books.

Geertz, C. (1973). *Interpretation of cultures.* New York: Basic Books.

George, G. (2014). From the editors: Rethinking management scholarship. *Academy of Management Journal, 57*(1), 1–6.

Gergen, K. (1994). The limits of pure critique. In H. W. Simons & M. Billig (Eds.), *After postmodernism: Reconstructing ideology critique* (pp. 58–78). London: Sage.

Gergen, K., & Gergen, M. (1991). Toward reflexive methodologies. In F. Steier (Ed.), *Research and reflexivity* (pp. 76–96). London: Sage.

Ghoshal, S. (2005). Bad management theories are destroying good management practices. *Academy of Management Learning & Education, 4*(1), 75–91.

Gibbs, R. W. (Ed.) (2008). *The Cambridge handbook of metaphor and thought.* Cambridge: Cambridge University Press.

Giddens, A. (1984). *The constitution of society: Outline of the theory of structuration.* Cambridge: Polity Press.

Gioia, D. A., Corley, K. G., & Hamilton, A. L. (2012). Seeking qualitative rigor in inductive research: Notes on the Gioia methodology. *Organizational Research Methods, 16*(1), 15–31.

Glaser, B., & Strauss, A. (1967). *The discovery of grounded theory: Strategies for qualitative research.* New York: Aldine De Gruyter.

Gond, J. P., Cabantous, L., Harding, N., & Learmonth, M. (2016). What do we mean by performativity in organizational and management theory? The uses and abuses of performativity. *International Journal of Management Review, 18*(4), 440–463.

Gower, B. (1997). *Scientific method: A historical and philosophical introduction.* London: Routledge.

Grant, D., & Oswick, C. (Eds.) (1996). *Metaphor and organizations.* London: Sage.

Gray, G. C., & Silbey, S. S. (2014). Governing inside the organization: Interpreting regulation and compliance. *American Journal of Sociology, 120*(1), 96–145.

Grey, C. (2010). Organizing studies: Publications, politics and polemics. *Organization Studies, 31*(6), 677–694.

Grey, C., & Sinclair, A. (2006). Writing differently. *Organization, 13*(3), 443–453.

Grodal, S., Anteby, M., & Holm, L. A. (2020). Achieving rigor in qualitative analysis: The role of active categorization in theory building. *Academy of Management Review,* published online.

Guba, E., & Lincoln, Y. S. (1994). Competing paradigms in qualitative research. In N. K. Denzin & Y. S. Lincoln (Eds.), *The Sage handbook of qualitative research* (pp. 105–117). Thousand Oaks, CA: Sage.

Guba, E., & Lincoln, Y. S. (2005). Paradigmatic controversies, contradictions, and emerging confluences. In N. K. Denzin & Y. S. Lincoln (Eds.), *The Sage handbook of qualitative research*. (3rd ed., pp. 191–215). Thousand Oaks, CA: Sage.

Gunning, T. (1997). From the kaleidoscope to the x-ray: Urban spectatorship, Poe, Benjamin, and Traffic in Souls (1913). *Wide Angle*, *19*(4), 25–61.

Habermas, J. (1972). *Knowledge and human interests*. London: Heinemann.

Hammersley, M. (2011). *Methodology who needs it?* London: Sage.

Harley, B., & Cornelissen, J. (2020). Rigor with or without templates? The pursuit of methodological rigor in qualitative research. *Organizational Research Methods*, 1–23.

Hass, L. (2008). *Merleau-Ponty's philosophy*. Bloomington, IN: Indiana University Press.

Hatch, J. A. (2002). *Doing qualitative research in education settings*. Albany, NY: State University of New York Press.

Heidegger, M. ([1927] 1996). *Being and time*. Albany, NY: State University of New York Press.

Hesse-Biber, S. N., & Leavy, P. (2011). *The practice of qualitative research*. Los Angeles, CA: Sage.

Holmes, D., & Marcus, G. (2005). Refunctioning ethnography: The challenge of an anthropology of the contemporary. In N. K. Denzin & Y. S. Lincoln (Eds.), *The Sage handbook of qualitative research* (3rd ed., pp. 1099–1114). Thousand Oaks, CA: Sage.

Holstein, J. A., & Gubrium, J. (1997). Active interviewing. In D. Silverman (Ed.), *Qualitative research* (pp. 113–129). London: Sage.

Holt, R., & Sandberg, J. (2011). Phenomenology and organization theory. *Research in the Sociology of Organizations*, *32*, 215–249.

Hunter, S. T., Bedell-Avers, K. E., & Mumford, M. D. (2007). The typical leadership study: Assumptions, implications and potential remedies. *The Leadership Quarterly*, *18*(5), 435–446.

Jackson, B. K., & Parry, K. (2008). *A very short, fairly interesting and reasonably cheap book about studying leadership*. London: Sage.

Jaggar, A. M. (1989). Love and knowledge. *Inquiry*, *32*(2), 51–176.

Jarvie, I. C., & Zamora-Bonila, J. (2011). *The Sage handbook of the philosophy of social sciences*. London: Sage.

Johnson, D. M. (1992). *Approaches to research in second language learning*. New York: Longman.

Jorgenson, J. (1991). Co-constructing the interviewer/Co-constructing 'family'. In F. Steier (Ed.), *Research and reflexivity* (pp. 210–225). London: Sage.

Kenny, K. (2018). Censored: Whistleblowers and public speech. *Human Relations*, *71*, 1025–1048.

Khaire, M., & Hall, E. V. (2016). Medium and message: Globalization and innovation in the production field of Indian fashion. *Organisation Studies*, *37*(6), 845–865.

Kincheloe, J., & McLaren, P. (2005). Rethinking critical theory and qualitative research. In N. K. Denzin & Y. S. Lincoln (Eds.), *The Sage handbook of qualitative research* (3rd ed., pp. 303–342). Thousand Oaks, CA: Sage.

Klein, N. (2000). *No logo*. London: Flamingo.

Knapp, M. S. (2016). The practice of designing qualitative research on educational leadership: Notes for emerging scholars and practitioner-scholars. *Journal of Research on Leadership Education*, *12*(1), 1–25.

Knights, D. (1992). Changing spaces: The disruptive impact of a new epistemological location for the study of management. *Academy of Management Review*, *17*(3), 514–536.

Knights, D., & Clarke C. A. (2014). It's a bittersweet symphony, this life: Fragile academic selves and insecure identities at work. *Organization Studies*, *35*(3), 335–357.

Knights, D., & Morgan, G. (1991). Corporate strategy, organizations, and subjectivity: A critique. *Organization Studies*, *12*(2), 251–273.

Knorr-Cetina, K. (1981). *The manufacture of knowledge: An essay on the constructivist and contextual nature of science*. New York: Pergamon Press.

Köhler, T., Smith, A., & Bhakoo, V. (2019). Feature topic for ORM: 'Templates in qualitative research methods'. *Organizational Research Methods*, *22*(1), 3–5.

Kreiner, K., & Mouritsen, J. (2005). The analytical interview: Relevance beyond reflexivity. In S. Tengblad, R. Rolli & B. Czarniawska (Eds.), *The art of science* (pp. 153–176). Malmö: Liber.

Kuehner, A., Ploder, A., & Langer, P. (2016). Introduction to the special issue: European contributions to strong reflexivity. *Qualitative Inquiry*, *22*(9), 699–704.

Kuhn, T. (1970). *The structure of scientific revolution*. Chicago, IL: University of Chicago Press.

Kunda, G. (1992). *Engineering culture*. Philadelphia, PA: Temple University Press.

Lakoff, G., & Johnson, M. (1980). *Metaphors we live by*. Chicago, IL: University of Chicago Press.

Langley, A., & Abdallah, C. (2011). Templates and turns in qualitative studies of strategy and management. In D. Ketchen & D. Bergh (Eds.), *Research methods in strategy and management* (pp. 105–140). London: Emerald.

Lather, P. (1991). *Getting smart: Feminist research and pedagogy with/in the postmodern*. New York: Routledge.

Latour, B. (1986). The powers of association. In J. Law (Ed.), *Power, action and belief: A new sociology of knowledge?* (pp. 264–280). London: Routledge & Kegan Paul.

Law, J. (2004). *After method: Mess in social science research*. London: Routledge.

Linnaeus, C. (1735). *Systema naturae*. Leiden: Lugduni Batavorum.

Locke, K., & Golden-Biddle, K. (1997). Constructing opportunities for contribution: Structuring intertextual coherence and 'problematizing' in organizational studies. *Academy of Management Journal, 40*(5), 1023–1062.

Locke, K., Golden-Biddle, K., & Feldman, M. S. (2008). Making doubt generative: Rethinking the role of doubt in the research process. *Organization Science, 19*(6), 907–918.

Lok, J. (2020). Theorizing the 'I' in institutional theory: Moving forward through theoretical fragmentation, not integration. In A. D. Brown (Ed.), *The Oxford handbook of identity in organizations* (pp. 732–749). Oxford: Oxford University Press.

Manicas, P. T. (1998). Explaining the past and predicting the future. *American Behavioral Scientist, 42*(3), 398–405.

Maranhao, T. (1991). Reflection, dialogue, and the subject. In F. Steier (Ed.), *Research and reflexivity* (pp. 235–249). London: Sage.

March, J. G. (2005). Parochialism in the evolution of a research community: The case of organization studies. *Management and Organization Review, 1*(1), 5–22.

Martin, J. (1981). A garbage can model of the psychological research process. *American Behavioral Scientist, 25*(2), 131–151.

Maxwell, J. A. (2012). *Qualitative research design: An interactive approach.* Thousand Oaks, CA: Sage.

Merriam, S. B., & Tisdell, E. J. (2015). *Qualitative research: A guide to design and implementation* (4th ed.). San Francisco, CA: John Wiley.

Meyer, J. P., & Allen, N. J. (1987). A longitudinal analysis of the early development and consequences of organizational commitment. *Canadian Journal of Behavioral Science, 19*(2), 199–215.

Meyer, J. W., & Rowan, B. (1977). Institutionalized organizations: Formal structure as myth and ceremony. *American Journal of Sociology, 83*(2), 340–363.

Miles, M. B., & Huberman, M. A. (1994). *Qualitative data analysis: An expanded sourcebook.* Thousand Oaks, CA: Sage.

Miller, A. (1995). Building grounded theory within educational psychology practice. *Educational and Child Psychology, 12*(2), 5–14.

Mills, C. W. (1940). Situated actions and vocabularies of motives. *American Sociological Review, 5*(6), 904–913.

Mills, C. W. (1959). *The sociological imagination.* Harmondsworth, UK: Penguin.

Mir, R., Willmott, H., & Greenwood, M. (Eds.) (2016). *The Routledge companion to philosophy in organization studies.* London: Routledge.

Mol, A. (2010). Actor-network theory: Sensitive terms and enduring tensions. *Kölner Zeitschrift für Soziologie und Sozialpsychologie, 50*(1), 253–269.

Morgan, G. (1980). Paradigms, metaphors and puzzle solving in organization theory. *Administrative Science Quarterly, 25*(4), 605–622.

Morgan, G. (1996). An afterword: Is there anything more to be said about metaphors? In D. Grant & C. Oswick (Eds.), *Metaphor and organizations* (pp. 227–240). London: Sage.

Morgan, G. (1997). *Images of organization*. Thousand Oaks, CA: Sage.

Müller, S. M. (2016). Becoming the phenomenon? An alternative approach to reflexivity in ethnography. *Qualitative Inquiry, 22*(9), 705–717.

Nagel, T. (1986). *The view from nowhere*. Oxford: Oxford University Press.

Nyberg, D., & Sveningsson, S. (2014). Paradoxes of authentic leadership: Leader identity struggles. *Leadership, 10*(4), 437–455.

O'Leary, J., & Sandberg, J. (2017). The practice of managing diversity revealed: A practice-theoretical account. *Journal of Organizational Behavior, 38*(4), 512–536.

Olesen, V. (2000). Feminism and qualitative research at and into the millennium. In N. K. Denzin & Y. S. Lincoln (Eds.), *Handbook of qualitative research* (2nd ed., pp. 158–174). Thousand Oaks, CA: Sage.

Ortony, A. (Ed.) (1993). *Metaphor and thought* (2nd ed.). Cambridge: Cambridge University Press.

Parker, M. (2000). *Organizational culture and identity*. London: Sage.

Patriotta, G. (2017). Crafting papers for publication: Novelty and convention in academic writing. *Journal of Management Studies, 54*(5), 747–759.

Pinder, C., & Bourgeois, V. (1982). Controlling tropes in administrative science. *Administrative Science Quarterly, 27*(4), 641–652.

Pinker, S. (2015). *The sense of style: The thinking person's guide to writing in the 21st century*. New York: Penguin.

Ploder, A., & Stadlbauer, J. (2016). Strong reflexivity and its critics: Responses to autoethnography in the German-speaking cultural and social sciences. *Qualitative Inquiry, 22*(9), 753–765.

Potter, J., & Wetherell, M. (1987). *Discourse and social psychology: Beyond attitudes and behaviour*. London: Sage.

Pratt, M. G. (2008). Fitting oval pegs into round holes: Tensions in evaluating and publishing qualitative research in top-tier North American journals. *Organizational Research Methods, 11*(3), 481–509.

Pratt, M. G., Kaplan, S., & Whittington, R. (2020). Editorial essay: The tumult over transparency: Decoupling transparency from replication in establishing trustworthy qualitative research. *Administrative Science Quarterly, 65*(1), 1–19.

Pratt, M. G., Rockmann, K. W., & Kaufmann, J. B. (2006). Constructing professional identity: The role of work and identity learning cycles in the customization of identity among medical residents. *Academy of Management Journal, 49*(2), 235–262.

Putnam, L. L., & Boys, S. (2006). Revisiting metaphors of organizational communication. In S. R. Clegg, C. T. Hardy, B. Lawrence & W. R. Nord (Eds.), *The Sage handbook of organization studies* (pp. 541–576). London: Sage.

Raadschelders, J. C. N. (2011). The future of the study of public administration: Embedding research object and methodology in epistemology and ontology. *Public Administration Review, 71*(6), 916–924.

Reay, T., Zafar, A., Monteiro, P., & Glaser, V. (2019). Presenting findings from qualitative research: One size does not fit all! In T. B. Zilber, J. M. Amis & J. Mair (Eds.), *Research in the sociology of organizations* (vol. *64*, pp. 1–24). Amsterdam: Elsevier.

Reed, I. A. (2011). *Interpretation and social knowledge: On the use of theory in the human sciences*. Chicago, IL: University of Chicago Press.

Reed, M. (1990). From paradigms to images: The paradigm warrior turns post-modern guru. *Personnel Review, 19*(3), 35–40.

Rhodes, C., & Carlsen, A. (2018). The teaching of the other: Ethical vulnerability and generous reciprocity in the research process. *Human Relations, 71*(10), 1295–1318.

Richardson, L. (2000). Writing: A method of inquiry. In N. K. Denzin & Y. S. Lincoln (Eds.), *The Sage handbook of qualitative research* (2nd ed., pp. 923–949). Thousand Oaks, CA: Sage.

Ricoeur, P. (1978). Metaphor and the main problem of hermeneutics. In P. Ricoeur, *The philosophy of Paul Ricoeur* (pp. 303–319). Boston, MA: Beacon Press.

Ritzer, G. (1980). *Sociology: A multiple paradigm science*. Boston, MA: Allyn and Bacon.

Rivera, K. (2018). 'Use your feelings': Emotion as a tool for qualitative research. In C. Cassell, A. L. Cunliffe & G. Grandy (Eds.), *The SAGE handbook of qualitative business and management research methods* (pp. 450–467). London: Sage.

Roethlisberger, F. J., & Dickson, W. J. (1939). *Management and the worker*. Cambridge, MA: Harvard University Press.

Rorty, R. (1989). *Contingency, irony and solidarity*. Cambridge: Cambridge University Press.

Rosen, M. (1985). Breakfirst at Spiro's. *Journal of Management, 25*(5), 463–480.

Rosenau, P. M. (1992). *Post-modernism and the social sciences: Insights, inroads, and intrusions*. Princeton, NJ: Princeton University Press.

Sandberg, J. (2005). How do we justify knowledge produced within interpretive approaches? *Organizational Research Methods, 8*(1), 41–68.

Sandberg, J., & Alvesson, M. (2021). Meanings of theory: Clarifying theory through typification. *Journal of Management Studies*. 58(2), 487–516.

Sandberg, J., Loacker, B., & Alvesson, M. (2015). Conceptions of process in organization and management: The case of identity studies. In R. Garud, B. Simpson, A. Langley & H. Tsoukas (Eds.), *The emergency of novelty in organizations* (pp. 318–344). Oxford: Oxford University Press.

Sandberg, J., Rouleau, L., Langley, A., & Tsoukas, H. (2017). *Skillful performance: Enacting capabilities, knowledge, competence and expertise in organizations*. Oxford: Oxford University Press.

Sandberg, J., & Targama, A. (2007). *Managing understanding in organizations*. London: Sage.

Schaefer, S., & Alvesson, M. (2020). Epistemic attitudes and source critique in qualitative research. *Journal of Management Inquiry, 29*(1), 33–45.

Schmidt, F., & Hunter, J. (2014). *Methods of meta-analysis: Correcting error and bias in research findings.* London: Sage.

Schön, D. (1979). Generative metaphor: A perspective on problem-setting in social policy. In A. Ortony (Ed.), *Metaphor* (pp. 254–283). Cambridge: Cambridge University Press.

Schwarz, G., & Stensaker, I. (2014). Time to take off the theoretical straightjacket and (re) introduce phenomenon-driven research. *Journal of Applied Behavioral Science, 50*(4), 478–501.

Schwarz, N. (1999). Self-reports: How the questions shape the answers. *American Psychologist, 54*(2), 93–105.

Searle, J. (1984). *Mind, brains and science.* Cambridge, MA: Harvard University Press.

Searle, J. (1979). Metaphor. In J. Searle (Ed.), *Expression and meaning: Studies in the theory of speech acts* (pp. 76–116). Cambridge: Cambridge University Press.

Sekaran, U. (2000). *Research method for business: A skill building approach.* New York: John Wiley.

Sennett, R. (1999). *The corrosion of character: The personal consequences of work in the new capitalism.* New York: Norton.

Shiner, L. (1982). *The invention of art: A cultural history.* Chicago, IL: University of Chicago Press.

Silverman, D. (2006). *Interpreting qualitative data* (3rd ed.). London: Sage.

Smircich, L. (1983). Concepts of culture and organizational analysis. *Administrative Science Quarterly, 28*(3), 339–358.

Smith, J. K. (1998). *Social science in question: Towards a postdisciplinary framework.* London: Sage.

Smith, J. K., & Deemer, D. (2000). The problem of criteria in the age of relativism. In N. K. Denzin & Y. S. Lincoln (Eds.), *The Sage handbook of qualitative research* (2nd ed., pp. 877–896). Thousand Oaks, CA: Sage.

Solnit, R. (2001). *Wanderlust: A history of walking.* London: Verso.

Stake, R. (2005). Qualitative case studies. In N. K. Denzin & Y. S. Lincoln (Eds.), *The Sage handbook of qualitative research* (3rd ed., pp. 443–466). Thousand Oaks, CA: Sage.

Starbuck, W. H. (2006). *The production of knowledge: The challenge of social science research.* Oxford: Oxford University Press.

Steen, G. J. Dorst, L., Berenike Herrmann, J., et al. (2010). *A method for linguistic metaphor identification: From MIP to MIPVU.* Amsterdam: John Benjamins.

Stevens, M., Armstrong, E., & Arums, R. (2008). Sieve, incubator, temple, hub: Empirical and theoretical advances in the sociology of higher education. *Annual Review of Sociology, 34*(1), 127–151.

Strauss, A., & Corbin, J. (1994). Grounded theory methodology: An overview. In N. K. Denzin & Y. S. Lincoln (Eds.), *The Sage handbook of qualitative research* (pp. 273–285). Thousand Oaks, CA: Sage.

Suddaby, R. (2006). What grounded theory is not. *Academy of Management Journal, 49*(4), 633–642.

Suddaby, R., Hardy, S., & Huy, Q. N. (2011). Introduction to special topic forum: Where are the new theories of organization? *Academy of Management Review, 36*(2), 236–246.

Suppe, F. (1979). *The structure of scientific theory*. Urbana, IL: University of Illinois Press.

Swedberg, R. (2014). *Theorizing in social science: The context of discovery*. Stanford, CA: Stanford University Press.

Swedberg, R. (2016). Before theory comes theorizing or how to make social science more interesting. *British Journal of Sociology, 67*(1), 5–22.

Swedberg, R. (2020). Using metaphors in sociology: pitfalls and potentials. *The American Sociologist, 51*(2), 240–257.

Sword, H. (2017). *Air & light & time & space: How successful academics write*. Cambridge, MA: Harvard University Press.

Symon, G., & Cassell, C. (2012). *Qualitative organizational research: Core methods and current challenges*. London: Sage.

Thrift, N. (2008). *Non-representational theory: Space, politics, affects*. London: Routledge.

Timmermans, S., & Tavory, I. (2012). Theory construction in qualitative research: From grounded theory to abductive analysis. *Sociological Theory, 30*(3), 167–186.

Tourish, D. (2019). *Management studies in crisis: Fraud, misconduct and meaningless research*. Cambridge: Cambridge University Press.

Tourish, D. (2020). The triumph of nonsense in management studies. *Academy of Management Learning & Education, 19*(1), 99–109.

Van de Ven, A. H. (2007). *Engaged scholarship: A guide for organizational and social research*. New York: Oxford University Press.

Van de Ven, A. H. (2016). Grounding the research phenomenon. *Journal of Change Management, 16*(4), 265–270.

Van Hulst, M., Ybema, S. B., & Yanow, D. (2017). Studying processes of organizing ethnographically. In A. Langley & H. Tsoukas (Eds.), *The Sage handbook of process organization studies* (pp. 223–236). London: Sage.

Van Knippenberg, D., & Sitkin, S. B. (2013). A critical assessment of charismatic-transformational leadership research: Back to the drawing board? *Academy of Management Annals, 7*(1), 1–60.

Van Maanen, J. (1979). The fact of fiction in organizational ethnography. *Administrative Science Quarterly, 24*(4), 539–550.

Van Maanen, J. (1988). *Tales of the field*. Chicago, IL: University of Chicago Press.

Van Maanen, J. (Ed.) (1995). *Representation in ethnography*. Thousand Oaks, CA: Sage.

Vannini, P. (2015). Non-representational research methodologies: An introduction. In P. Vannini (Ed.), *Non-representational methodologies: Re-envisioning research* (pp. 1–18). New York: Routledge.

vom Brocke, J. et al. (2009). Reconstructing the giant: On the importance of rigor in documenting the literature search process. *ECIS 2009 Proceedings*, paper 161.

von Glasersfeld, E. (1991). Knowing without metaphysics: Aspects of the radical constructivist position. In F. Steier (Ed.), *Research and reflexivity* (pp. 12–29). London: Sage.

Weick, K. E. (1989). Theory construction as disciplined imagination. *Academy of Management Review, 14*(4), 516–531.

Weick, K. E. (1992). Agenda setting in organizational behavior: A theory-focused approach. *Journal of Management Inquiry, 1*(3), 171–182.

Weinstein, J. (2000). A (further) comment on the difference between applied and academic sociology. *Contemporary Sociology, 29*(2), 344–347.

West, C., & Zimmerman, D. H. (1987). Doing gender. *Gender and Society, 1*(2), 125–151.

Willig, C. (2011). *Introducing qualitative research in psychology: Adventures in theory and method.* Buckingham: Open University Press.

Willmott, H. (2011). Journal list fetishism and the perversion of scholarship: Reactivity and the ABS list. *Organization, 18*(4), 429–442.

Wilson, E., Mura, P., Sharif, S. P., & Wijesinghe, S. N. R. (2020). Beyond the third moment? Mapping the state of qualitative tourism research. *Current Issues in Tourism, 23*(7), 795–810.

Winch, P. (1958). *The idea of a social science and its relation to philosophy* (2nd ed.). London: Routledge.

Wray-Bliss, E. (2002). Abstract ethics, embodied ethics: The strange marriage of Foucault and positivism in labour process theory. *Organization, 9*(1), 5–39.

Yin, R. K. (2014). *Case study research: Design and methods.* Thousand Oaks, CA: Sage.

Yob, I. M. (2003). Thinking constructively with metaphors. A review of Barbara J. Thayer-Bacon, 2000, *Transforming critical thinking: Thinking constructively.* New York: Teachers College Press.

INDEX

Page numbers in **bold** indicate tables.